WRITE
& GET PAID

REVISED and EXPANDED

Anthony Tinsman

Freebird Publishers
www.FreebirdPublishers.com

Freebird Publishers
221 Pearl St., Ste. 541, North Dighton, MA 02764
Info@FreebirdPublishers.com
www.FreebirdPublishers.com

Copyright © 2017, Revised 2020
Write & Get Paid by Anthony Tinsman

All rights reserved. No part of this book may be reproduced in any form or by any means without the prior written consent of the Publisher, except in brief quotes used in reviews.

All Freebird Publishers titles, imprints, and distributed lines are available at special quantity discounts for bulk purchases for sales promotions, premiums, fundraising, educational, or institutional use.

ISBN: 0-9996602-1-7
ISBN-13: 978-0-9996602-1-8

Printed in the United States of America

Disclaimer: While the publisher strives to make the information in this book as timely and accurate as possible, the publisher makes no claims, promises, or guarantees about the accuracy, completeness, or adequacy of the contents of this book, and expressly disclaims liability for errors and omissions in the contents of this book. References in this book to any specific organization, law, party, process, or service, or the use of any trade, firm, or corporation name are for the information and convenience of the public and do not constitute endorsement, recommendation, or favoring by the publisher.

Dedication

This book is dedicated to anyone who has ever contemplated picking up a pen and laying down words in hopes of becoming a writer.

Introduction

"The instruction we find in books is like fire, we fetch it from our neighbors, kindle it at home, communicate it to others, and it becomes the property of all." – Voltaire

The best way to hone your message is to listen to your readers. I learned this during the period I ran a bi-weekly column called "Dear Tinny: Demystifying the Law, Craft and Business of Publishing." My specialization became advice giving. I did not "sell" any one method but worked to clear up misconceptions and unblock paths for authors. Once all of those columns were compiled, it made *Write & Get Paid* a must-have for troubleshooting authors' careers.

Feedback from readers is unanimous: No matter whether your career is well-established or just starting, this essential guide is a powerful tool to get your creations out of the note pile and into the backlist. The life-changing advice is easy to apply immediately. One reader in Illinois, Jason, wrote that *Write & Get Paid* lifted him out of a 20-year slump. He has now self-published two eBooks, writes a daily word quota, and plans his career appropriately. Readers have actually put it on their desk beside a pencil, pen, recorder, and keyboard. And now it is even better.

NEWLY REVISED
I have taught workshops and lectured for almost a decade, and writers need to hear this again and again: "You don't need to be led by the hand." This updated edition answers writers' commonly asked questions and offers expanded chapters on setting reasonable expectations for their career. It also delves into creating predictable freelance routines that fit any lifestyle. Plus, it lays out even more dynamic ideas and resources to get the job done.

Some of the changes address new topics of interest and concern, including how to deal with piracy and infringement, publicity problems, identifying the life hacks that open up the internet and social media, and teaching authors how to develop short-term income into continuous, long-term income. Pick and choose from the step-by-step instructions to begin exploring opportunities specific to your career goals.

MORE INFORMATION
It is a pleasure to know that some readers who purchased the original edition highlighted it completely! Now you will need a new highlighter, because over 100 authors are quoted on issues ranging from the personal revelations that occur while writing, to public decisions made while wearing the CEO hat. You won't find these gathered anywhere else. Their insights, like my own, were chosen with the knowledge that your full understanding is what matters.

I began my journey at 8 years old, staring at bookshelves and magazine racks, wondering how to get my creations up there. I have learned a lot since then, won awards, published numerous books, and been featured on Google Finance, Simon & Schuster, the *Huffington Post*, and international venues. That is all fine, but what keeps me grinding forward are the writers who have approached me with copies of my old blogs in hand: "Your Book Marketing Plan" or "The Portable Office." It is like carrying a certain type of fire that gives off warmth more inspiring than pixels can convey.

TAKE CONTROL
Every chapter shows you what your career can become.

PART 1 introduces the basics, providing an explanation of what works and setting a foundation for you to begin exploiting the value of your writing.

PART 2 shows you how to go from idea to rough draft to finished manuscript, covering the perspective of an editor on the importance of the subject and detailing the various methods of organizing the creative process.

PART 3 details the nuances of the business, the best way to stand out, developing a taste for a mercenary mentality, and the importance of considering what sells.

PART 4 delves into the specifics of the art, such as crafting better dialogue, genre, and a strong plot, and developing your narration skills by reading with purpose.

PART 5 helps you maneuver considerations on distinguishing your name, creating an effective website, an objective look at the use of pen names, and getting social with readers.

PART 6 examines the process of working with a publisher, goes in depth about independent publishing tools, and presents a variety of methods for creating multiple streams of income from each book.

PART 7 maps the world of online book promotion, the most effective strategies, services, and standards that get readers' attention, and reveals less well-known options that are catching on in a big way.

PART 8 reveals the inner workings and outer limits of free speech, use of copyright-protected materials, as well as strategies for stopping piracy and keeping your name unblemished throughout your career.

PART 9 pinpoints the essentials of operating your business, where to find good help among companies and experts, and preparing your estate so your writing makes income long after you're gone.

Start with page one and work your way through, or pick a topic to assist you in your current work. Apply the durable details within, and you might discover new ways to refresh business strategies, open doors to readers, or gain new understanding on exactly what it takes to craft compelling manuscripts. Whatever method you choose, this book will give you a complete picture of how to write and get paid.

WRITE & GET PAID

Table of Contents

INTRODUCTION

PART 1 **GET STARTED** — 3
1. Perfection is the Enemy — 5
2. Plan Ahead — 9
3. Opportunity for Authors — 17
4. Mentors — 21
5. Standard Practice — 27
6. Irresistible You — 33
7. Get Your Money — 39

PART 2 **THE CRAFT** — 43
8. Kick Start the Creative Process — 45
9. Outline — 51
10. Revise — 57
11. Edit — 63

PART 3 **THE BUSINESS** — 69
12. Understand What Sells and For How Much — 71
13. Exploit Markets — 77
14. Utilize the Mercenary Marketplace — 83
15. Follow the Markets — 89

PART 4 **STYLE** — 95
16. Read with Purpose — 97
17. Write Better — 101
18. Write Faster — 107

PART 5 **HUSTLE** — 113
19. Basic Platform — 115
20. Penetrate Your Market — 123
21. Brand Yourself — 129
22. Publicity — 135

PART 6 **BOOKS** — 145
23. Going with a Publisher — 147
24. Independent Publishing — 151
25. Exploit Subsidy Rights — 161

PART 7 **BOOK SELLING** — 169
26. Pro Tools — 171
27. Book Reviews — 181
28. Content Sharing — 185

PART 8 **THE LAW** — 191
29. Get it in Writing — 193
30. Consequences of Free Speech — 205
31. Protect Yourself While Writing — 211

PART 9 **THE END** — 221
32. Life as an Author — 223
33. Good Help and Where to Find It — 229

i. Write & Get Paid Exclusive Quiz — 233
ii. The Writers Manifesto — 235

ABOUT THE AUTHOR — 237

PART 1
GET STARTED

Chapter One

"You start out a phony and become real." – Glenn O'Brian

PERFECTION IS THE ENEMY
Publishing is an exciting path to prosperity. With a bit of work, a yearning that starts as "I want to write a book" can become a major source of income. The arc from author to running a global media empire is driven by a similar characteristic. Learn on the job. Success is determined by how well you organize the traits writers are celebrated for. Come up with ideas. Write a lot. With a bit of fearlessness, success can blossom.

To wrangle the big checks, you must consistently create value with your words. The best way to do that is not to try too hard. One of the most diversified authors of our time, David Morrell, hit it big with his first novel, First Blood. It spawned the Rambo franchise of movies, toys, and even a Saturday morning cartoon. Morrel kept going, wrote plenty of other books, and worked as a Professor of Literature, screenwriter, and writing instructor. His secret is that he grew his income by taking opportunities as they came, regardless of whether he had the training to do it or not.

Morrel's advice to writers was simple enough: "I found that if I didn't strive for perfection, if I somehow got through whatever I was struggling with, the next thing became a little easier. Motion became my purpose. I gave myself permission to make mistakes, reassuring myself that, when it was finished, everything would be made right."

Believe in doing your best, not in being perfect. If you spend all your time stumbling after perfection, your writing and your career will always come up short. The alternative is not only superior, it's also easiest. Loosen up; study your craft and the business of writing. Work, however, makes you feel comfortable.

DEFINE SUCCESS
How do you measure success? Are 50 five-star reviews on Amazon enough? What about fan mail from readers you've never met? Or should you cut the bologna and measure success by income? Probably a little of each, but definitely the latter. It helps to think like Baseball legend Yogi Berra: "If it doesn't make dollars, it doesn't make sense." Measuring income is a concrete sign of where you are on the learning curve.

You don't have to be rich to be successful. If your income covers your overhead with enough left over to buy the groceries this month, that's successful. Keep at it, and eventually you'll redefine success. Making a full-time living as a writer is nothing to rush into. Can your family survive on your income? Is your overall well-being better off or worse than a more conventional career? Success can be a hybrid, slowly progressing towards more time writing.

- Embrace low-stress jobs that jumpstart good writing habits.
- Promote your eBooks, publish shorter eBooks, and build a backlist.
- Work at home editing other people's manuscripts for $2.00 a page.
- Do PR for other people, like selling books and music reviews for $250 each.

To get in the right mindset, smash these fairytales immediately.

- A Master of Fine Arts (MFA) is mandatory.
- You're either born with talent or you're screwed.
- Editors will seek you out, and publishers will handle all promotion.

Above all else, finish your manuscripts. A lawyer once advised me, "You shouldn't think about how you'll win a million dollars. You have to win first. Then win one dollar. A hundred. A thousand. Then a hundred thousand." You can set any number you want as your goal. Just don't forget that learning on the go means taking what you can get.

Success to some people could be embodied by winning an award. Most MFA programs inspire students to produce books capable of winning prizes. As nice as that is, you need to think about how valuable it is, really? Having won a PEN/Fielding Dawson prize myself, I can say it helped my confidence and maybe got a few editors to consider manuscripts. Unfortunately, by itself it didn't add another comma to my bank account. I rarely mention the prize anymore because working with people is what pays the bills, not tooting my own horn about the past.

COPY ROLE MODELS BUSINESS SENSE

Your role models can teach you more than the craft of writing. Think about it. We learn to read and write by copying down the alphabet. Musicians learn to play by practicing scales. Painters learn to paint by reproducing masterpieces. Done seriously, copying the masters can lead to mastery of a larger set of skills, useful in the art and the business. You can learn more than a few tricks from your heroes. Study them a little more deeply, look into their lives, and their business models. Their strategies empower your ability to grow.

Mixing and matching writing with service or by maintaining multiple writing careers is the best way to keep your options open. Success is based equally on exploiting opportunities as well as perseverance. The lines blur where they intersect, but the point is often mistakenly called luck. I like to think of it as something different, something we all have in common, a willingness to learn and develop whatever skills it takes to succeed. These strategies could work for you:

1. *Nonfiction books with multiple products, speaking, and consulting* – Nonfiction makes money from book sales as well as the "backend" information products. Motivational DVDs, professional speaking, and consulting/coaching services are a potential gold mine. The book acts more like a business card, raising the status of the author. It's the other services that make up the majority of the cash flow.

Here are just a few authors you may have heard of who are making a fortune this way:

- Robert Kiyosaki, 'Rich Dad, Poor Dad' (finance) seminars and consulting.
- Jordon Belfort, 'The Wolf of Wall Street' (investing), speaking events, and consulting.
- Chris Brogan, 'The Freaks Shall Inherit the Earth' (branding), speaking and online courses.
- Robert McKee, 'Story' (writing), online video memberships, multi-day workshops.

2. *High volume book releases* – Karen S. Wiesner has published 12 series, ranging from three to a dozen books each, including bestseller *Incognito*, for a total of 101 books. Wiesner is not the only writer profiting from high production. Authors who build a "backlist" can see explosive sales when consistent readers discover them and dive in. From Douglas Preston and Lincoln Child's *Pendergast* series, to Kate Jacobs' Friday Night Knitting Club, the most successful ones focus on serials, books that are either numbered (#1, #2, #3) or released in the same category (mystery, thriller, how-to, etc.). It has become commonplace for super-producers to release shorter books, novellas, and short stories as fast as they can. Readers gobble it up.

3. *Sporadic books with teaching/speaking/freelance writing* – Writers like John Irving (*The World According to Garp*) and Ian McEwan (*Atonement*) make as much money from their books as they do teaching at the Iowa Writers Workshop. Literary writers spend more time polishing the language in their work. If they decide to turn literature into a career, they make most of their income from teaching creative writing, applying for grants and prizes, or from another writing career like journalism or freelance writing.

Emulating successful role models gives you a glimpse of their minds, a view of their perspective. Some of their understanding can be pulled into your work. Read self-help books around writing and mindset and listen to podcasts and motivational audios. Analyzing someone's brain for business gets you there in the shortest distance possible, because it's impossible to emulate someone's mysterious, creative side. Besides, some business geniuses made lots of money without any exceptional writing talent.

TAKE THE NEXT STEP
Let readers guide your career. Their votes are counted by sales. Tailor writing for their markets, adopt a style they find attractive, and cover subjects they consider interesting. The income will make you feel a whole lot more successful than perfect little posers who keep their masterpieces snugly in their heads. This straightforward strategy works for serious writers who want to take things to the next level.

Wherever you are, it is not far to get where you would like to go.

"I'M NEW TO THIS."
Nobody's first piece wins a Pulitzer Prize or a $30,000 endowment, but it can bring you 5 cents a word, and that isn't too shabby. Do anything to get a first draft done. Once you've worked with an editor, you'll learn how to improve your writing. If you publish, sign contracts, and market a finished product, then guess what? You will get better, try new things, accept failure, and pivot as necessary.

Tamara Linse was a self-professed "lazy scaredy-cat writer-baby" who spent a lot of time pretending to write. "I'd sit down to write, and hours would pass as I aimlessly strolled the Internet." When her twins were born, she wanted to be a good example, so they would follow their dreams. She downloaded a free desktop timer (xnotestopwatch.com) and worked for 10 minutes here and there. "A miracle occurred," she said. Two novels, plus short stories and essays, resulted. Oh, then she shopped for an agent and got one.

Ideas are popping into your head every day. What are you doing with them? The creator of the Twilight Zone, Rod Serling, explained the state writers must avoid. "A writer," he said, "is a frustrated actor, reciting his lines in the auditorium of his skull." To beat this, authors give common advice for keeping your ideas flowing onto paper, from Earnest Hemmingway to Anne Lamott, they advocate that it is okay to write "shitty first drafts."

Getting your ideas down in some form (paper or pixel) puts it in a medium where it can be immediately worked on. Use Write or Die software. Set word counts. Do National Novel Writing Month (nanowrimo.org). Just get across the finish line. Everything gets easier with a manuscript in your hands.

"I AM A SKILLED PROFESSIONAL."
With enough experience, you are not just ready, but capable of taking control of your future. Moving to the next step may mean going full-time, running your own publishing company, or simply carving out a proper chunk of time for the business of writing. The more serious you get, the more things will naturally start happening. Plan your writing time, and before long, you'll reach a tipping point in your productivity.

Roger Morris edited his college newspaper; then, a favorite English professor invited him to review a novel without pay. It appeared in the *Charleston Gazette*. "That free review led to a paying job at the newspaper." Fifteen years later, Morris freelances full time as a national columnist and contributes regularly to *USA Today*.

Keith Richards, legendary guitarist of the Rolling Stones, noted he had more ideas for songs than ever after writing his first hit ("The Last Time"). "One thing feeds the other," Richards said, "you might be having a swim, or screwing the old lady, but somewhere in the back of your mind, you're thinking about a chord sequence or something related to a song, no matter what is going on. You might be getting shot at, and you'll still be 'Oh! That's the bridge!' and there's nothing you can do. You don't realize it's happening."

Active writers have a sort of radar. You might hear a piece of conversation across a room, and that's the spark for a story. Take lots of notes. Over time, you'll notice a big change. The more you keep notes of these ideas, the more you'll find that these ideas increase. You'll learn how to share your ideas with a range of people in ways that make them more attractive. Turn that ear to other authors and you'll soon be getting ideas about the art and business of writing.

"I HAVE ATTAINED A CERTAIN LEVEL OF MASTERY."
Juggling the writing, marketing, and production side, as well as strategizing, scheduling, and more, is not something that just happens. There are not many life hacks that can guarantee to turn you into a focused CEO. You have got to push your limits and learn as you go. Increase your sensitivity to opportunities by pondering all sorts of writers and media. Whether it is "Old time American transcendentalist individualism" personified by Thoreau or the pop sci-fi of Shonen Jump, it can teach you about new venues and pleasures.

Treat every personal experience as a building block. Adam H. Graham, a Swiss backpacker who did part-time travel writing, found assignments built on one another. Looking back at his ascent, he said, "My first *New York Times* piece changed the way editors thought of me and opened a lot of doors. I suddenly had a voice." With that voice, any number of directions or reinventions is possible.

The line between success and failure is a blur because it is easy to bounce back. Even international multimedia giants like Nippon Ichi, producer of the PlayStation series Disgaea, perform well despite critics and bad reviews. They listen to fans and feed them spin-offs – light novels, manga, and serialized fiction. At any stage in their career, authors have unlimited chances at success. It is as easy as telling yourself, "Relax a little." Then let the words flow.

✎ Writers Manifesto No. 1 – Don't let perfection interfere with what's possible.

RESOURCES
Author – Mar Lafferty, podcast "I should be writing," bit.ly/1nvJubv

Chapter Two

"The best way to predict the future is to create it." – Peter F. Drucker

PLAN AHEAD
Whether authors get up early or stay up late, as long as they produce there is no question about what the results will look like downstream. The simplest plan is to write daily, fitting it in among mowing the lawn, balancing a checkbook, home repairs, and gainful employment. A good word diet can turn occasional assignments into steady income. Novelists like Tom Lucas don't play games; his mission statement: "Butt in chair until I write 1,000 words – every day." That's the beauty of a word diet. It can start easy – 500 words a day – and build into a four-digit quota.

Admittedly, creative people tend to prosper with a little disarray. Author Alton Brown emphasized this when he explained his success: "I find the only way I can advance my originality is by having a certain amount of whirlwind." But if your office looks like it was struck by a tornado, then it's self-defeating. Think it through organizationally; ultimately, authors need to record all activity, incoming and outgoing. You have got to be clear about who owes, who's paid, what you've written, deadlines, and so on. Using a daily planner or productivity app like Evernote gives your word output a boost by making order out of madness.

When you succeed daily, every aspect of your publishing career escalates. The writer, still afraid of rejection, begins sending work everywhere and monitors each submission. A full-time freelancer makes a schedule to tap into their community. Administering the paperwork is also a diet. Log stuff as it happens, experiment with different systems and tools. The right mix can turn you into a writing machine.

Laying out a binder for tracking sheets, research notes, marketing research, proposals, resumes, and samples of sales literature increases your access to information that can easily get lost in the jumble. Even then, I still use a pocket flip book to take notes and cross out daily chores. It only takes a few minutes to make a list of must-dos and then figure in my writing goals. All this makes the actual work a piece of cake, and most authors agree that it's life-changing.

THE ACTUAL PLANNER
A planner can be as simple as a wall calendar or as involved as a 3-ring binder with tab-separators. I've used both, evolving towards a hybrid. Being organized means my creative energy doesn't get sapped when I stop and figure, "What was I supposed to do today?" or "Didn't I have a deadline for this?" or "Is this project going to help me reach my goals?" The answers are a few pages away, prioritized from repetitive tasks to the most time-sensitive projects.

The relief allows the creative valve to open. It took me a while to get organized in a way that addressed all the responsibilities that have piled up as my career has grown. Learning how to make the goals clear, steps simple, and information relevant was a matter of experimentation. Perhaps you'll find a store-bought planner is all you'll need. I found that having control over the arraignment led to the best results.

Here's the layout I use:

- Monthly Calendar
- Accounting Sheet
- Submission Tracker
- Publication Log
- Contacts
- Project Planner
- Special Contacts
- Goals Sheet with Action Steps

MONTHLY CALENDAR
Check your calendar each morning to ensure that you hit your targets. Marking a calendar is a unified representation of your goals and is an essential part of an effective planner. This outlines when you are to act. There's usually enough space to add a variety of notes.

ACCOUNTING SHEET
Just as important as figuring out your costs and expenses is being able to anticipate income. A clear record of debts and assets is a better way to be prepared to deal with your writing career and issues. There are several forms that pros use (balance sheet, income projection, profit and loss), but even plain accounting sheets work.

Income/Expense	Comment	Amount	Date

Assets	Debts

	Income Projection		
S			
M			
T			
W			
T			
F			
S			

SUBMISSION TRACKER
At their peak, writers send out a lot of requests, proposals, and manuscripts each week. With so much incoming and outgoing correspondence, they need to track each piece to ensure timeliness. This means recording when it was sent, received, and accepted, including room for comments that can be helpful in the future.

SUBMISSION TRACKER Date from to

Title	Market	Contact	Date Sent	Date Returned	Date Accepted	Date Published	Payment Received	Comments

PUBLICATION LOG

A publication log is important for writers and their partners. It serves three purposes: 1) the formal publication you accomplish puts in chronological order, 2) selecting, at a glance, the right publication to support pitches to editors, and 3) managing the sources shared with audiences in your bio. It's also valuable because it forces you to review results in an itemized way that puts your goals into perspective.

Title	http://	Date	Market/Theme

CONTACTS

A thorough contact page is a powerful tool. It gathers email, phone, and physical addresses. You don't want to rely on only one means of communication with important contacts. Phone numbers change, emails get buried, and people move. A contacts page is also handy if you want to ask specific questions or remember someone's birthday, just jot them down alongside their info. The next time you're in touch, these notes can help you craft messages that make a connection.

PROJECT PLANNER

My project planner is organized in a diagram. Work that serves the same market belongs in the same diagram. This grants some perspective on current and long-term goals and presents a clear picture of market penetration.

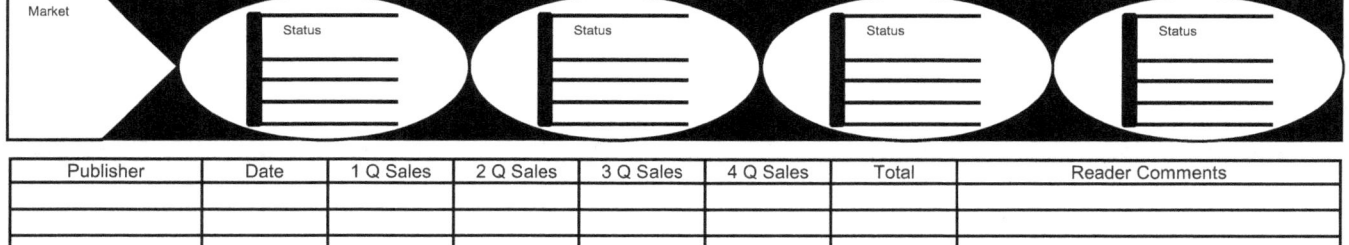

Publisher	Date	1 Q Sales	2 Q Sales	3 Q Sales	4 Q Sales	Total	Reader Comments

SPECIAL CONTACTS

This section contains information from the contact page but serves a separate purpose. These contacts have agreed to work with you, are currently working with you, or have done so in the past. Perhaps you intend to utilize their specialties (PR, reviews, book cover design, etc.), so this should contain a note about what you have in mind for each person. I categorize these by profession, in alphabetical order, making editors, publishers, and publicists easier to find.

GOALS SHEET WITH ACTION STEPS

This section is simply a checklist on a grand scale. It serves as a practical outline for important tasks and identifies gaps, so you can make each goal actionable. Leave room for notations for what resources you'll need and special objectives. It keeps your progress in balance and running smoothly.

Date	
ACTION STEPS	**TOP PRIORITY**

ON THE RADAR

WRITE
WITH FOCUS

READ
WITH PURPOSE

BUILD
YOUR COMMUNITY

PROGRESS

Think about the results you want and work backwards until you figure out what initial steps must be taken. It's also a good idea to make a personal plan (similar to a business plan) to organize daily routines as they relate to achieving your goals. By identifying where you'd like to be in one, three, or even five years, it's easier to put relevant tasks in your planner.

FINANCIALS
You can play around with figures and income projections, and it's all based on a best guess. It's easier after you have some sales, can add up the checks, and compare everything on a balance sheet. At its most basic, the financial part of your plan should answer these questions:

- What are your income sources?
- Are you 'Ramen Profitable' (able to pay a few small bills with your income)?
- If not, how long will it take to reach that state?
- Where would you like your income to be in 5 years?
- What do you have to do to reach that future state?

There are all sorts of tips and tricks you can put into practice, but for the sake of simplicity, let's consider what a relatively successful book's income looks like. The average book sells between 250 and 3,500 copies in its lifetime. Here's an example for a self-published book:

One book priced at $2.99, at 70% royalties, makes $2.00 per copy. Estimated sales = 100 per month = 1,200 copies a year (believe it or not, that's a top seller!). Total income per year is $2,400.

If you budget $1,000 for editing and cover design, your profit will be $1,400 in the first year. Assuming nothing changes, which is an inflexible way of thinking, you can carry the $2,400 per year going forward.

You will need 10 books selling at this rate to make $24,000 per year. Most people would agree that even that isn't enough to live well in the U.S. and Europe.

To increase income, you need more books, or more copies of each sold, or a higher profit per book, or multiple streams of income from shorter work. The trickles of cash flow can add up. It takes high production to make higher income, just be realistic about the math (words = manuscripts = sales X year). It'll take trial and error to find the sweet spot in your schedule, but that's all just part of the process of making your plans materialize.

WORD DIET
The advice goes "write every day," but it's like a weight loss program. You'll go through many different word diets before finding the one best suited to you. Consistency is key. Stephen King usually writes ten pages a day, but sometimes up to twenty. Bob Meyer, *New York Times* bestseller, writes by the hour, dedicating the morning to it, and spends afternoons running his business.

With time, it gets easier to avoid things that get between you and writing. If I'm making new pages, I write for a couple of hours a day, usually in the morning. If I am editing or polishing, I may go longer. I procrastinate, but I also write nearly every day. One way or another, I am working from about ten to six. There are bad days and good days, but they are mitigated by preparing each evening, laying out what I'll need, so in the morning I get a fresh start.

Once you've got your process figured out, keep adjusting it as needed; eventually, a routine will emerge. Pulitzer Prize winner Barbara Tuchman wrote her first drafts in longhand on a yellow legal pad with everything messed up and xed out. She followed with drafts on a typewriter, triple-spaced, ready to be scissored apart and scotch-taped back together in a different sequence. Customarily, she worked for four or five hours at a stretch, without interruption. Otherwise, the detail-oriented work would become too much to manage.

PRODUCTION SCHEDULE
To increase production, consider what sells. Shorter books, or novellas, are a means of exploiting Constant Readers and the ease of purchase brought about by eBooks. In fact, authors mix and match selling short works between longer books. One of the most successful contemporaries using this strategy is H.R. Ward, whose romance novellas are independently published every few weeks. She's sold over 4 million books to date and hit the *New York Times* bestseller list eleven times in 2013. She writes short fiction because it takes less time to get more products in front of readers and reach her financial goals.

From a scheduling standpoint, this takes as much practice as it does discipline. In order to maximize output, writers must consider how their day-to-day activities affect their ability to produce. For example, writing after going for a jog might leave a person drained and writing poorly. In this case, moving the time reserved for writing sooner, or jogging till after, would be worth looking into.

Ultimately, you have 8 hours plus 8 hours plus 8 hours in a day. In other words, each day grants you equal parts for work, private stuff, and rest. The daily time spent on writing should be as much as possible, while not interfering with life itself. Once a schedule takes root, amazing production is possible. Here are some questions to help you plot out an effective production schedule.

- How many manuscripts do you need to write this year (books, short pieces, social stuff)?
- How long does it take you to write each type of manuscript?
- When do you need extra time in your plan?
- How much advance notice do you need to give editors?

Keep in mind that not every project begins as, or needs to be, book-length. Sometimes they can be broken down into small pieces and grow naturally over time. The role model for exploiting an idea in this way is Ray Bradbury. His book *Fahrenheit 451* took one week to turn into a novel. The story, however, originally began as a one-act play that was later expanded into a short story, "The Fireman." Then he wrote the book. Each iteration brought in a little more income than the last.

Successful authors and productivity are linked together like mother and fetus. While a Daily Planner is effective, keep your eyes open for tools that let you work on the fly. Organize around the need to streamline the creative process. Woody Allen, the comedian and filmmaker, once hauled out boxes full of one-liners and ideas to make a point about the production requirements of a busy pro. You can amass stuff in the same way or keep it in the cloud! Apps like Office Time, Things, and Evernote sync up with phone and desktop so you can add ideas to separate folders (fiction ideas, nonfiction ideas, business ideas, etc.) and check up on things when you're settled.

Making production their business is what guides prolific authors:

- Steve Scott released a nonfiction book a month, for a total of 40.
- Billy Wilder wrote a script directly for the screen each year for 48 years.
- Nora Roberts (also writing as J.D. Robb) writes a book every 45 days, for a total of 67.
- R.L. Stine, bestselling children's author of all time, can write several a month.
- Roger Morris publishes food and travel columns each week, 1,200 and counting.

These awesome numbers are the result of a lifetime of writing. Each of these authors started with one project at a time, slowly increasing their skill and speed. When the creative juices are flowing, amazing things can happen. Most of us can write a book a year, as well as the small stuff that keeps a platform growing. But with a refined process, you might aim for a ranking among the top lifetime achievers:

- Isaac Asimov, over 500 books
- Enid Blyton, over 600
- Barbara Cortland, over 700

SET WORK ORDERS
Another excellent way to manage day-to-day writing is to build a system similar to what restaurants use to fill their orders. After the wait staff scribble down what the customers want, each order has important details and needs to be completed in a timely fashion. You are the chef. Instead of snatching an order slip from the kitchen window, you scratch them out of your Daily Planner.

I prioritize work by deadlines and write a plan. The plan covers my platform content, which needs work orders for every piece I intend to write that year, and for larger projects that stand alone. These plans organize important details about each manuscript and its market, when they'll be ready, and a short list of editors I can submit to in case my first choices aren't interested.

WORK ORDERS FOR BOOKS
Books benefit from special care. I make a separate plan for book projects that are either accepted in advance, ghosted, or are likely to be published because of their market. The first step is to identify what distinguishes the book and makes it appealing.

- For Nonfiction:
  - What are the problems that your manuscript is trying to solve?
  - How are the questions going to be answered?
- For Fiction:
  - What are the themes and characteristics of the manuscript?
  - What are some similar manuscripts?
- In General:
  - What category/genre does it fit into?
  - What themes crop up in your manuscripts?

I make orders in two groups, one for the book and one for what I'll use to promote it. I gather piles of notes and list research or questions I have that will help me compose the manuscript. I attach them to the plans and figure out a schedule.

WORK ORDERS – THE BOOK
After making an outline and getting clear about the market, I'll go one step further before beginning a project. It is helpful to itemize the process of producing the actual book. Research, formatting, illustration requirements, rough draft, typing, proofreading, revision, cover letter, submission, and contract sticking points all become a checklist. From this, a clear image of the book's length, unique angle, and tone makes it easy to tear into, because I can prioritize and know what to knock out first, second, and third.

WORK ORDERS – ABOUT THE BOOK
This covers the promotional materials I'll use when marketing the book. I like to come up with seven items. A sample review and news release are pure boilerplate. Articles are next, coming up with them gets easy, they can expand or spin-off a book's content. A sample interview is last, writing all the Q&A, and having a specific author in mind who may be willing to work with it. Each of their outlines is attached to the plan in order of deadline.

This system allows you to find the right information during work, and specific material is utilized to compose each manuscript. Second, it allows you to review projects in advance of deadlines. Third, if it is prepared well, arguably any editor would be able to coordinate with you if you sent them your schedule.

PORTABLE OFFICE

The actual writing may take place at your coffee table, bedside, or on a patio surrounded by roses. Work according to where you're comfortable. A serious writer, however, doesn't sit around waiting for inspiration to strike. Whether you are chasing a lead, on tour, or traveling back and forth to work, the tools you need to write can be put all together in a go-bag. It's the best way to be prepared. There's also the added confidence that comes from feeling the weight of your go-bag; it tells you, "it's time to go to work."

A portable office can be customized to fit any environment:

- *On the Go*: A basic kit would include your planner, tablet or laptop, memory card, notepad, highlighter, and pens. Depending on what you'll be doing, a portable scanner may aid research. A solar charger or car adapter may be useful if you find yourself off the grid.

- *Photojournalist:* A specialized kit for multimedia production may include a tablet or laptop, a camera, a lens, and cleaning equipment. A notepad, highlighter, pens, mini recorder, memory card, and business cards are just a few examples of what you can add.

- *Inmate:* No matter your environment, it's easy to think ahead, a typewriter ribbon, a pack of 8.5 X 11 paper, a project folder, white-out, batteries, a notepad, a highlighter, and pens held inside see-thru or clear cases that can pass inspection from guards.

Get a well-made attaché, briefcase, or gym bag that will protect your gear. Organize the contents of a portable office to make it stand up in your environment. Things like a one-use poncho or waterproof bags to protect your electronics, and cases or tubs with snap lids to hold small and easily tossed about items. Keep your tools on hand because you may have an auditorium packed with listeners at 10:00, but at 8:00, you still have an appointment with a word diet. It ensures you don't waste time and can focus on what you need to do: write.

RESOURCES
Business and Productivity Apps:
- culture.code.com/things
- evernote.com
- officetime.net

"Watch what you write. It could come back to reward you." – Dan Poynter

Chapter Three

"If you think adventure is dangerous, try routine." – Paulo Coelho

OPPORTUNITY FOR AUTHORS
To arrive at success, master the economy of your craft. First, try to think less about producing one potential bestseller. Instead, shoot for steady paychecks. Your odds increase with short works being published regularly. Lastly, whether it is blogs, articles, or interviews, they keep you ranked high on search engines and in front of readers.

Take your ideas and subdivide them into many short pieces. Length equals time, and the number of publications you achieve determines your income. Do the math: a 15% royalty on a 60,000-word novel (selling 7,500 copies) is sometimes less than a flat $250 for a book review, which can be knocked out in a day. Alanna Nash admits, "I seldom make any money off a book." That said, you build your reputation, and books command attention. "It enhances your worth in the magazine market," Nash says.

You can publish articles, reports, newsletters, and many other short forms by matching the piece to the right venue. It draws attention to your book and brings in new clients who may hire you for writing-related services. And those small pieces can always be recast into a book or syndicated elsewhere.

PUBLICATION VENUES – A ★ RATING SYSTEM
    1. *Paper Net* ★ – The underground venue of fan zines and extremist newspapers called the Papernet is a novelty, not a way to make a living. A few publications identify themselves as "radical" and thrive off the distinction. Called Zines, these periodicals can be professional like *Slingshot* (slingshot.tao.ca), *JND Ads and Contacts*, and *The Rusty Razor*. But most are just slapped together. After placing ads with several of these publications, I noticed almost no book sales. Numerous stories and interviews only drew in a handful of letters from college kids and a few sexual advances from neglected freaks, writing, "Do you have nice feet?"

Here's a taste of what counts as radical:

- Organizing a protest, march, rally, or riot
- Primitivism (like living in a wooded Canadian commune)
- Communist rants against "Amerika"
- Anarchy (train hopping, slumming, etc.)
- LGBTQ extremism
- Squatters' rights (living in abandoned buildings)
- Rape culture on campus (is it a real problem?)

You'll find sources by visiting local bookshops, especially those with a "radical" publication section. It may be called a Zine Distro (magazine distributor) or have a cool name like Wyman's Library. Just imagine the surprise upon entering the backroom of a novelty shop. Instead, you'll find back issues. Amid the dozens of monthly newspapers and newsletters, it's easy to find contacts for reviewers, to place an ad (free), and build relationships with some influencers.

2. *Blogging* ★★ – First, let's distinguish between a mom-blogger using WordPress read by her neighbors and girlfriends, versus a professional blogger whose site is rated on Technorati. There must be a flow of traffic and commerce. The best way to do that is to do whatever it takes to get some followers (blog tours, giveaways, memes, contests, or maybe Search Engine Optimization). Once you have a backlist of blogs and followers, it's easy to negotiate your continued blogging success.

Blogging is a way to build credentials when you have none. All sorts of companies need writers to produce content for their sites and interact with readers. Play your cards right and you can get started at .5 cents a word. If everyone likes your stuff, it's feasible to jump to $0.10, $0.15, or even $0.20 per word. But you must get results. That means when you're not blogging, you're networking to bring in new readers (giveaways, memes, contests, all over again). It's time-consuming, so make sure all parties are being adequately compensated ($).

Blogging can become lucrative if you work through the initial setup and get absorbed by associate and affiliate programs. They'll pay you per click or per sale from the advertisers they route to your site. Payments could scale up from $1 to $100,000 depending on your performance.

If you're talented, it pays to start producing multimedia content to take full advantage of these programs. Adding a YouTube channel to your services is a great way to develop multiple streams of income and establish a brand. Producing podcasts (online radio) and VLOGS (video blogs) can increase your income as well. (Just write some decent scripts before production.) Worst case, you can use the work as a portfolio and fish for work as a freelancer, contractor, or consultant.

3. *Activity Journals* ★★★ – Exactly what it sounds like. Local and regional publications like newspapers or tourist guides are good places to start. When you are up for it, publications like *Outdoor Life*, *Bon Appétit*, and *Condé Nast Traveler* are always on the lookout for interesting pieces. The pay scale dips and climbs because a high-class magazine like Conde' Nast serves affluent subscribers, whereas Extreme 4X4 serves a bunch of grease monkey rock crawlers. A good article can sell for a few hundred or a few thousand.

One way to stick out is to invest in a good digital camera. These days, even mobile phones have top-quality camera features. Provide pictures with each article, relying on action shots. Acting as your own photographer keeps the copyright simple, so all permissions and payments come to you instead of multiple contributors.

Activity Journals have other cool opportunities, specifically writing product reviews. Manufacturers send magazines free products for review all the time. Once you've established yourself as a reliable contributor, many editors can be persuaded to send you new products (camping gear, telescopes, emergency car jumpers, etc.). You use the product (snap some photos), write a review, and keep the stuff. Sometimes you get paid as well. If you become their "go-to" contributor, a debit card may be issued by the publisher to cover minor expenses (remember always get a receipt).

4. *Publishing Houses* ★★★ – Not all publishers are created equal. Large or small, they focus on eBooks, paperbacks, and hardbacks (600,000 new ones each year). They are busy releasing everything from graphic novels, cookbooks, how-to, you name it. Professional houses hire a cover illustrator, an editor, a book designer, and maybe a publicist. But smaller houses can't afford all that. You see books with blemishes and websites that go days or weeks without attention. But even big publishers have their problems, like Putnam, which is hard to reach, effectively stonewalling readers.

This inattention means they are busy doing other stuff. To make the most of what happens behind the scenes, just be open-minded. Other than receiving a quarterly check for your book, there are opportunities to get paid working for a publishing house. Here are some typical services:

- Typing $1.00 to $1.50 per page (depending on format, like if the original is handwritten)

- Editing $2.00 to $5.00 per page (depends on the level of editing required)
- Sales literature $0.5 to $0.10 cents per word (back cover, blurbs, news release, etc.)

Most houses need competent, cheap labor. They have books lined up for editing held up because the editor(s) are still working on other projects. If you have the skills, you can make a few hundred bucks on each project by helping carry the load. By the way, it never hurts to build a close partnership with your publisher.

5. *Literary Magazines/Journals* ★★★ – These are literary publications operated by colleges and universities that are also in business. They are easy to spot by their names. *Kenyon Review*, *Seneca Review*, *Sows Ear*, *Image*, *Slipstream*, you get the gist. They all lean one way or another, focusing on poetry, essays, or fiction.

They offer prestige, not money. What that means in laymen's terms is that the material is so intelligent that only a small number of people pay for it, like a thousand or so. But it looks good on your bio, and besides a few free copies for publication, you may rub elbows with a young editor on their way to a big publishing house. Additionally, bibliophiles truly appreciate excellent writing. Take that and the $50 you might squeeze out of them and feel satisfied.

Modern universities do it all online, largely to increase accessibility. You'll find many opportunities for biography-building with literary publication. Things like the Pushcart Prize and Best of the Web anthologies can really open your work to hypertext. Plus, they come in a range of hip editing focuses. Names like Shadowbox, Brierty, or The Grind attract more readers, or "hits," than traditional print. That bodes well for finding readers and editors and positioning yourself for maximum profit.

6. *Online Magazines* ★★★★ – Online magazines have a large appetite for good writing. Most cannot afford an in-house writing staff; they depend on no-overhead freelancers for more content than ever before. The popular ones make money through advertising, but they got popular because a tribe of viewers comes to their site to check out new content. It's a food chain; in order to keep the ad revenue, they must feed content into the fire.

They excel at attracting bloggers, freelancers, and other professionals because they are relatively easy to please. It's called a "low barrier to entry." Queries can be sent and answered in minutes. Researching and fact-checking are faster than ever, thanks to the Internet. Good writing gets published, and reliable contributors get top placement on the home page or bookmarked (Editor's Pick, Top Pick, Daily Special, etc.). The catch is that awesome placement is all you get. Online magazines rarely pay contributors. Writers have to work a system to get a paycheck.

Good online mags are syndicators, which means that other sites visit them daily seeking content they can borrow. The system allows sites to link up and publish an excerpt of the content. You simply find people who want that level of publicity and charge them to write and publish it online.

After establishing yourself on a good site, like *Blog Critics* (ranked 75 by Google) or Huffington Post (ranked 22 by Google), you can solicit work from bands, authors, companies, or whoever. Charge them for a one-shot publicity service. The prices are negotiable. It's all profit, so even if you bid low, there's no loss. Something like this:

- Book review, published on site with 5,000 unique viewers = $100 to $300
- Music review, published on site with 75,000 unique viewers = $250 to $400
- Author Interview, published on site with 225,000 unique viewers = $250 to $500

Another perk to having easy publicity at your fingertips is the ability to barter with clients. You can advertise your services on Fiverr or find work on social media and chat rooms. Being a top contributor to an online magazine also grants you bargaining power when dealing with publishers, since you can publicize your books as well as their entire backlist. Just be assertive, get paid up front, tell them "No money, no publicity."

7. *The Slicks* ★★★★★ – Glossy paper magazines haven't died off yet, amazingly. They have gotten skinny and modernized with online content to keep readers interested. There are 100,000 to 1,000,000 readers for these mega magazines, which makes the advertising effective (most of the profit from magazines comes from selling ad space). *GQ*, *The Atlantic*, *The New Yorker*, and *Rolling Stone* have been around for decades; they evolve and survive and continue to showcase new talent. They pay well. For example, *Playboy* used to pay up to $3,000 for a feature article, sometimes paying expenses to research the material.

Seth Ferranti, the LSD kingpin who lived as a fugitive for years, got his writing career on the map by getting published in big magazines. He interviewed notable criminals and pitched articles to *Crime Magazine*, *Rolling Stone,* and national newspapers. It didn't happen overnight, in fact, Ferranti vents about it, "How'd I do it? I kept pushing it on them."

It's best to develop an inside connection for each venue. During the course of your career, you'll link up with editors and agents who have acquaintances, just ask them who they know and ask for help presenting your work. If that doesn't work, call and pester editors *mano e' mano*. Just have a great angle for your article. It's worth some patience because publication in a major venue will boost your reputation overnight.

✏ Writers Manifesto No. 2 – Original doesn't equal interesting.

RESOURCES
PR Contacts and Research:
- Profnet.com

Chapter Four

"Coming together is the beginning, keeping together is a process, working together is success." – Henry Ford

MENTORS
The right mentor can launch your career into orbit. You can't learn all the tricks of the trade from books and message threads on Goodreads. That's like reading about circumnavigating the globe and then jumping on a 40-foot schooner and trying it. If you survive, it'll be a great story to tell. If a seasoned hand guides you, however, you are much more likely to achieve your goals. What you need is a mentor, someone who understands where you're coming from and where you'd like to go.

YOU ARE NOT AN ISLAND
A few hours chatting with members of an online writer's community may help you find professionals with spare time. Writers like talking about, well, writing. Strike up critical conversations, "Hey, what do you think about this concept?" It can lead to big picture moments. They see your work in general terms, whether the story is interesting, whether it's marketable, and so on. You can also push for some assistance: "Hey, who wants to swap work?" Help each other work out pesky details, such as fixing awkward sentences and clumsy scenes. If you keep working with people, eventually, you'll find help with your career.

Go a step further and look for opportunities to mingle. Each year, there are dozens of weekend writing workshops across the country. These are usually advertised on authornation.com, and in magazines like *Writers Digest* and *The Writer*. Choose a weekend program near you and give it a try. You don't have to submit a story to get in, but you might have to pay a fee.

At these events, authors give seminars every hour. The topics vary. Sometimes agents and editors show up. It's a good way to make contacts and gain experience. Look for gatherings that match your interest, like the Horror Writers Association, the Mystery Writers of America, the Western Writers of America, and the Romance Writers of America conventions. Odds are you'll meet people who will benefit you in the short and long term.

Here are some common personalities:

    1. *The Scout* – Editor Lisa Bain, who over the years has commissioned hundreds of pieces first for *Esquire* and now for *Glamour*, says, "Part of the process when we have an idea is really trying to find somebody whose skills will match it. Is reporting the right thing? Is voice the big thing? I mean, we really have to figure out what it is that we're looking for and how we match it up."

When she had a special piece, her writer of choice was Stephen Fried, someone she'd stayed in touch with ever since meeting at a writing conference. "I needed somebody who was a good reporter – it was something that was going to be heavy on style. I mean, I didn't want it to read like a newspaper. I wanted it to be very vivid and alive."

Is this the voice of a mentor? In a way, yes. Like other editors who are always on the lookout for interesting writers in regional magazines, she had followed Fried's work in *Philadelphia Magazine* and later in *GQ* and had already been developing a professional relationship with him. Sooner or later, the right project would come along. This one seemed a perfect fit.

In conceiving the piece and trying to match it to the ideal writer, editors like Bain are creating the chance for something more lasting. The rest depends on execution. When people like Bain step up with advice and challenges, it is an act of passive mentorship.

    2. *The Tease* – Sometimes the cocktail, otherwise known as "motivation," contains a heavy dose of spite. I'll tell you right now, I got screwed over by my PEN mentor. They never wrote back. I taught myself. When a real writer was finally around, I had already learned the ropes, but there was always new stuff to learn.

In New York City, down Broadway, the grinding midday traffic crawls past the PEN American Center. My anti-mentors. It looks like a regular skyscraper. The same can be said for the office of shaving razor manufacturers and soap companies. What makes PEN stand taller are its principles?

PEN sponsors professional writers from around the world. They operate prestigious literary awards, and they even run a Prison Program, which has distributed over 20,000 copies of a free book, Handbook for Writers in Prison, since 1971. One of which is mine.

I first heard about PEN in 2006 while looking over a resource listing for writers. I have been and always will be grateful for their organization. PEN makes new writers earn placement in their mentoring program by winning one of their contests. I sent in a story and it won, got on the list, and got a publishing credit.

The cash prize and publication in Fortune News immediately updated my writer biography, and I started hitting up publishers with proposals. A mentor would have been helpful, but the award gave me a sense of who I could be as a writer. Now my story is told, I consider us square.

    3. *The Sheppard* – A button-nosed woman with shoulder-length auburn hair looks out of place surrounded by a bunch of convicts. Zoe Mullery didn't seem to mind. She smiled, facing a room of nineteen imprisoned writers and more than sixty free world guests for promotional photos taken by inmates working for the San Quinten News (one of the few prisoner-run newspapers in the world).

Mullery had worked to convince prison officials about the rehabilitative impact of writing, and in turn, the Brothers in Pen meetings have thrived. She spends even more time working in the community to engage writers. It is a real undertaking to win them over, get them cleared to enter the prison, and meet the men.

Guests travel San Quentin's lower yard, past gates and wire-topped fences, a basketball game, and men doing pushups and stretches military style. Deep inside the institution, guests can attend the Brothers in Pen public reading. Fortunately, it's well-organized and only high-quality writing is presented.

Mullery began by quoting Tobias Wolf, who visited the reading years ago, as well as *Huffington Post* correspondent, Ella Turner, and volunteers from NPR. "We are storytelling animals." Wolf wrote a foreword to one of the prisoners' anthologies. "It's how we organize the past and try to make sense of it. To see patterns our action and interaction create, to see how these patterns break or repeat them, even in the stories of others, we can begin to recognize ourselves."

Shepards like Mullery give writers opportunities to meet professionals and improve their craft. The meetings pick up most people's spirits. It allows everyone who attends to bond through shared interests and realize that they aren't alone.

    4. *The Buddy* – Dumb luck can grace us all like it did Dannie Martin, a bank robber, junky heroin addict and longtime federal prisoner who in his own words was "a criminal by any definition." In 1986,

after many years of self-education, he decided to turn his gift of sharing stories with other prisoners and dish it out to local newspapers. He struck gold with the *San Francisco Chronicle*.

The editor, Peter Sussman, was impressed by Martin's perceptive commentary on AIDS in prison, addiction, and the inner workings of America's criminal justice system. Martin wrote 50 eloquent and revealing profiles of prison life, exploring racism, brutality, inadequate health care, harassment, and other bad conditions that caused the sensible white readers to groan, "My God, what are they doing to these men?" That was the beginning of a problem.

The prison administration got tired of all this negative attention and called Martin's writing "criticism." They retaliated by stripping Martin naked and putting him in a solitary cell. The hole: A deep, dark pit where he was allowed to write one letter a week. This could have ended right there. But Sussman and Martin had bonded – first a mentor, then a buddy, now a friend. Sussman took up the fight to free his once-mentee from the hole. And this turned out to be the fight of their lives.

What followed was a high-profile First Amendment lawsuit. As Martin framed the issue, "I committed bank robbery and they put me in prison. That was right. Then I committed journalism, and they put me in the hole, and that was wrong." With Peter Sussman's unyielding support, they got lawyers involved to seek justice. Martin's freedom (within the prison, anyway) came down to settling two constitutional questions:

- Does a convict have a First Amendment right to publicly define himself and his surroundings?
- Does the public have a First Amendment right to hear a prisoner's viewpoint?

The answer was obvious. They won. Martin was released back into the general population, and the two wrote and published a book about the experience. It just goes to show how far some writers are willing to go for each other. While your mentor might not bail you out of a deep, dark hole, they can help you write what sells and get paid. If they're your buddy, they may drink a beer with you and lament about your new rejection slip or congratulate you on your new contract.

     5. *The Conspirator* – So, how did a regular guy end up publishing exclusive interviews with Noam Chomsky, or speaking about journalism at Duke and Dartmouth? I mean, he must be connected, right? The answer is yes. Paul Wright is a major journalist today, but he didn't get his mentor until he'd hit absolute rock bottom.

Flashback. A twenty-year-old military policeman drove around the corner, eyeing the side streets for activity. He wasn't on the job. He was looking to come up on some crack cocaine. One week away from completing his service, Wright was out of money and tried to rob a dealer. The dealer drew his own gun on that honky. Paul Wright shot him first.

Next thing you know, Wright was stripped of his prior expectations of life. He discovered a new daily regimen of being given orders, fed three meals a day, going to the commissary, and it went on and on for 17 years. In the Washington State Reformatory, nothing happens out of thin air. Wright's achievements were fertilized by his own gutter mentor, Ed Mead. Ed was a real character. Mead was a short man who met the definition of a typical convict. He also insisted he was a political prisoner, which was more propaganda. He was involved with organizations that litigated prison conditions, but his heart was into something else. He liked making cheap zines or radical newspapers.

Mead's cell was littered with strips of paper and paste bottles forming parts of radical zines called The Chill Factor, The Red Dragon, and The Abolitionist. Many have since inspired spin-offs among the new generation of Marxists, aka communists. Wright was inspired by Mead's work for several other reasons.

First was that quickening interest, "You mean I can *make* this stuff?" Meads' brand of journalism was going somewhere (not just on top of trash cans), exposing a segment of the population that had ceased to gather public interest with the passing of the Civil Rights movement, women's liberation, and the Vietnam anti-war rallies. The U.S. was entering a state of decompression. Angry people felt left behind.

Wright and Mead bonded because they were veterans. Journalism felt like a crusade, so they took to it like drug addicts on a new high, which it essentially was. In 1990, still adjusting to prison life, he founded *Prison Legal News*. It was typed, photocopied, and all ten pages reached twenty-five potential supporters. The budget was $50.

The Washington State Reformatory administration took notice quickly after Wright published an article about "slave labor" in state factories where prisoners produced materials for political campaigns and packaged Microsoft software. A trip to the hole and censorship ensued, but only drove them to keep on fighting. The two conspirators fought the system from inside until 2003, when Wright was released.

Today, Wright's publishing empire is widely known. *Prison Legal News* passes through 75,000 readers and gets delivered to over 1,000 libraries each month, with critical articles about the Criminal Justice System. Wright likes the hard stuff; he always has several lawsuits going against various correctional facilities. PLN brings in money and operates as an advertising tool. It's become a beacon for sexy photo sellers, pen pal ads, and lawyers fishing for clients. Several of the books advertised in every issue are written by Wright and a host of contributors, like the infamous Mumia Abu-Jamal. Even my books have been advertised in it. No small thanks to Ed Meads' conspiratorial mentorship.

     6. *The Spouse* – The publishing business requires a special set of skills. Its more than just the ability to differentiate from talking about it and getting it done. You need someone who will call your bluff and say, "No. Honey, we can't just spend our retirement on this stuff." Sometimes the best motivator is a real partner: Your spouse.

New York Times bestselling author Kimberla Lawson Roby got started self-publishing her first book, *Behind Closed Doors,* in 1996. After fourteen rejections from literary agents and editors, her mother and husband encouraged Roby to form her own publishing company.

"I read every book I could on the subject, and my background helped me make a business plan and a marketing plan. In 1996, I printed 3,000 copies, and then my husband [I'm not the risk taker in the household] and I had to admit, I think he believed in it more than I did. He said, 'You've got to give your two-week notice, because if you don't give this 100%, I don't think you're going to be successful with it.'"

She's been writing, promoting, and speaking full-time ever since. It might not seem like that ground-shaking of an event, but encouragement comes from many folks. Mentors know us; they may or may not know the details of your interest, but can usually guide your approach because they know you. If you have a spouse like this, trust me, many people are going to be jealous.

     7. *The Counselor* – Earnest Hemingway is known for a masculine writing style, but he didn't arrive there on his own. Since childhood, he'd dreamed of becoming a writer. Things just never came together. He grew up (wrote a little), enlisted and drove an ambulance in World War 1 (kept a diary), and was wounded badly (became a poet). All he had to show for it were night terrors and writing that wasn't very impressive.

Frustrated with his civilian job as a reporter working for the Kansas City Star, Hemingway took an assignment in Paris, where luck found him in the shape of a counselor. Gertrude Stein was a literary sensation and took an interest in him. She reviewed his writing, saying it was filled with "no good description." They worked on it enough that a few months later, while reporting on a peace conference in Switzerland, Hemingway showed his unpublished stories to a fellow journalist, who was so excited about it that Hemingway wrote back to his wife, Hadley, in Paris.

Disaster struck because Hadley packed a trunk full of her husband's original writing (and the carbons) and stuffed it into the luggage compartment on a train headed for Switzerland, but the trunk was stolen. It took a while before Hemingway wrote again. This time, he applied Gertrude Stein's advice more stringently. By then, he'd met other famous writers, one of whom was Ezra Pound. Pound took Earnest under his wing and counseled him with a bold warning that unless he started producing publishable work he'd be stuck as a reporter his whole life.

Apparently, that's what he needed to hear because Hemingway's first novel came fast and furious, and when it arrived in bookstores, it sold out. A Farewell To Arms (1929) was thought to be based on Hemingway's life, but it wasn't. He used his reporter skills and the tips from Stein and Pound to interview veterans, read old newspaper articles, study histories, cite maps, and borrow details he couldn't come up with on his own from whatever travel guide was lying around. This was the formula he used for all his books afterwards, owing vital parts of his process to his counselor.

✎ Writers Manifesto No. 3 – Choose a lot of role models, it gives you more people to steal ideas from.

WHY NOT, GIVE IT A TRY, BECOME A MENTOR
It should be enough of a reason to mentor someone because it feels great when a mentee finally writes and gets paid. If that isn't enough, then think about this: taking an active role expands your wisdom about the business and the craft. We learn more from teaching others. People find themselves in all sorts of weird situations, and blessed ones. Which gives us a pool of wisdom gained from watching other people screw up instead of ourselves.

There are plenty of selfish reasons to do it. Editors don't want to publish you all the time. They want fresh voices and ideas. Groom writers and feed them to editors. I scout talent to keep relevant, and so my next piece will get published, Quid Pro Quo. It's a great deal for everyone.

Becoming a mentor is a form of symbiotic behavior; success raises the status of all parties. It's these efforts that make us better writers, and perhaps better people. It shows everyone who needs to see that you have stood at a fork in the road staring at the signpost long enough. Make the smart decision about who you're going to be; it's sort of inspiring.

The sign reads:

<< Coach Potato << [ ] >> Creator >>

RESOURCES
Writers Organizations:
- Academy of American Poets, poets.org
- American Crime Writers League, acwl.org
- American Independent Writers, americanindependentwriters.org
- American Medical Writers Association, amwa.org
- American Screenwriter Association, atanet.org
- Education Writers Association, cwa.org
- Horror Writers Association, horror.org
- The International Women's Writers Guild, iwwg.com
- Mystery Writers of America, mysterywriters.org
- National Association of Women Writers, naww.org
- National Association of Science Writers, nasw.org
- Organization of Black Screenwriters, obswriter.com
- Outdoor Writers Association of America, owaa.org

- Poetry Society of America, pw.org
- Romance Writers of America, rwanational.org
- Science Fiction and Fantasy Writers of America, sfwa.org
- Society of America Business Editors and Writers, sabew.org
- Society of American Travel Writers, satw.org
- Society of Children's Book Writers and Illustrators, scbwi.org
- Western Writers of America, westernwriters.org

Chapter Five

"If you make life easy for editors, they will give you coverage." – Torri Lousier

STANDARD PRACTICE
Every industry has its standards and procedures, its cautions, and the norm. To become successful, become familiar with this list of "Do's and Don'ts." Authors who sign a lot of contracts are masters of proper formatting. It tightens editors' focus from the first page. Provided that what authors have sent matches their market, good form balances the decision with what really matters: the writing's quality.

The standard for manuscripts is concrete and pretty much universal. It's all about the way text is arranged on the page. There are, of course, misfits out there. So be sure to download submission guidelines from publishers before sending in your work. Correct formatting gives your work additional professionalism. Not a bad reward for fudging some margins and changing fonts.

Entering a contest is particularly sticky, since some contests demand that you place the title of the submission on each page but not the author's name. This is meant to prevent judges' favoritism. Other special formats make less sense, like editors with idiosyncratic demands, such as placing your full contact information in the right-hand corner of a cover letter. Try to charm the tyrants by doing what pleases them.

FIRST CONTACT
It's proper business etiquette to include a cover letter with any submission. A standard business letter format works: full name and contact information, date, addressee, short body with a professional closing like "Sincerely" and a list of any attached documents. Since most editors accept electronic submissions, it's tempting to just message back and forth before dumping your manuscript. You should avoid this sloppy impulse.

There are supplemental documents that pop up in guidelines. Stuff like "query before submission," "include synopsis," or "send proposal and first three chapters of manuscript." These items help editors cross out a mental checklist. The actual documents are not a big challenge to make.

- *Query* – A query is a letter that inquires if editors are interested in an idea for a piece and will greenlight the project. Try to pitch it in one sentence, like so: "They say (noun) is only trying to resolve (complication), can (angle or twist) be that simple?"

- *Synopsis* – A strong synopsis runs about a page long and simply turns your boilerplate blurb into a spoiler alert. That's right, save everyone some time and give away that amazing outcome you have created. If it is nonfiction, detail your unique credentials for the piece.

- *Proposal* – A proposal runs as long as it needs, but should be as short as possible. It mostly details the author's platform, sales history, and any market research about the project. Tip: If the proposal's "voice" matches the manuscript, editors can fall in love before they consider the actual work.

Improper formatting is a sign that you probably didn't get the other parts right either. It's sort of a test. It's like the Venue Contract that bands make promoters sign before agreeing to make an appearance. These agreements ensure necessary technical needs are met; however, the more outrageous parts are what become famous.

Shocking demands include:

- Six helium-filled sex dolls shall be in the band lounge area (AC/DC).
- 1,000 M&Ms, sorted by color, placed in different bowls in the dressing room (Van Halen).
- 10 bottles of Goldschlager shall be chilled in ice in the dressing room (Drake).
- One White Anaconda with snake handler shall be available (Nicki Minaj).

At first appearance, these could be brushed aside as the ego trip of prima donna rock stars and nothing more. The weird parts are actually a test. If a promoter doesn't fulfill each provision in the agreement, the band will turn around and walk away. There are usually dozens of pages with technical requirements for sound, lighting, and stage equipment in these agreements. If the promoter can't supply a bowl of M&Ms, then they probably didn't make sure all the breakers are on. If everything wasn't completed, then the show could be a disaster.

Editors and publishers set strong guidelines to smooth out the submission process. When writers ignore them, they throw a wrench in the machinery, causing delays and frustration. The process is usually the same, but double-check. Most times, you will send a query letter first, then a few messages to hash out details, then the actual manuscript. Though this is the normal procedure, a few special conditions exist. Adjust your strategy accordingly:

- *Agent Only* – Exactly like it sounds. Not from an agent? Not interested.
- *First Time Authors* – Some publishers do, others do not, work with new talent.
- *No Unsolicited* – A pitch must be accepted first, then send a manuscript.
- *Accepts Unsolicited* – They will look it over, along with a large volume of work.

Unless they specify differently, my standard query letters are sent via email. The "subject" of the email needs to grab an editor's attention, so I address it to a specific editor. The following is a sample.

SUBJECT: Attn: Editor, Steve Hussy – Tinsman's Fiction Submission
(When the email is opened, it reads like this:)

Re: Idea from the author of *Life With A Record*

Anthony Tinsman
P.O. Box 26040
Beaumont, Texas 77720
07-28-2019

Steve Hussy
Editor, *The Savage Kick*

Dear Mr. Hussy,

I'm finishing up a new book. It's a how-to, a lot of information targeted at writers, namely interviews and profiles of writers, publishers, and the like. So, I have exclusive stories and other interviews that weren't used in the book just lying around.

Are you interested in true crime stories that go outside the crack-kingpin and hustler-thug templates? I have a couple: a con man, a scrip-writing Doc, a sealed-lip lifer, and a couple of others to top it off.

I think the angle would refresh some readers. Let me know if not, please give me some direction.

Sincerely,

/s/ Anthony Tinsman

I submit most of my pieces on a highly secure email system called TRULINCS. The proper format for each submission is followed, as well as the need for a cover letter. It used to be that all my submissions were done via U.S. mail, so I'm in the habit of attaching or mentioning previous correspondence with editors. It helps to jog their memory about the details of the piece and whatever special conditions we've hashed out.

✏ Writers Manifesto No. 4 – All those submission guidelines were meant for someone.

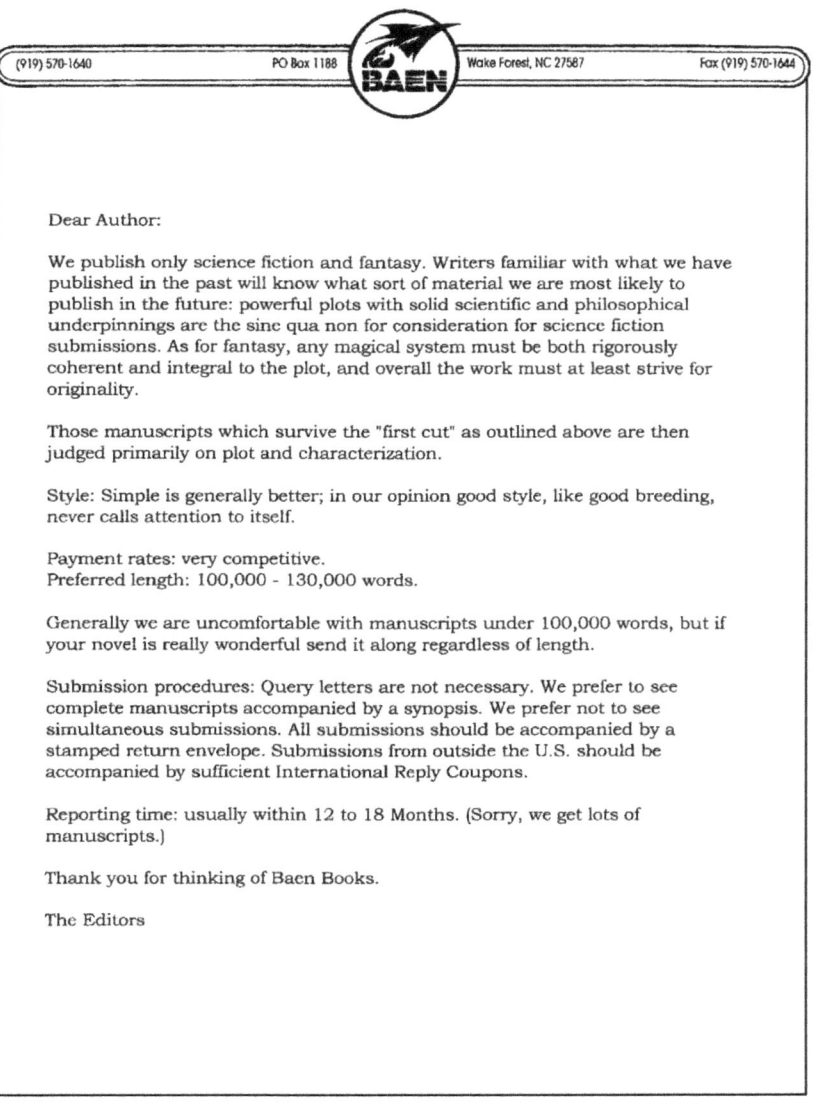

STANDARD LENGTHS

Publishers have set concrete lengths for each type of manuscript. The system is based on the estimated word count. Most people assume manuscripts are measured in pages, but text can be formatted to fill a page with 250 to 800 words per page. The page count is irrelevant.

Here's what editors will expect:

- *Book-length Manuscripts*: Books of 25,000 words minimum, typically 75,000 to 90,000 words, and as long as 130,000.
- *Novella*: A short novel or a long short story, approximately 7,000 to 15,000 words.
- *Short Story, How-To, Vignette, etc.*: A complete short story or a vignette intended to realistically depict an interesting moment in life, 700 to 1,500 words.
- *Serial*: Published in installments, fiction is often broken off at suspenseful spots, whereas articles offer a combination of information and advice on doing something in steps, usually 750 to 1,500 words.
- *Picture Book*: A type of book aimed at preschoolers to eight-year-olds that tells a story using a combination of text and artwork, usually 500 words.
- *Young Adult (YA)*: Offers a high level of interest for readers of low reading level, typically 60,000 to 90,000 words.
- *Graphic Novel*: A story in graphic form, using comic strips, or a heavily illustrated story of 40 pages minimum.
- *Chapbook*: A small booklet, usually paperback, of poetry, ballads, tales, typically 25 to 100 pages.
- *Screenplay*: A manuscript detailing scenes and sequences of a film, typically 90 to 120 pages.

STANDARD FORMATS

1. *Book-length Manuscript*
    - White paper, 8.5" X 11"
    - Numbered pages
    - Title of book and author's name on top of each page.
    - Double-spaced
    - 1" margins
    - 12 Point Type (New Times Roman, or Plain Text)

2. *Poetry*
    - 10 to 80 lines

3. *Screenplays*
    - A script that will sell is expected to be almost, if not exactly, 120 pages. The basic structure includes an introduction listing each of the characters who appear in the script. The story itself is completed in three acts, but it helps to think of a screenplay in four equal parts. Act I, cover pages 1 through 30, the Midpoint consuming 30-60 and 60-90, and Act III taking us to page 120. Why 120 pages? One page usually equals one minute of screen time.

4. *Stage Plays*
    - List of characters
    - List of sets

5. *Electronic (Publisher)*
    - Jpg
    - No email with attachments

6. *Electronic (Printer)*
    - Book Designer

- Adobe Acrobat
- Jpg

TIME MATTERS

Submission periods make or break more good work than anything else. Work must be prepared in advance of special issues, a release, or a contest. Once you know an editor's timeframe, mark your calendar and deliver before it is due. Timeliness applies after a submission as well. Give editors at least 30 days to review it before expecting a response. It is okay to follow up at any time, but progress is made when authors only ask for the same consideration they show. I usually mention a recent (and relevant) publication, and then ask if they have decided to use my work yet. That is the pattern that will not only open the door but keep it open.

SPOTLIGHT ON RECOVERY MAGAZINE
"Giving a Voice to the Therapeutic Community"
9602 GLENWOOD ROAD, #140
BROOKLYN, NEW YORK 11236
Phone: 347-831-9373   E-mail: rgraham_100@msn.com

September 26, 2015

Mr. Anthony Tinsman
P.O. Box 3000
Forest City, AR 72336

Dear Anthony,

I don't recall receiving a contract for While You Were Sleeping, one is enclosed. I also edited your version of While You Were Sleeping and enclosed a copy for you to review.

I received your picture and your bio, thank you very much. I was able to scan your picture for my file and I am returning it to you.

Congratulations on all your accomplishments.

Please sign the contract and return it to me.

Sincerely,

Robin Graham
Robin Graham
Founder/Publisher

Chapter Six

"Professionals sell then write, while amateurs write then try to sell." – Gordon Burgett

IRRESISTIBLE YOU
Being irresistible to editors and clients is a dance of sorts; it takes grace, grit, and teamwork. Editors want to work with writers who are accurate and who submit on or before the deadline. A big picture attitude also helps. Travel writer Stirling Kelso makes a point to remember editors' special interests and forwards related articles and notes to stay in touch. "This keeps you front-of-mind for more assignments." When it is time to sell, Kelso sends an email with "three concise article ideas." That opens the door in most cases.

It's okay if you've finished a manuscript already. Pitch it. Worst case, you can always rewrite it to match an editor's focus. The process can be boiled down to this: work with editors to please their audience. They'll remember you for it.

Master the art of pitching ideas. Take notes with the goal of adding angles to your idea list. Explore angles, lean on them, have fun – you never know where an interesting slant will come from. It is not unusual to match venues and possibly editors at the same time. Adam H. Graham found success with it: "I think it's the originality of my ideas that led to part of my editorial appeal." The experts say that if you pitch 5 to 10 articles for every one published, then you are on target. But your accuracy will improve, especially with practice.

You want to convince them that you are, in fact, the goose that laid the golden egg. Think of each submission as a way to market yourself as a professional. Help out the photo editor. Use tact with overly zealous fact-checkers and become their "go-to" person when another writer fails to deliver. Start by examining your work. Does this Travel Quiz fit this magazine? Is this essay too topical for that website? To dance well, your work must be at its strongest, as well as your sense of match-making.

PROCESS OF ACCEPTANCE
Editors' tastes are well defined by their previous publications; it pays to track that. Companies change, tastes evolve, and contacts get promoted. Publishing is as fluid a lifestyle as anything else. It's important to keep up with changes (even after you sign a contract) to see what opportunities have opened up or possibly closed.

Consider the submission process from an editor's perspective. Imagine 1,000 random manuscripts, emails, and letters hitting your desk each year. They consist of bills, proposals, outlines, hate mail, and sample chapters from writers who want you to publish their rough draft. You judge them by a quick scan. Most meet their end in the same ritual:

- Pull staples and paper clips.
- Feed into the shredder.
- Print, sign, and mail the rejection letter.

When a well-pitched submission finally grabs an editor hard enough to spill their coffee and the word "eureka!" to involuntarily come out of their mouth, then they know what to do – add it to an equally impressive stack of people who can do the job. Tailored submissions that fit an editor's interests are the best way for authors to get on top of the pile.

Most writers refer to *Writers Market*, an annual publishers' directory and website, which helps distinguish venues and their pursuits, but that shouldn't be your only source. Directories can give you an address and some basic information about publishers, but don't overlook the best way to get to know and talk to other authors. They are busy doing the same thing you are. Share information and add newcomers you discover to your contacts.

Once you get the swing of categorizing all the confusing information publishers dump about themselves, it gets easier. Cut right to the meat, like how many books did they publish last year? As the questions keep going, clarify your metrics. How is my idea unique, or how does it contribute to their catalog? Do I understand their audience? We all want affirmative answers, but to make a match, authors need to weigh all the facts.

IT TAKES TWO TO TANGO
A professional letter just explaining who you are, an author open to opportunities, can get you what you ask for. As I've discussed elsewhere, you can even introduce new writers if they are a good fit, while letting a company know that you're also interested. Before drafting your letter, it's good to get the facts and familiarize yourself with their catalog (backlist). Publishing is a simple business, don't pester with irrelevant or obvious questions, but if you have specific ones that aren't clear in their materials, don't be afraid to ask.

Since I've met most of my publishers with a letter, I usually describe my circumstances, and the impossibility of going online and simply downloading their guidelines (I'm in prison and all that). I ask them to mail me a copy, usually with a SASE enclosed. It's a practical way to test the waters, because if they simply respond "Go to our website," I know they'll be hard to reach in the future. However, if I receive a copy and maybe a note or letter, then I know there is potential to make a good deal, at least we begin with an understanding of my strengths and weaknesses as an author.

It helps to plan writing goals throughout the year, prioritizing which outfits should be targeted first, second, and third. Usually, I won't touch a manuscript until I've identified three or four companies. For example, a Science Fiction short story could be entered in a contest first. If it doesn't place, it can be submitted to magazines, and the success of all that will determine if it would be worthwhile to give it a book-length treatment and pitch to publishers. Through each stage of the process, I'm cross-referencing deadlines and guidelines, ensuring that I can take advantage of each opportunity while doing only as much work as necessary.

This all gets plugged into my planner, and work orders are arranged. Regardless of the approach, maintaining publisher information gives authors a tool when they get ideas. It's easy to search through it, counting the actual publishers who'll be genuinely interested. If there aren't many, you'll have to think strategically. The good news is that you only need one company to become interested in your idea.

The longer you gather information, the more confidence you'll gain as a writer, which takes you a notch closer to reaching the goals you've set. This takes a lot of stress out of finding the right publisher for the next piece you write. Most exciting of all, as your career morphs and grows, you'll have a list of helping hands in the publishing community who can help break open doors to venues you don't even know exist.

DON'T MAKE A BAD IMPRESSION!
Regardless of whether you want the attention of an editor, agent, or client, you'll have to get through the initial screening. Then you'll have your opportunity to impress. The authors I know get it done because they treat another person's time as respectfully as their own.

When I review submissions, either as an editor or consultant, I'm blown away by the range of bad impressions good writers can make. I've reduced the worst offenders into five categories. It doesn't matter if their submission made it through to the initial culling; these personalities end up in the rejection pile.

1. *Panhandlers* – Haven't used any recognizable format in their letters or manuscripts, yet they expect you to hook them up regardless of the submission process. Conveys:

- Sloppiness
- Inconsideration
- Unaccountability

2. *Crumb Chasers* – Beg for a deal, but don't understand what standard provisions are. Plus, they act as if publishing their book is privileged and you'll owe them a favor.
Conveys:

- Lack of Respect
- Selfishness
- Confusion

3. *Damn Fools* – They think they're the best writer in history, but they've never been published. Lacking in depth and content, they demonstrate a complete misunderstanding of markets.
Conveys:

- Poor Temperament
- Unreasonableness
- Arrogance

4. *Schemers* – The creativity devoted to convincing you of their brilliant idea only works if you do all the work for them. If left to them, nothing would ever materialize.
Conveys:

- Untrustworthiness
- Laziness
- Unreliability

5. *Heartbreakers* – Their agent, editor, or book doctor is determined that you look at their stuff, and their talent is obvious. They are gifted. This leads you to ask, "How are we going to promote you?" They expect you to do all the work.
Conveys:

- Distraction
- Awkwardness
- Lack of Commitment

Often, there isn't a shortcut for hard lessons; the only way past is through. "One should learn from rejection, or at least decide whether there is something to learn from each one." Celia Blue Johnson found that career-changing moves were often small things that didn't seem all that important at the time. Especially rejections, but she adapted. "Once I reevaluated my approach based on negative and positive responses I received, I found success as a writer."

Cloudbank
PO Box 610
Corvallis, Oregon 97339
www.cloudbankbooks.com

Dear Contributor,

Thank you for your interest in *Cloudbank*. We've considered your work carefully, but it does not meet our needs at this time. Please check our website for information about our next issue, as well as submission information for future issues and future contests.

If you'd like to subscribe or purchase a copy of the current issue, please use the coupon below.

The Editors

We all have off days. Stuff happens, but overall, you've got to be a team player. If you're better in person, institute a video chat. Be fun and professional when you communicate. If need be, take a day off. It's better to appear busy than to stick your foot in your mouth. Or stick to using the U.S. mail for a steady stream of correspondence through sending cards, business letters, and important documents, frequently. It's worth a little extra effort because a good working persona will carry you through deals that'll make other writers jealous.

WIN SOME, LOSE SOME
When you don't get stellar results, it's important to take responsibility. Someone trusted you and took a spill. Use innovative techniques like deprecating humor, owning past mistakes (as lessons learned), and being open to suggestions. These techniques help you later on to build a reputation as a professional.

Be fair with clients and editors. Keep them in the loop when opportunities arrive. Holler at them, "Hey, I'm working with an editor for a good site; I'll mention you in an industry profile." Giving your relationships value will always be rewarded. One day, some of your contacts may be your friends. It's okay if every project doesn't always pay out; it's your approach that makes you irresistible.

One novel in particular has terrorized my career. I've submitted it to dozens of publishers: in packets with a query letter, in packets with a business plan and resume, in packets containing a few chapters, and others with the full manuscript. Amazingly, I've had three publishing agreements, and the book has yet to be published. Each company either went out of business or was sold.

The person I ghostwrote the novel for doesn't want to self-publish, even though he can muster 150,000 followers on social media. I was stuck, expected to shop around the book for infinity. After a heap of rejections and three good deals gone sour, it was my belief that he'd gotten his money's worth. I told him if he wanted to self-publish, we could move forward with that; otherwise, I was done. He opted to leave it in my hands, hoping that I'd cross paths with a niche publisher later down the road. Either way, I was off the hook, and I still have a good relationship with my client.

Roll with the punches. Not everything is going to go your way. Of course, you can't predict when a great deal is going to fall into your lap either. When I pitched the idea for *Life With A Record,* the editor said, "No." They had had trouble selling self-help books. We talked about a completely different book, and I started researching for that instead. Two weeks later, the editor hits me back:

> "Disappointment!"
>
> "What happened?"
>
> "An online advertiser called Access Package declined to represent our books."
>
> "Ouch."
>
> "They said they'd look at a self-help book if we had one. Lol. Maybe you should write it?"

The self-help book was just an outline when I pitched it. It's no different than pitching a blog, really. You can either do it or you can't. That book came together fast, in eight months it was on Amazon with preorders coming in – proof that the best thing for you to do, rain or shine, is to keep dancing.

✎ Writers Manifesto No. 5 – Deliver your manuscript like a dozen roses, smile a lot, be funny, and get down to business.

Chapter Seven

"Nothing works, and nobody cares." – Woody Allen

GET YOUR MONEY
When you finish a job, there are three options for actual payment: pre-publication, post-publication, or a royalty on a set schedule. The art of looking for work is the bread and butter of any successful writing career. Jobs do occasionally land in your lap. But work usually comes because you were out there pushing your services. Call it freelancing if you have to, professionals call it their business. The goal is to build a reputation as a hustler, a writer unbound by the restraints of procrastination or vanity. Once people know they can rely on you, they'll go out of their way to have you write for them.

Jobs are easy to find; they are advertised everywhere. If you're just getting started, there are opportunities with organizations like Patch.com. They have over 860 "hyper local" affiliates who hire bloggers to report on local news like city council meetings. It pays $50 to $100 per gig. Or you can fish around online, where magazines have been reborn as pixels representing over 100 consumer and trade markets.

Just contact the editors and pitch your services. Eventually, one will offer you a paying assignment. If not, they will take your work for free. Then it's up to you to locate a client who wants publicity in that market and charge them a fee. It's pure simplicity, but in real life, you may have to follow up to get paid for the work you do.

WRITE MAD, MAIL CALM
My friend, John Lee Brook, a freelance professional and best-selling author, writes to me ranting about his experiences. All his messages read like this: "I have to email the people that owe me money for writing things for them." In between wishing me well, getting over a bug (he tells me to take lots of Vitamin C), he just complains and gripes about not getting paid fast enough. Recently, he griped about his payment for an article in the cultural section of the L.A. Weekly. His full rant is educational, examine it:

"I don't know why it's so hard for people to pay the writer! It's like pulling teeth with most people. Only a few pay promptly. One guy even pays ahead. The jerk at *Downtown L.A. Weekly* owes me a measly $80 and has excuse after excuse. They were converting their payment system. Then they had to do their taxes. Then he asked me for my PayPal, so he could pay me that way. Of course, no money ever arrived. I now suspect they are broke. Either that or he's just a jerk."

All this over a measly $80. The reason I bring this up is to illustrate a very important point about freelancing. Writing isn't an employee/employer relationship. If you're working for McDonald's and the manager "forgets" to pay you for a month, then you have grounds for a lawsuit. Writers are more like contractors whose options are limited to "lien" or "repossession." If an editor (whom you've already signed a deal with) drags their feet on a payment for months, who are you going to call?

You can't just let people owe you. That $80 might cover the light bill. More likely, the utilities are covered, but it would sure buy some nice cigars. Don't waste your time threatening lawsuits; both of you know that it isn't worth the $300 filing fee to put a civil claim on the docket sheet at your local courthouse. Instead, pester, needle, and prod (as kindly as three times a week allows) until it's clear to them that it's easier to pay you to get you off their back.

THE ART OF PLAYING DIRTY

I sold a story to a magazine called *Spotlight on Recovery*; it was only worth $44.45, but I wanted it. I signed the final proof copy and waited for publication (payment upon). I wrote the editor and asked how things were going. They sent me a copy of the magazine; I waited some more. I wrote another letter asking about the money. I waited some more.

After 5 months, I was fed up. I dumped my last and first correspondence on my counselor's desk, and she looked at it. "What do you want me to do?" she asked. I smiled. I wanted to make a "free" phone call to the editor. The thing was, my counselor would have to identify herself as a Department of Justice employee, allowing an inmate to make an unmonitored call.

The words prison and "unmonitored" have a rattling effect on most people. It had the desired effect. With a copy of my contract in hand, the editor agreed that payment was overdue. "We're a small operation; I can't afford to pay you more." The editor told me, a little jarred. I could have guilted her into giving me more, but I only wanted my $44.45. The cash arrived a week later, via Western Union. You should see how much trouble I've unleashed to get $1,000. It's all a part of the hustle.

As a writer, you'd better stand up and take your own side and get what is rightly yours. After an editor sees that, not always, but usually, you'll have an excellent relationship. That's how it went with Spotlight on Recovery and pretty much every magazine I've been published in after.

If publishers don't pay up front, it can be difficult to get paid at all. Save yourself a lot of trouble and keep track of your agreements and deadlines for payment. Organize your daily planner so a portion of each day can be dedicated to running down people who owe you. Stay ahead of deadlines by sending friendly reminders. If you get boned, hopefully your piece is online floating around in cyberspace. There's value in that. You can use it to moonlight for clients or hunt down new assignments and demand payment up front for another piece.

What other dirty tricks might get you paid? When editors burn you, the cat isn't out of the bag. Give them a bold ultimatum. Pay up or you'll troll them, drag their name through the mud by writing a series of watchdog articles focusing on their sketchy business practices. What if they don't pay even then? Should you follow through with the threat? Probably not.

Consider what your reputation should be. It's best to avoid smearing clients because it will weigh on the minds of future clients. If they feel you might lash out at them, they will just avoid you. Sometimes you have to eat the loss, pester, and be creative about getting a check, and move your career forward by seeking out a more reputable clientele. If things are truly lost, don't let it stall progress. Write another piece and roll the dice. You'll get paid more often than not.

✎ Writers Manifesto No. 6 – The only form of harassment not recognized in a court of law is that of a writer demanding payment.

Write & Get Paid

05-19-09

Dear Mr Tinsman,

Our apologies for the delay in mailing out your award check. Our accounting department has been experiencing delays. We are writing to assure you that the requests are there and the check will be mailed promptly as soon as it is printed.

Separately our Mentorship Coordinator is pairing winners with Mentors, and will be in touch shortly.

Thank you for your patience,
PEN Prison Writing Program

PART 2

THE CRAFT

Chapter Eight

"You can't connect the dots looking forward, you can only connect them looking backwards." – Steve Jobs

KICK START THE CREATIVE PROCESS

Writers have honed their craft the same way since before Homer penned the Odyssey: write daily, read a lot, and get organized. To get the work across the finish line, there is a definite process. You must take notes and then outline everything. Incorporate a strong plot. Then write a quick rough draft and ruthlessly revise each manuscript until it sings a tune that pleases readers. The first step is coming up with the guts of a manuscript.

NURSE YOUR IDEAS TO GOOD HEALTH

One day, you have a daydream, or you open the newspaper, and something gives you an idea … a tenth of an idea, really … a hundredth of one. You think about it while you take a shower, walk the dog, or get stuck in traffic. A few additions occur to you. Day by day, you continue the process, going about your routine while slowly developing your idea. In search of the next piece of the puzzle, aspiring writers ask what their idea is supposed to be – a book, an article, or a poem?

This is how it works for everyone. Sometimes it leads to great stories. It happened in 1990 while a young English teacher traveled on a train from Manchester to London. She was living on welfare, recovering from a divorce, and trying to raise her daughter Jessica. The idea? It was a big what-if: "What if trains took us to magical places?" That young teacher was J. K. Rowling. And the magical place turned out to be a wizarding school named Hogwarts. But not all at once.

When you get the initial idea, you nurse it with lots of questions. What's the setting? What research do I need? You talk about the project with a friend, a spouse, or a child. The conversations help to focus on what you want to do and lead you toward the turning points in the story. Often, you're not even aware that you're thinking about it; your subconscious is doing the work. J.K. Rowling developed Harry Potter by testing during story time, tucking her daughter in for the night. Some ideas caught, others didn't, and over time, the right tone emerged.

At some point, everything coalesces and fits together like a jigsaw puzzle. Then it's time to make an outline. Try to be objective about it. Try to figure out which format will sell best. Like, should your idea be a screenplay or a series of essays or a video game. Then get to work.

Your idea may not become a mega-bestselling franchise like the one J. K. Rowling created. It may not produce the fastest-selling book in history (*Harry Potter and the Goblet of Fire*). It may not employ a small village of filmmakers for the better part of a decade and make you the 13th wealthiest woman in England, ahead of Queen Elizabeth. But your idea can become something valuable, get published, and get you paid.

MEAT AND POTATOES

The first priority is to anchor your ideas by writing them down. No other concerns are relevant until that happens. Kregg P.J. Jorgensen, a Vietnam Special Forces veteran, was a columnist for *Behind the Lines* and interviewed other vets for stories of supernatural occurrences and humor. While he checked that each vet had actually served, some of the vets wanted their identities to be kept secret. Jorgenson said, "It wasn't a problem. My notebook is full of pages of chicken scratch, which is my handwriting. Even I sometimes need to go over it a few times before I finally recognize what it said. Secrets were really secret."

Concepts for dialogue or plot might get your heart racing when they pop into your head, but if you don't jot them down, the nuance becomes murky. Take notes and review them, do your best to separate your ideas into two groups: fiction (big lies) or nonfiction (factual). Once you make the distinction, you can guide the rest of the creative process so that it matches the best market.

FICTION

Perhaps you want to write novels and short stories. Fiction is a competitive market because it's entertainment. Music, movies, games, and other spectacles vie for consumers' attention and money. To keep up, the lines between fact and fiction have blurred. Genre has turned into 'faction', the trend began with so-called nonfiction novels by Truman Capote and Norman Mailer, and ended up with scripted reality shows like MTV's *Jersey Shore* and YouTube's *Lonely Girl 15*.

The Five Hallmarks of Fiction:

1. It has a plot incorporating archetypical themes.
2. Fiction is entertainment, so it should strive to fascinate readers.
3. Because of the purpose of escapism, it is released from the restraints of reality.
4. It contains a sense of deep human understanding.
5. Fiction shows serious attention to the craft of writing.

Where does fiction begin? Consider your mind. No matter how clear-cut or simple the events we're trying to relate, the minute we decide to write, we embellish. We misremember, reimagine actual events, giving them a different emphasis, a dramatic flair. The subconscious is always transporting us from boring real-life situations into pleasurable fantasies ... sometimes nightmares.

Let's emphasize the word "disguised." Fictional stories don't explicitly address your psychological concerns. They can be metaphors or daydreams. Some stories insist on being told; the imagination won't rest until the images and characters that linger there are brought into the light.

Out of all the possibilities, Stephen King chose horror, and he took over the genre. His breakout hit, "Carrie," arrived when the shockwaves of Vietnam, feminism, and the sexual revolution of the 1960s reverberated throughout society. A male author exploring the psyche (and menstruation) of a high school girl was as controversial and edgy as you could get. Did King plan it that way? No. He overheard a high school janitor talking about installing tampon dispensers in the girls' bathroom, and the story just grew in his mind. With his twists, the story became a statement about bullying, religious repression, and being a little different.

A critic once asked Stephen King why he writes horror. King's response was, "What makes you think I have a choice?" In his book *On Writing*, King describes the brutal poverty of his childhood and the twelve miles he hitchhiked each Saturday to a movie theater that specialized in horror movies. It was a distraction from being broke all the time. The horror novels, stories, and comic books he compulsively read fulfilled the same function. Made-up horror helped lift some of the burden. Why would he write some other kind of stories when he could relive the relief he'd gotten as a boy? Go with what moves you.

Here are the major fiction genres:

- Erotica
- Fantasy
- Horror
- Humor
- Literary
- Romance
- Science fiction
- Thriller

Be fiercely loyal to the genre you choose. Focus on the process (putting words on the page) and craft (writing techniques), and maybe you'll make readers feel what you do. People read fiction to escape reality. They may be coping with disaster: a divorce, a fire, a flood, a crippling car accident, a loved one's death, the loss of a job, or maybe just boredom. Life is boring – diets, raising kids, walking pets, changing oil, watching TV, peeing – boring, boring, boring. Your fiction must deliver the excitement they crave.

NON-FICTION

Nonfiction is defined not by what it is but by what it is not. It is not fiction. Duh! It is also not poetry, or a libretto, or a lap dance. It's like defining classical music as non-jazz. Or sculpture as non-painting. Readers have a clearer picture of the purpose of nonfiction: informational instruction. Factual writing comprises 90 percent of all publications. It sells as how-to, do-it-yourself, self-help, history, travel, cookbook, and on and on. Developing your own nonfiction ideas is a matter of logically organizing the facts about the subject and writing a narrative with your distinct style.

The Five Hallmarks of Non-Fiction

1. It has a subject and a deeper subject.
2. Because of the duality of the subject, nonfiction is released from the usual journalistic requirement of timeliness.
3. Creative nonfiction is narrative, it always tells a good story.
4. It contains a sense of reflection on the part of the author.
5. Nonfiction shows serious attention to the craft of writing.

The word nonfiction tells you all you need to know. Not fiction. "I consider myself a storyteller," said Bob Reiss, author of several novels and two books of nonfiction and a correspondent for *Outside* magazine. "And I distinguish between stories I make up and stories I find out." Creative nonfiction is the stories you find out, captured with a clear eye and alert imagination, filtered through a mind passionate to know and tell.

Good nonfiction can change lives, whether it's a step-by-step tutorial about building a patio or the discovery of an ancient city. *The Iliad*, by Homer, was long considered to be "only" myth. Until one reader, Henrich Schliemann, used it as a nonfiction document to discover the actual remains of Troy. It was kind of a big deal. Troy is a real place, after all, even if it was fought over by mythical gods and goddesses. Poetry and history together – creative nonfiction.

Nonfiction satisfies a hunger for the "real" and our need to make sense, make order, out of chaos. Reality provides us plenty to write about (politics, hobbies, philosophy, etc.). When you write nonfiction, you are appealing to the most diverse writing market there is. You'll be able to locate editors and readers for almost any subject you write about.

GATHER PIECES OF THE PUZZLE

The common advice about writing is, "Write what you know." Many writers get stuck following the advice. Jack London wrote about his adventures in Alaska. Steinbeck traveled with the Depression-ravaged

"Okies" as they left their dust-bowl homes and struggled across the country toward California and what they hoped would be the promised land. Tucker Max relived his college whoredom.

If you have a dramatic profession, like a paramedic or a deep-sea explorer, by all means write about what you know. That's what forensic anthropologist Kathy Reichs did when she wrote the *Bones* series. So did author Patricia Cornwell, who once had a clerical job in a medical examiner's office.

The problem with "write what you know" is that for most of us, life seems ordinary. How are you supposed to write something interesting if you have an ordinary life? Students consider this advice and lament, "I don't have any ideas." Then it turns into "I don't have anything to write about!" and "Nothing interesting has ever happened to me." Yeah, well, maybe it's time to forget what you know about.

Write with your emotional knowledge, if not actual experience. There is tremendous power in using your perspective. Roger Nygaard affirms that the biggest cliché, write what you know, actually means write what you feel. He said, "I never got a job as a CIA agent, never went into the Marines, never became a fireman or a cop, didn't go on the road and get arrested or sell cars. Your own life is often the best place to start." However, for this to work, you must be honest and dig deep. It's all about telling your truth, whether you're writing about your life growing up in a small town in the Midwest, or saving the world from an alien attack. Readers will respond to the truth. They'll get caught up in it.

There are a couple of methods I use to kick-start the creative process. With fiction, it's as simple as modifying a set of playing cards. Divide the cards into four or more equal piles. Label the backside in each group to distinguish a category, like "Relationships" or "Hobbies." Think of a variety of nouns that symbolize alternatives, then write one per face side. Shuffle the piles separately and pick a card from each. The random details won't always go together, but this method provides a lot of inspiration.

Categories can include some of these.

- Occupation – Doctor, taxicab driver, waitress, engineer, soldier, etc.
- Physical trait – big teeth, tall, overweight, prosthetic limb, etc.
- Prop – locket on a broken chain, studded leather collar, salt and pepper shakers, etc.
- Story point – a mysterious stranger arrives, they get fired, a long-lost friend calls, etc.

With non-fiction, I use a method that focuses on theme and attribution. The idea is that themes like fashion, design, travel, marketing, ask-a-pro, ethics, tech, and many others give you a general direction, while attributions like comparison, tips sheet, and interview nail down the exact approach. These can be mixed and matched for a nearly endless supply of ideas. Once you have the framework, it's just a matter of filling in the blanks and coming up with an angle.

Here are three solutions.

1. *Live It Then Tell It* – Journalism is built upon reporting the facts. But by incorporating a personal perspective into the narrative, it gains depth, as well as giving you a vector to fill in the word count. That's how Hunter S. Thompson pioneered Gonzo Journalism. It revealed his interior life, becoming as much a part of the story as the subject Thompson was covering. Apparently, if you do enough drugs, break enough laws, and thumb your nose at the status quo, you can share lucid adventures. He said:

"The job of a writer, it seems to me, is to focus very finely on a thing, a place, a person, act, phenomenon, and then, when the focus is right, to understand and then render the subject of that focus in such a way that it suddenly appears in context, the readers context, regardless of who the reader happens to be, or where."

In James W. Hall's *Hit List*, an examination of the biggest hits of the 20th century, Hall reveals that readers love an insight into another reality. Authors who live it then tell it can introduce fascinating details into their work. Kathryn Stockett's *The Help* gives us that by pulling back the curtain on the world of black maids in the 1960s. Garth Stein's *The Art of Racing in the Rain* (156 weeks on the *New York Times* bestseller list) gives us Formula One racing. It's easy to deliver because authors can access their insight at any time.

When you live it, then tell it, there is no wrong approach. Populated by elegant brownstone mansions and fashionable carriages parading down Fifth Avenue, Edith Wharton's books were also full of mundane events that readers could relate to. She provided eyewitness accounts of what it was like in part of Manhattan's repressive, secretive high society. But Wharton pulled from her own struggles, like divorcing her hot-mess husband and moving to France. By the way, this all took place in the last third of the 1800s. But Wharton is still a mainstay in Ballentine's *The Classics* collection.

2. *Research Your Way to Become an "Expert"* – Writers don't have to be experts in a particular field to write about it. If they had to be, we'd have no novels, ever. Consider this: *New York Times* bestseller James Patterson writes fast-paced detective novels, yet he is not a detective. If he wrote a nonfiction book about detectives, he would probably rely on actual facts, interviews, and ride along with the boys in blue. But he would still not be a detective.

Elizabeth Sims, nonfiction guru and author of crime and mystery series, says, "In all genres, audiences love to hear stories about the research you did for your book." Readers who hear how it will change their life, or make them think in a new way, or teach them something astonishing are more likely to spend their hard-earned money on a book. Sims holds rooms spellbound at bookstores and conventions by revealing a few things about her process. One time, "I relayed how my friend, a surgeon, educated me in how it feels and sounds to set a broken bone."

Facts are important, in fiction and nonfiction. Research is vital to making a credible book. But you don't have to travel to Indonesia and China gathering materials for your prose like Li-Yong Lee (whose father's flight as a political prisoner drew their family across Hong Kong, Macao, Japan, and America). The masters used maps, interviews, and imagination to paint pictures of places they had never seen. It's that easy, you can do it too.

     3. *Interview People for Details* – When I needed details for a city in my PEN/Fielding Dawson prize-winning short story, A Selfish Discovery, I asked people, at random, where they were from. I went cell to cell, hit them up in the chow line, and blended in with strangers on the yard (a scary prospect for some). At first, I just paid attention to each person's ability to clearly describe their city. Did anything stick out? Could a detail be used to demonstrate something about my character? Were they passionate about the city?

Eventually, I found a person with the right chemistry, a 40-something reprobate with long red hair, a gap in his teeth, and demonic tattoos. Jack Flash had lived in Colorado and knew all sorts of history about the place. From hang gliding on the updrafts at a peak in the mountains in Golden, to the college kid hangouts and the names of strains of cannabis like "Northern Lights" (though that had nothing to do with my story).

I took notes about the way the Rockies appeared to hover on the horizon as you drive into Golden. I led with questions. "I bet it was beautiful the first time you saw that." I pushed for details about the restaurants and bookstores around a college where my story took place. Piece by piece, I got way more facts than I needed. Only someone who'd lived there would know a certain rock formation was called the Devil's Thumb, right? It looks like a giant thumb hitching for a ride. I used all of it in the story. These details made my story come to life. It works the same for everything you'll write.

All sorts of sources are available. Go! Crawl through library stacks. Carry out midnight raids on the internet when the tourists have all pulled off the information superhighway. Without delay! Track down fascinating people and interview them until they say something extraordinary. Fill up some notebooks, date and label them. Stock your memory with images, sounds, smells, recollections of places, and people's faces and odd remarks made in passing. Now! Go wherever the story leads as often as you need to fill in the pieces of the puzzle.

✎ Writers Manifesto No. 7 – Quickening interest is nature's way of telling you to take more notes.

Chapter Nine

"There are three rules to successful writing: (1) have something to say, (2) know how to say it, and (3) be able to sell it." – David Hellyer

OUTLINE

Agatha Christie's winding mysteries gave readers an important clue at the beginning. Be impressed, but there is no supernatural genius involved. Instead, it's a whole lot of craft. First comes a note pile, then it's arranged into elaborate outlines for each story. Outlines are essential to keep you on track. A good outline has numerous benefits. It can resuscitate stalled writing, unify loose scenes, and give you a clear estimate of an idea's potential.

Francine Pascal noticed that her idea was huge. It started when her creative energy was sparked by a casual comment from a friend, "Why no soap operas for teenagers?" In no time, she had a story about twins Jessica and Elizabeth. "I sat down and wrote a (character) bible and the first 12 stories. It went quickly because it was such a fertile idea," Pascal said. She called it *Sweet Valley High*.

Pascal then oversaw a team of ghostwriters who worked off the detailed outlines she created. "The story outlines weren't chapter by chapter, more like acts: you get from here to here, then you get from here to here." Pascal's beloved series ran for 20 years and sold 150 million copies worldwide. By the end, her plots featured everything from forbidden love to evil doppelgängers. What made it work on a fundamental level was the author's ability to make an outline.

TOO COLD

The purpose of an outline is to test the cohesion between the plot (or subject) and the major scenes. A good reason to keep it loose is that outlining can cause you to lose a sense of urgency to tell the story. But this can be taken too far. Ernest Hemingway insisted that a writer shouldn't talk about a story before it was written. He felt that too many good ideas ended up in the air rather than on the page, and worse, that the emotional release of talking about a story took away the pressure of needing to write it.

Too skimpy an outline, however, can lead to difficulty. Lisa Jewell, author of 16 novels with a combined 2 million sales, doesn't outline at all. "I'd rather be freewheeling," she says. That explains why she thought her first novel was going to be a dark psychological thriller but found herself going much lighter. In fact, 15 of her books are "chick lit." Her refusal to outline makes projects tough to finish, but Jewell powers through. "I go in with the best intentions," she said. "But the minute I start putting plans in place, I feel trapped."

TOO HOT

There are a variety of outlining techniques to chart the major parts of every manuscript. Blogs or books it doesn't matter. Having a map for the introduction, body, and conclusion is essential, especially when you have deadlines. The trick is learning what amount of detail works best for your project.

A writer I know, Jordan Davidson, made these really detailed outlines for his novels. They had subcategories with large and small caps, letters, and roman numerals. It resembled a corporate report.

The following is a piece of Davidson's outline:

Chapter One

A. Khaled is warned that his bodyguard is actually a cloned cyborg working for the Indonesian government.
    a. He stalks her at night, observing her "recharge" in her quarters, and sees:
        i. that her eyes flutter beneath the eyelids
        ii. that she stands ramrod straight
        iii. that she remains in uniform.
    b. She admits nothing the next day when he confronts her.
        i. She tells him what matters is the rebellion he is supposed to be leading.
    c. She contacts her Indonesian agency and prepares a shipment of APCs (Armored Personnel Carriers).
        i. They will need them to raid the Capitol.
    d. Khaled watches her leave, knowing he is her slave and that he loves her.

With his signature smugness, Davidson asked me, "Well, Tinsman, are you jealous?" I told him these sorts of outlines are soul-grinding. Writers need room for spontaneity. He was insulted at first, but came around to press me for what I thought made a "good" outline.

"Think of yours like a movie, they'd play an orchestra in the background."

"What's wrong with that?"

"Boring."

"And why is yours any different?"

"My rule is – It's got to have a rock n' roll soundtrack."

Outlines should excite you. Keep your outline as simple as it can be and still do its job. Of all the methods to choose from, it's a Goldilocks decision. Two tightly detailed and it's restrictive; too loose and it's almost useless. When they are just right, outlines fill in the gaps in your manuscript and keep the momentum going once you start writing.

JUST RIGHT
"The most important thing is brainstorming. Brainstorming is simply sitting down with a large piece of blank paper and a pencil," says bestselling author John Lee Brook. "In the center of the blank paper, write the topic or the title of the book." When Brook does this, he circles the word, then writes everything he wants to include in the book, using either a phrase or a single word. This gives him a quick outline or a sequence of topics.

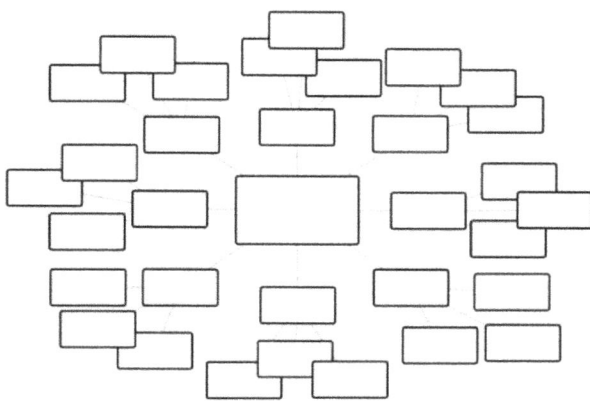

The next step is to make a preliminary Table of Contents (TOC). It charts the beginning, middle, and end, broken up into ten or twelve chapters. This can change. It definitely will move around as you write the book. But right now, you just need to arrange the most important pieces.

Table of Contents

INTRODUCTION

PART 1 GET STARTED
1. Perfection is the Enemy
2. Plan Ahead
3. Opportunity for Authors
4. Mentors
5. Standard Practice
6. Irresistible You
7. Get Your Money

PART 2 THE CRAFT
8. Kick Start the Creative Process
9. Outline
10. Revise
11. Edit

PART 3 THE BUSINESS
12. Understand What Sells and For How Much
13. Exploit Markets
14. Utilize the Mercenary Marketplace
15. Follow the Markets

PART 4 STYLE
16. Read with Purpose
17. Write Better
18. Write Faster

PART 5 HUSTLE
19. Basic Platform
20. Penetrate Your Market
21. Brand Yourself
22. Publicity

PART 6 BOOKS
23. Going with a Publisher
24. Independent Publishing
25. Exploit Subsidy Rights

PART 7 BOOK SELLING
26. Pro Tools
27. Book Reviews
28. Content Sharing

PART 8 THE LAW
29. Get it in Writing
30. Consequences of Free Speech
31. Protect Yourself While Writing

PART 9 THE END
32. Life as an Author
33. Good Help and Where to Find It

i. Write & Get Paid Exclusive Quiz
ii. The Writers Manifesto

CARDING
Once you have a rough outline, it's easy to add details for non-fiction, sort, shuffle, and mark notes, arranging them into lists or piles for each chapter. What I do is paperclip together information that I plan to reference. Then I begin to fill in the gaps: it's as simple as marking the notes "are there statistics for this?" or "mention this subject in the introduction."

Fiction can be a little different, since you are making it up. I use index cards when I have them; otherwise, I tear a piece of paper into four squares. About a hundred cards should do it. I review my notes and write "Part One: Steve realizes it's a zombie apocalypse for the hundredth time." If I have details in my note pile for this part, I'll add them on other cards, scene by scene.

Chapter 1 looks like this:

- Card #1 reads "He drives around (describe city at night, no electricity) and goes to the bar because all the roads are blocked."
- Card #2 reads "Bar is empty (looks lived in, trashy) finds one bottle of booze, feels fear, starts drinking."
- Card #3 reads "Sees some drunks (zombies) staggering outside, drawn to the bar. He finally sees they're corpses. Freaks."
- Card #4 reads "Barely makes it to the car (attacked) and climbs in. It has a breathalyzer! It won't start. Zoms surround the car."
- Card #5 reads "Comedic relief – he gets it to start, finally (didn't drink that much) and races off, messing his pants."
- Card #6 reads "Crashes into Zom, wakes up dazed. Car totaled. Blocks from home. The reader realizes Steve is an amnesiac."
- Card #7 reads "Steve climbs out, sees body, thinks hit-and-run, and flees on foot. Home is a fortress, he faints."

I wrote the original version of that book in one week using the carding method. The subconscious writer was telling a story that pressed upon and invaded my thoughts. Sometimes I needed the cards, other times I just flowed for 20 pages straight and crossed out any good scenes I'd used from the pile. Each card may yield only a sentence or may fill several pages. The trick is to keep the writing flowing. When you feel like you don't know what to write next, review your cards and see what connections you can make to the scenes that are coming next. Remember, you shouldn't be a slave to your outline; it's only a guide.

Pulling a stack of these cards out of my gym bag always surprises students. They are marked 1, 2, 3 or A, B, C with brief notes scribbled on them. I use this for books and short articles. You can stick them on a wall or lay them out on the floor and get an impression of how a manuscript flows.

I always slap a few cards down on each desk in the front row. Students begin to see how all that information would be too much to keep track of with a notepad (or, heaven forbid, only in your head). If a piece of information looks out of place, just pick it up and move it. Hell, you can move that card/information anywhere you want, maybe to chapter one or even the trash can.

STORY BOARDING
Large projects can be hard to outline using typical methods. The story arcs in a comic book series, a video game, or a screenplay are convoluted unless they are staked out in clear progression. Create a flowchart and use it to figure out the turning points in your story. It works well for series where each character has their own drama unfolding. To see how this could apply to what you write, it helps to disassemble masterfully told stories.

Here's an example: The FX series *The Americans* follows a family of KGB spies working in Washington, DC. It evolved numerous subplots and characters over 5 seasons. Plots develop and conclude, so new plots must be constantly reintroduced, leading into the next. We see plots about the Jenkins children's turmoil over spy training and the messy rift between agents using their bodies to steal information, as well as maintain a marriage. Plots expand to show us their rival, Stan, their neighbor who works at the FBI. His job, his life, and his hunches are always getting closer to capturing the spies he's tasked with stopping.

How do they maintain continuity amid all the complex plots and subplots in a story like that? The writers use a method for plot organization developed by the executive vice president and publisher of DC Comics, Paul Levitz. He designed a grid assigning scenes like Plot A, Plot B, and Plot C.

- The A plot is the main story. – The Jenkins steals blueprints for a submarine propeller.
- The B plot is important but doesn't receive as much time as the main story. – Stan gets a new partner at the FBI office.
- The C plot is like little "pop-ups" that keep a lesser plot relevant. – At home, the Jenkins daughter begins to question her mother's absences.

Levitz used a chart to keep everything prioritized. You can make one of your own and outline multiple plots. Here's what one looks like.

Issue #1	Issue #2	Issue #3
A Main characters survive crash. ≡ACTION≡		A Pug convinces the crew to educate Ace, investigate reports.
B Crew posts bail, Pug in drunk tank, Jack gives refuge.	B Ace & Pug find crash site, find surprise ≡FIGHT≡	C Dee gives Ace his first lesson: weapons.
C Ed recieves update.	C Ed explains it to [illegible] lesser of two evils.	D Dee meets Ed, recieves new mission.
	A Squad inspection. Seargant Major introduces Warren Oates (LW 3)	B Interceptor gets new assignment, attention in office. ≡FIGHT≡

Issue #4	Issue #5	Issue #6
B Ace encounters Sig. Major's Squad ≡FIGHT≡	A The crew help Ace hide out, he's a handful.	
D Dee's mission makes her inside military secrets.	B ≡ACTION≡ Outlanders aid partners in battle against creatures.	B Outlanders intelligence agency makes discovery.
A Suzy glimpses the encounter (Ace vs. [illegible]) and begins an investigation.	C Glitch gives Ace lesson in engineering.	C Jack gives Ace a part time job.
		A Mimi lives! Advises crew into action. ≡ACTION≡

Now, here's where it gets interesting. After the A plot has resolved itself, the B plot is promoted to the main story. Everything else gets promoted as well, and a new plot is created. Called the Levitz paradigm, it was inspired by soap operas, which have multiple plots going at once, and has since been used in various derivatives by screenwriters and novelists for the past 50 years.

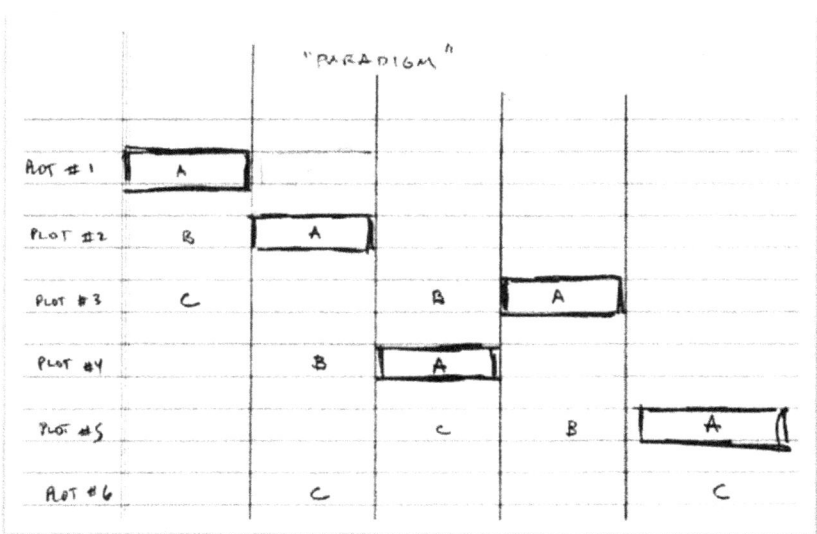

✏ **Writers Manifesto No. 8 – The best stories choose you, you don't choose them.**

Chapter Ten

"I always hit some point where I know the book is awful and cannot be saved. I ignore this. I keep writing." – Lori Devoti

REVISE
The power of a good story can outlive technological leaps and changes in society, making lifelong fans who seek out more of your creative fruits. The more time you spend revising and rewriting your work, the stronger it gets. You can build a shack or a mansion with your words; it's up to you.

Quality speaks for itself. One of the best stories told in gaming history was the epic quest in the classic PlayStation hit *Final Fantasy 7*. It was tweaked and polished over the years, involving multiple development teams and radical changes mid-production. The revisions paid off, earning FF7 a role as a touchstone of gaming design (mini games within the game) and storytelling (a large "epic" arc, subdivided by episodic back stories and missions). It sold so well that it was repackaged, and it sold just as well again. It had been worked on until it had a balance that can't be faked. Fans even petitioned to get the game ported to modern consoles with rebooted graphics.

When the balance is off, you get something that struggles to sell. Pick any summer popcorn flick, and they will have equal parts flashy special effects and vapid storyline. Predictable. That's not necessarily a good thing to emulate when your writing needs to sell consistently. Fortunately, there's a tried and true process for making finished writing more dynamic: revision.

Writers Manifesto No. 9 – You'll get to The End many times before you are finished.

GOOD WRITING IS REWRITING
Sorry to burst your bubble, but writing is never a graceful leap from height to height. You don't write a book or an essay. You write an exchange between characters – a paragraph, a scene – it jells and becomes more than the sum of its parts. It's been compared to the architecture of buildings. Think of your manuscript as a collection of building blocks. The act of moving those blocks around to form a better whole is what distinguishes professionals from everybody else.

Writer and director Roger Nygard advises, "Every time you feel that the manuscript is done, put it down for a week or a month, and then come back to it and you'll see it's not done because it's never done. Writing is rewriting. You're constantly re-writing." Revision means having a new vision for your work. Done right, it balances and tightens the elements in your writing.

To get the first blocks in place, we all have different preferences. Some writers feel comfortable making an outline, others just blow through pages (like me), peeking at notes when they get stumped. There is no right or wrong way. The one thing everyone ends up doing, however, is common: subdivide, or move one block at a time.

MAKE PLENTY OF TIME FOR REVISION

Sometimes we fall in love with characters, scenes, dialogue, or bits of narrative, and refuse to get rid of them, at the expense of muddying everything else. It's better to tell one story with as much force as possible. In Rebecca Miller's original draft of the screenplay Personal Velocity, there were more stories going on than she could use. Once she found the heart of her script, she was left with only three. A friend suggested, "Why don't you just write a movie about those characters?" She ended up doing it, and it became the film Angela. She was glad she did it. "Sometimes you just take the fingernail off the giant, and the fingernail is your story."

Handwritten notes in my doctor's prescription chicken scratch go through a transformation, from notepad to manuscript, pretty quickly. When I reread the rough draft, each paragraph is loaded with flaws. I immediately start marking it up. The pages get loaded with crossed-out sentences, circled portions swing into new locations, and tiny amendments (new sentences, questions to myself, notes like "Need more research here," stuff like that) squeeze into the margins to fill in the gaps. It's an eyesore, which is then rewritten into a clean version.

Then the process begins all over again. It goes on for as long as it has to; who cares if it's 3 times or 20? The finished product is tightly written. My process applies to every form:

Poetry

1. Write one page, two tops.
2. Subtract until abstractions are clear, delete or reposition anything that gets in the way of making it flow.
3. Compare existing notes with similar thoughts and expressions, and use the strongest passages.
4. Proofread, set aside for a few weeks, reconsider every line, until they pop, sizzle, and deliver a punch to the gut.

Blog

1. Write one or two pages.
2. Do research on the facts cited, double-check any contacts (addresses, phone numbers, websites, etc.), summarize the findings, or add quotes.
3. Reorganize the paragraphs so the beginning and conclusion are in harmony.
4. Recast sentences into their most vigorous composition, leading from one to the next with gusto.
5. Edit, proofread, and finish.

Book-length Manuscript

1. Write 60 to 100 pages.
2. Reviews sections fill in gaps of fiction (character development, plot, etc.) or nonfiction (instructions, examples, etc.) up to 200 pages.
3. Rewrite, recomposing sentences to transition between sections.
4. Review and add sensory details, do research, and establish emotional anchors in the story (love, greed, etc.). Increase word count to the desired length (60,000 – 90,000 words) by creating new scenes or chapters.
5. Subtract to make clear, delete, or reposition to improve flow.
6. Edit, proofread, and finish.

The thing that guides my process is the knowledge that every piece of writing tells a story. And every story has these three things: a beginning, a middle, and an end. It becomes easy to knock out pieces of writing that aren't working when you subdivide a manuscript to make it less imposing and move forward to the next phase of the process.

MOVE THE BUILDING BLOCKS

With almost no variation, storytellers have followed the three-act structure since Greek philosophers Cicero and Aristotle identified it as a way to keep stories in balance. The three-act structure is so familiar that we use it intuitively, making up bedtime stories for our children: the princess gets in peril, goes on an adventure, finds something fantastic (maybe love or empowerment), and defeats the wickedness. That's basically the same story for Star Wars, Mary Poppins, and The Sound of Music. It's so imitable that it's been passed around by every writer from Shakespeare to John Grisham.

Here's how classic storytelling works:

Act I (A-B)
   Objective: Introduce characters, setting, and main conflict.
   Act I opens with action and drama. With fiction, the most important goal is to portray all the parts in motion. The hero is plunged into a situation where it is "sink or swim." They meet a lively cast of characters and a villain worthy of opposing them. With nonfiction, you provide an overview of the subject and the expected results. As soon as the reader understands the essentials, Act I is finished.

Act II (B-C)
   Objective: Escalation of conflict, character development, and plot.
   Act 2 is a non-stop escalation of conflict and character development. This is 80 percent of your finished product. Fiction's goal is to escalate the drama to such a point where a conclusion is inevitable. A love interest that cannot be had and a dependent that desperately needs the hero round out the tale, leading into Act III. Nonfiction is busy too, with the expansion of details about its subject until the most complicated details can be discussed. When you've reached a climactic plateau, Act II is finished.

Act III (C-D)
   Objective: Conclusion of main conflict.
   Act III contains the brief but intense resolution of all major conflicts. The story gallops along with barely a breath in between: we know the hero's wellbeing, maybe their life, is at stake. Plus, if they do not win, death and suffering (or nearest equivalent) will continue. Fiction usually follows a short fourth act where characters' stories are tied up after the climax. Nonfiction may provide information about advanced strategies, information, or sources. The conclusion of Act III always looks the same: "The End."

Whatever the proportion, the elements have to feel in balance with one another. The three acts do that naturally – AB and CD not too long or short in relation to BC – everything giving the parts of a story a sense of movement. Don't get worried about perfection (it is the enemy, remember). Instead, construct it intuitively and fine-tune it in subsequent revisions until you reach the final draft.

Even the smallest forms (like individual essays) follow a mini AB > BC > CD > structure. The length of these smaller parts has changed over the years. The thick chapters of the nineteenth century have dissolved into flash-bang chapters influenced by the rapid pace of content consumption. They tend to avoid lengthy (boring) exposition and jump straight into the purpose of the scene, then get out of the scene and into the next without lingering for a drawn-out conclusion. It skips the beginning and ending by jumping from middle to middle.

FINE-TUNE THE FLOW

You can identify points in the story that aren't flowing as well as they could. Do readings of your manuscript as you rewrite and refine it. There's no denying that hearing your words read aloud is a great way to quickly learn what's working, what's not, and what needs to go. It's easier to find and change clunky lines, remove lines that aren't needed, or write new lines to expound things better. Dialogue especially benefits from readings. Ensure that the finished stuff clips along. It's worth doing serious surgery on your work before subjugating readers to it.

There are plenty of "artful" structural techniques writers can't seem to resist. The goal of most tricks is to dazzle readers, maybe add impact to a mystery, romance, or literary theme. Not all of these techniques work as we'd like. The worst offender is the flashback. The very name indicates the problem. By definition, flashbacks impede the forward movement of the story. Sometimes you just need to cut to the chase.

Once or twice is sometimes necessary, but for some writers, these devices are as contagious as the flu. So, how do you fix these problems? Stop justifying them. The flawed structure causes the flow to stumble.

- *Make things interesting.* Let the reader connect the scenes. Usually, a clunky structural technique is a writer's admission that a scene isn't very interesting. If the scene won't be interesting by itself, then it probably won't be interesting crammed into other scenes, so for clarity, cut it.

- *Don't muddy back stories.* If your characters have a lot of disguised flashbacks while sitting (driving, drinking, sleeping, etc.), then the plot has become tangled. If past events are so important to the story, rearrange the plot and start with them. Everything you present in writing must move the story forward, unless you have a powerful reason for turning us backward, which is rare.

- *A side story is sometimes good enough to lead a story.* Your best bet is to open with action. Start each scene with the strongest event that will grab the readers' attention. Ask yourself over and over again, "What is the event that sets the story in motion?" Often, the answer is an event that will require a flashback to explain what's happening; pay attention to the flashback, because that often is the opening scene.

SUBTRACT, SUBTRACT, SUBTRACT

Edgar Allen Poe wrote several essays about writing, two of the most influential are "The Philosophy of Composition" and "The Poetic Principle." Poe had a notion called "unity of effect and the single sitting." Basically, Poe was worried about the attention span of his readers. In reading an epic (especially a 19th-century epic, like say *Paradise Lost*), our attention inevitably wears out. He made the following observations:

- No matter how brilliant the passages, we can't appreciate all of them.
- As we tire, we fail to catch the good lines.
- The epic becomes dull in spots.
- Finally, we skim entire pages looking for something exciting to quicken our interest.
- Then we stop reading.
- When we come back, our attention is challenged as we try to reenter the story in the middle of an event.
- Gradually, we become in tune, and the thing seems brilliant again.
- We can even re-read stuff that seemed dull the day before, and it's not dull anymore; in fact, it's amazing.
- Then the process of falling appreciation happens again.
- And we're asleep with the book on our chest before we know it.

Troubled by these observations, Poe wondered how he could write something that wouldn't suffer from the limited attention span of readers. His advice (like William and Strunk's in *The Elements of Style*) was to avoid big words and to keep the work short. Because only in works designed to be read in a single sitting could a writer expect the reader to appreciate the artistry of the composition.

Experts tell us that people's attention spans are getting shorter and shorter. It used to be a joke that MTV's frantically paced music videos were the norm. Those were 3 to 4 minute videos. Today, if a YouTube video doesn't grab you in 20 seconds, it's over. You might point out that "Those types of people aren't determined readers." True enough, but even Constant Readers have trouble finding sustained blocks of time in which to absorb a book. The phone rings. The bladder insists. Because of this, the flow is fractured. How do you fix this? Keep it short.

There are other benefits to doing short work. Like, you can make more money. Take, for example, an interview I did with Dustin Costa (founder of several publishing companies, lately NexGenInk). The length (and scope) of the interview was too long to run in its entirety. I broke down the information into several shorter pieces and submitted them to various sites as exclusive content.

Instead of one drawn-out interview, I subdivided and revised until I had an interview, a profile, a news release, and an industry watchdog article that highlighted NexGenInk. It was easy to sell to Costa; he wanted as much publicity as possible. It was easy to sell to editors because they wanted to cover "hot" new personalities, just with their own exclusive content. Most importantly, readers got something short, which meant more of them fully appreciated the subtle nuances I had worked hard to create, and more of them acted on it. Everyone was happy.

The same works for books. Skim the latest offering by James Patterson. The chapters are a page or a page and a half at most. Study the headers and sub headers in this chapter, breaking up information into sound bites. Easy to read. Easy to dog-ear and resume later. Utilize these techniques during revision, no matter what you write, and you will get the best results.

Write & Get Paid

Dear Mr. Tinsman, Enclosed is a printed copy of Dustin Costa's novel Squirrel Days. I apologize if the printing is a bit rough around the edges ~ I wanted to get it sent out to you as soon as possible, for your review. I will also mail you a printed copy of the cover design in its current form, or have the designer mail it to you directly, if that's determined to be the more efficient course of action.
Thank You Very Much,
Vanessa

Vanessa Nelson
PO Box 5548
Sacramento, CA 95817

Chapter Eleven

"Earlier writing looks soft and careless. Process is nothing: erase your tracks." – Annie Dillard

EDIT

Some authors get frustrated and try to publish too early or slap stuff together, which always has negative results. Make no mistake, well-written work is rewritten work. It's like a magic trick. The magician practices every day so that one performance goes off right. When he learns a new trick, he messes up a lot before it comes off smoothly. Take time to iron out the tangled sentences, dialogue, and grammar that got past you. When you reach the point where removing a single word could undermine everything else, it's done. It will get you paid.

Editing is a skill that goes beyond a mastery of grammar, syntax, and spelling. The techniques are an art form, from reading a manuscript aloud to gauge its flow, to testing alternative writing to see if it strengthens your work as a whole. At a professional level, you can also make good money editing another person's work. People pay anywhere from $1.00 to $3.50 a page for standard editing, and up to $7.00 a page if you have to contribute some writing. Either way you look at it, you can't afford not to become an editor.

REFINE MANUSCRIPTS IN SMALL BITES

Rereading, rewriting, and reconsidering your words helps break down the process into small steps. It's like musicians playing small gigs and entertaining on street corners to make it, then building up to bigger and bigger gigs. As you knock out each part, excitement will overtake you because you're writing will impress!

My quickest books were written for other people. This is no mystery. I was paid up front and wanted to get into the next paying job as fast as possible. I didn't care what it was about, and I wasn't worried about showing them the rough draft. The first draft is always bad. Perfection isn't even the enemy; it's an afterthought.

I've used a bunch of different methods over the years, but it always comes down to me grinding out the last chunks near the deadline. The clients hear this, "Look, I'm going to edit once, then let you read it. Then you tell me what you like, and your ideas, and we'll work closely on the second round. Then I'll rewrite it and we'll send it out to some proofreaders." After the proofreaders get through with it, we consider their critiques and advice.

I might edit some more or just tell the "author" it's time to send this to a publisher. The process is intentional: 5 easy steps. Editing begins after setting the manuscript aside for a few weeks and then re-reading it, evaluating it from a fresh perspective. You may decide it is finished, or you may change all the dialogue, cutting complete paragraphs, re-casting scenes, and ironing out continuity.

EDITING IN 5 EASY STEPS

It's easy to look back over a quick manuscript to consider its strengths and weaknesses. The process of proofreading, fact-checking, and other fine details can be knocked out in any order. However, the biggest improvements are made in a definitive progression.

STEP ONE – THE MACHETE EDIT

Just skim it over and over. Look for "hot spots" or great scenes. Some scenes are in place, or characters or associations have jelled, or the plot has solidified. Keep that – whatever has the most potential. You'll know it when it quickens your interest. Anything that doesn't, that bores you, circle it. You can wonder later, "Now, what's wrong with this stuff?" Find the heart of your piece.

This first rough edit is called content editing. Think of it as the first swing of your machete. It only gives a view of the number of words you have to cut in order to proceed. Hack the "band aids." Band aids are what you use to gloss over defects or superficial holes after the early revision.

The next machete hack targets significant additions and deletions. Sections should be rearranged, changing the focus or emphasis of each chapter and bringing the heart of your manuscript into tight focus. Search for continuity in the story, character development, or overall balance of the narrative.

I usually ask myself, "Is it gripping?" Even nonfiction, like this book, can't be boring. I'll go through the chopped remains of my original draft looking for pieces to rewrite as a foundation to fill in the gaps. No need to write something new if you can move an existing section.

At this stage, it's obvious certain parts don't have enough information, numbers, or facts. During this edit, you simply put a note in brackets or make a list to remind yourself, "I need a quote on page 114," or "What kind of car is she driving on page 203?" or "Can I make this a love story?" You can research and digress later. Keep hunting down things that disrupt your manuscript. Here are a few things to look for:

- Inactive scenes that don't further the main story, sub-plots, or characterization.
- Scenes that don't match the pace of everything else.
- Dialogue that doesn't show complications in the story or challenge the characters.

The goal of this edit isn't to make it "readable" or even to flow. It's meant to show you what writing you're going to keep (for now) and how much you need to rewrite, possibly from scratch. This step feels great, you finally get to go in and abuse the manuscript that's been beating you up. Show that thing who's boss.

STEP TWO – THE SCALPEL EDIT

Constrain yourself. During this edit, you are concerned with silly things. Like the relationship between paragraphs and sentences. Paragraphs and dialogue, paragraphs and paragraphs, subjects and chapters, everything is about flow.

Read it aloud and listen to the rhythm of the language. If you stumble, highlight the sentence for "surgery." When you come back, it may require one of these common fixes:

- Replace *inactive* verbs ("to have," "to be," "the fact that") with *active* verbs ("took it," "done it," "it just got real").
- Cut duplication, repetition, and big words. (You would literally cut either "duplication" or "repetition" from that sentence.)
- Replace "-ing" verbs with *active* syntax. *Not*: "He's writing a lot." *Rather*: "He writes a lot. It's graphomaniac."
- Question abstractions and generalizations. *Not*: "Is it well written?" *Rather*: "Is it grounded in sensory detail?"
- Check capitalization, punctuation, spelling, "quotations," abbreviations, etc., et. al., e.g.
- Never use a big word when a short word will work. *Not*: nincompoop, *Rather*: fool.

Nothing is ever perfect, but you don't want your editor seeing a million screw ups. Keep skimming over your book, tweaking it around sentence by sentence until it beams. Remember the reason why the grass is greener on the other side. It's because someone else is watering that grass. Editors are attracted to a greener manuscript. Groom your manuscript over and over again.

STEP THREE – SECOND OPINIONS

Is your edited manuscript a hotshot or a misfire? There's only one way to find out. Test your writing with readers. Readers are expert fact-checkers, proofreaders, and consumers! Most people are also interested in what their peers write. You should have no problem finding willing guinea pigs.

Accept their critiques. Be a good sport about their heartless remarks like "Did you think this was finished?" Smile when they hurt your feelings and tell you, "Man, your book put me to sleep and I don't want to finish it!" One reader plucked at my shirt sleeve, pinching it and releasing it quickly again and again, "It was like that, it didn't pull me in."

To balance her writing, Amy Holden Jones, scriptwriter of *Mystic Pizza* and *Indecent Proposal*, does a full draft and then has a very select group of people look at it. "If three or four of five people say, 'The end doesn't work for me,' then I know the end doesn't work." She listens to their opinions and is willing to work out any problems. Author Dylan Kidd has people read his work, but offers a little extra wisdom: "I generally have found that putting too much stock in feedback can get confusing." He says, "Unless the comments match something I already felt in my gut anyway or if every person has the same comment, then I know I have an issue."

People often find fault with one area of a manuscript and fail to realize that the blame for the problem lies elsewhere. The real problem doesn't always exist where it appears; it can be like a medical symptom. Someone can acknowledge that there is a symptom, but you should be very skeptical when they start talking about what the solution is or what the nature of the problem is.

You must strike a balance with feedback; readers' solutions are their solutions, but come up with other ones. Only you really know what you have to fix (maybe you can introduce something later, or sooner, or change the order of the chapters, etc.). Don't rush in, that's the only way to avoid the one downside of re-writing: sometimes something very good can be lost in the haste to make it better. Sometimes, the long way around, the long speech, the boring passage, is the better way to go.

The more people you get to give you feedback, the more honest it will be. A good critique often leads to changes, but it can be hard to distinguish a reviewer's real thoughts. That's why experienced writers ask people about behavior rather than opinions. The reason is that people's actions accurately represent their underlying attitude. And behaviors are easier to describe.

If you ask, "Did you like my story?" many people won't know what to say. "Yes" or "No" doesn't tell you where you can make it better. But if you ask, "Was it hard to put down?" then their answer is solid. Here are some questions that can tell you what areas of your manuscript need to be tweaked.

- Did certain chapters, sections, and portions make you yawn?
- Did certain parts cause you to speed up to see what happened?
- Did you have to look up any words in your dictionary?

By asking these types of questions, readers will give you close estimates. All you have to do is thank them for reading and giving their feedback. Remember the old writers' axiom, "The reader is the greatest collaborator." They do all the heavy lifting; they imagine scenes and characters that you've only written about!

STEP FOUR – NITPICKING

You've got all the parts stitched together. It's still not finished, like Frankenstein's monster, it needs a little more refinement before you unleash it on the world. This fourth round, I call Nitpicking. This is the name for the practice of cleaning up freshly sewn garments. After a garment has been sewn, it is picked over, plucking out stray threads and loose knots so its attractiveness is increased. Such is it with writing. There are pestering details, unsightly nuisances that are easy to deal with once you know you should pluck them out.

First, look for unsightly words – errors in tense, prefixes, suffixes, and adjectives. Then look over the entire work (like, "Could this button be sewn on any better than it is?"). Small changes can alter your entire manuscript, so go back over it after a round of changes to ensure your adjustments don't feel "off."

COMPOSITION
Composing in your own language conveys reassurance, authenticity, and acknowledges intelligence implicitly, thereby giving words more force. It also helps match the language readers expect in certain genres. It can also become part of a writer's style. Just look at the optimistic, slightly crude tone used in this book.

There are limits to writing like you talk. A book written in text or slang is confusing, though some people try. I mean, imagine a book written like: "btw becuz fmo I be over @ 11: p." What is that? Or "Ima put chrome shoes on my '79 Cadillac." *Some* people will get it, but *most* readers will not. And it will confuse the most important person in the Getting Paid chain of command: the editor.

The editor of the *Kansas City Star*, back when Ernest Hemingway still worked there, had his editorial preference stenciled on his door. It was good advice then, and still is. It instructed writers:

> "Use vigorous English. Be positive. Avoid the use of adjectives."

For the best results, read the *Chicago Manual of Style* and *The Elements of Style*. Both have extensive sections explaining the mechanics of good writing. My preferred writing manual is the *Hodges Harbrace*; this premier academic text explains everything from composing an essay to properly fixing a dangling participle. Here's the gist:

Grammar and Spelling
- Form the possessive of nouns with 's
- In a series of three or more terms with a single conjunction, use a comma after each term except the last.
- Enclose parenthetic expressions between commas.
- Place a comma before "and" or "but" introducing an independent clause.
- Do not join independent clauses with a comma
- Do not break sentences in two.
- A particular phrase at the beginning of a sentence must refer to the grammatical subject.
- Divide words at line-ends, in accordance with their formation and pronunciation. (knowledge, describe, atmosphere, religious, etc.)

Mechanics
- One paragraph to each topic.
- Begin each paragraph with a topic sentence, and end it in conformity with the beginning.
- Use the active voice.
- Put statements in positive form.
- Omit needless words.
- Avoid a succession of loose sentences.
- Express coordinate ideas in a similar form.
- Keep related words together.
- In summaries, keep to one tense.
- Place the emphatic words of a sentence at the end.

STEP FIVE – LISTEN TO EDITORS
If you aren't sure if your language and content are up to par don't worry, an editor will tell you. They operate defiantly. You may receive a "Request for Change" form that contains a sentence or paragraph

with a quick note, maybe as simple as "Please rewrite this." Or your entire manuscript may come back with a wide margin containing notes like "Good grief," or "I'm lost," or "Repetition?" When you aren't sure what they want, just ask.

It's a good sign when one actually has ideas and they took the time out of their lives to read your work. They aren't always right, so when an editor suggests a change that would alter the overall piece, stop and explain your rationale for why you used a technique in the first place. They'll listen. Consider an editor's suggestion before you snap at them. At the end of the day, you'll both reach a point where you throw your hands up, howl "Good enough for me!" and take it off life support. It's ready for the world to see.

✎ Writers Manifesto No. 10 – The art will happen when you aren't editing.

"Mother? Why are we running?" Anna shuttered her eyes against the sunlight; it also seemed a humble act considering the consequences for angering mother. Mother stepped high over the grass and pulled Anna's wrist. Anna resisted, surprising herself with the strength to break mother's grip. Mother stopped and Anna bumped into James, who giggled. Mother's shoulders raised and fell softly. The red cross on her uniform was darkened by sweat. She turned with her eyes held high, focusing on the school.

> **Comment [G1]:** Kelsey Akee: good shit

"Nigeria is invading us; we are at war, Anna" Mother said. For many months the state of Biafra had attempted to establish its sovereignty, not it had, but war was the price. She looked down at Anna. So many emotions overlapped her face, but Anna could not read something troubling in Mother's eyes.

> **Comment [G2]:** Kelsey Akee: us, We are at war, Anna. (more powerful)

> **Comment [G3]:** Kelsey Akee: now?

"Isn't it safe?" Anna despised the whine in her voice. It was so childish.

"You can't go back." Mother shook her head and continued her flight through the field. They broke through the grass and passed over tracks in yam field. The fields were leveled, ready for the rains after January. Following Mother over the lowed soil was easier partly because Anna forgot about poisonous spiders and snakes. Anna looked out across the wide field, concerned that the roads were so unsafe that mother had chosen a direct path, or maybe it was just mother over reacting. Anna had begun to question her parents' infallibility well before her 12th birthday, but she did not rely on second guessing them openly.

"Seconds?" Anna asked Chidi, speaking Igbo.

> **Comment [G4]:** Kelsey Akee: may want to insert asterisks to emphasize the separation. You used them when starting into Anna's story so you should use them when transitioning back to Chidi

Chidi was finished though, and excused himself.

"Auntie Hope is coming to see you off to college." Anna told him.

"Really?" Chidi smiled, he hadn't seen Auntie Hope since her husband, Uncle Uche, had died last year.

> **Comment [G5]:** Kelsey Akee: . He

Write & Get Paid

PART 3
THE BUSINESS

Chapter Twelve

"Everything that needs to be said has already been said, but since no one was listening, everything must be said again." – André Gide

UNDERSTAND WHAT SELLS AND FOR HOW MUCH

While taking into account the standard writing assignments (screenplay adaptation, book length, etc.), don't overlook the earning potential of short-form work. It's a good experience. Plus, it's the best promotional tool for book-length projects and writing-related services you may offer.

The need for content is like a bacterial explosion under a microscope. Editors want daily things like blogs, profiles, articles, and stories to feed their print and electronic publications. Readers gobble it up. But as soon as it's devoured, fatigue sets in, and they crave something fresh.

SHORT FORM FOR SALE

Thumb through a magazine or browse any e-zine, and it's unmistakable that writers must fine-tune topics, genres, and themes into specific forms. An interview is different than a political analysis in content and structure. The perspectives of each form are also unique, but they're all short: between 500 and 1,500 words. Anything longer than that can require a lot of pitching.

The prices included in this chapter are ballpark figures that I've used for years. Most publishers have a payment policy in place, but when there isn't any, I target what's presented here. Check a publisher's payment information before pitching a piece; you can sometimes get a higher rate if you have a reputation. If you want a more detailed price gauge, you'll find the best among directories like *Writers Market* (writersmarket.com). Just visit their site and select the tab How Much Should I Charge? Shoot for the low average; it's easier to negotiate.

All you have to do is find what pieces editors prefer for their publications and cast your words within the best form. Once you become familiar with the details of an investigative exposé versus a book review (and a dozen other forms), they become quick templates for your writing assignments. Grind out manuscripts, pitch them, and consider your prices.

Short work has its own rules that help editors determine how to fit it into their magazines, online journals, and so on. You've seen all of these forms before, but they're so common you may have overlooked the differences. Let's review:

Article ($10 to $3,000) – It's a general term for any piece that presents facts and information, tells a story, or explores an issue of real-world experience. There are expository and informational articles. Done right, these can be sold as a journalistic feature story that introduces the reader to a subject in some detail.

Essay (10¢ to 40¢ per word) – An exploration of intellectual or philosophical ground. In a column for *Esquire* called "Ethics," Harry Stein used to investigate all sorts of moral quandaries that cropped up in everyday life, from adultery to flattering your boss to get a raise. Every short piece can be sold off as either an article or an essay, they share elements.

Travel ($10 to $350) – A broad category ranging from a straight destination piece meant to arouse tourists to a reflective piece that uses details to portray the inner journey of the writer. Jan DeBlieu speaks with such a voice in *Hatteras Journal*, the memoir of her sojourn on a North Carolina island. "It was like falling in love," she says, recalling how the storm-washed landscape affected her. "And you know how when you fall in love with somebody, you end up just wanting to tell them everything and portray them as honestly and poetically as you can to other people?"

How To (15¢ to 20¢ per word) – A step-by-step primer for accomplishing something: training your dog, building a wooden boat, buying real estate. These pieces can be sold under "health and fitness," "self-help," or "general interest."

Nature ($10 to $1,000) – A fairly broad category that includes any writing about the natural world for a general audience. Like travel writing, the place may take on the role of a character (like Yosemite National Park or New York City).

Science and Technology ($100 to $1,000) – A piece requiring expertise, to present complex scientific and technical information in a comprehensible way. Stephen Jay Gould, a Harvard paleontologist, for example, regularly deciphers complex evolutionary issues in *Natural History Magazine*. Selling these pieces comes down to well-cited research (footnotes) and education.

Issue ($15 to $300) – Any piece that explores a topical issue, such as famine relief in Sudan.

Public Event ($15 to $350) – The detailed story of a public happening, such as John Hersey's account of the atomic bombing of Japan in *Hiroshima*, or *New Yorker* editor and baseball fan Roger Angell's accounts of the World Series for *Sports Illustrated*.

Political Analysis ($20 to $1,000) – Current events viewed through a lens of partisan (biased) perspective or broad examination of historical differences between political parties, political celebrities, and nations.

Investigative Expose ($10 to $3,000) – A piece that offers unrevealed truth about a public person, issue, or event. Such writing demands exceptionally dogged reportorial and research skills and usually relies far less on one lump sum of information, such as with informants. The majority of work will be done over endless hours in the library, online, and the Hall of Records.

Review ($15 to $500) – A reasoned and informed critique of a book, play, movie, concert, or other public document or performance, frequently using it to discourse on the art in general. See John Updike *Hugging the Shore: Essays and Criticism*, a collection of book reviews he wrote for the *New York Times Book Review*, which not only offers eloquent analysis of specific books but also stands as a history of contemporary writing.

Personality Profile ($50 to $1,000) – Just what it sounds like. Gay Talese went to Beverly Hills to interview Frank Sinatra, but Frank had a cold and couldn't see him. For six weeks, he followed Sinatra from the movie set to the recording studio to the night club, interviewing the people in his entourage, and came up with a telling, multifaceted portrait. It was a departure from the usual celebrity profile called "Frank Sinatra has a Cold." "I gained more by watching him, overhearing him, and watching the reactions of those around him than if I had actually been able to sit down and talk to him," Talese said.

Arranged Interview ($10 to $1,000) – The aim is similar to that of the Personality Profile, but the bulk of the piece is told in the subject's own words, either as a brief introduction followed by straight question and answer session, or a Q & A session interrupted at strategic places, so the author can make telling observations of the subject's physical demeanor, the setting, past events, etc. It is "arranged" because authors select portions of tapes or notes, often out of order, used for effect.

Personal Essay ($15 to $350) – A piece that offers one or more firsthand experiences from the writer's life, then endows that experience with a meaning that transcends the reader's personal interest in the author's life. See George Orwell's "Shooting an Elephant," in which he describes his action as a colonial officer in India: the events that culminate in his being obliged to shoot a rogue elephant in front of an unruly crowd provided him with a functional metaphor for colonialism. He had to do what he knew was wrong in order to maintain face (and power) with the natives, who vastly outnumbered him.

Memoir ($10 to $1,000) – Memory in words, and very closely related to the personal essay, although the meaning may be implicit in the memory. Or the meaning may derive from the glimpse it offers of a famous personality in an intimate moment. Sometimes the memoir takes on significance because the writer was a private witness to a historical event, such as the Holocaust.

Adventure Narrative ($15 to $1,000) – A dramatic true-life story. Often includes nature writing and shades into the personal essay.

LONG FORM FOR SALE
You can take any short piece and pipe in more words to sell it to a new market. Toss in new research, add stories, juice up a big plot, make up more characters, whatever. Your only consideration should be "Will a longer version get me paid more?" Or, will a longer version do what cannot be done in short form? It's important you know the answer, because one thing editors will constantly ask you is, "Can you shorten it up?"

As a successful graphomaniac, clients will defer to you, much like a mechanic at a greasy shop. You get a lot of questions and do a lot of bidding. Guesswork. Real work. One of the most common requests is "Would you write my book for me?" Tell clients to write it themselves or pay you $5,000 up front. Otherwise, charge $200 for a consultation session; review your notes and conclude that, "Yep. I still need $5,000 to write this."

Clients may not like the price tag, but some will go with it. They get a book, and you get compensated for your time. I make it clear to my clients: writing a good book is like building a mansion. It's a labor of love for the client, but it's a long-term obligation for the writer.

The same thing occurs when you pitch optimistic (perhaps hyperbolic) deadlines. Oh, sure I can complete a book in 6 months, but will it suck? Probably. Off chance it won't. If I spend as long as it takes to polish it up, I can pretty much assure a consistent seller. Long-form writing is a delicate thing. All the pieces of the mansion have to come together. Otherwise, it loses value.

It's a good idea to clear a hefty part of your schedule for a year when you take on these projects. Don't fret about the time; you'll make plenty of money from the writing that surrounds it: news releases, interviews, reviews, and whatever else clients want afterwards. Don't underbid. Don't set a fast deadline. Don't think, "Oh, I'm so good I can just do this at the last minute." Avoid making problems for yourself, and you'll do well writing long form.

Filler ($5 to $17 per page; or 10% to 50% royalties if published as a book) – Filler is a short book that may rely on kitsch more than insight. Or it may be a work of satiric genius. It's fast and dirty and makes it look way easier than it is. When I pitched *Write & Get Paid*, I told the editor it'd be a 200-page rehash of a previous book but for a larger audience. I'd bump up the technology, make it up to date, and add valuable information. They said it was an "easy reader." It essentially filled up their book catalog and wasn't a giant aggravation, so they said yes.

Biography ($5 to $17 a page; or 10% to 15% royalties if used in a book) – The best biographies take the structure of novels though unflinchingly truthful and accurate; they nevertheless present selected scenes from the subject's life in a manner that builds toward some kind of defining moment. The biographer Ron Powers said, "Biography flows from the early Sanskrit text, the sacred histories of

Buddha, the legends of Mohammad, the New Testament that illuminated Christ's life in the four Gospels." That's a pretty good sales pitch if you want to write a biography.

In my experience, I ghostwrote about Nigerian immigrants. Though truthful, many personal facts about the Biafra War were unanswered. I filled it in with research into the war's events (on a day-to-day progression from bombing to embargo) and developed the characters using fiction techniques, building their romance that became the core of the story.

Commentary ($50 to $1,000) – John Hershey's *Hiroshima* narrates the atomic bombing of Japan in 1945 and was first published in its entirety in a single issue of *The New Yorker* magazine. It was over 25,000 words, 100 pages plus, and was closer to a book than a magazine article. His commentary was built around five interviews with survivors: a child, an old man, a German Catholic priest, a mother, and a soldier. It documented the grizzly aftermath of radiation poisoning, mass confusion, and lingering casualties. The value of it is displayed in the lasting impact it made in the chants of protesters at anti-nuclear proliferation rallies. *Hiroshima* was published a few months later – you guessed it, as a book.

Book (Categorical; $5 to $17 a page; or 10% to 50% royalties if published under your byline) – Categories evolved out of long practice, tinkering and fine tuning until we all say, "My book is Current Events/Politics" or "It's Psychology/New Age." They are pigeonhole into whatever category seems to fit and what readers expect when they pick up a book in that genre.

Genre is slippery. It's used loosely, sometimes as interchangeably as bumper stickers. Within a genre, there are subgenres. But the categories are never as absolute as textbook writers would have you believe. New ones are popping up all the time.

The YA genre, or Young Adult fiction, is a relatively new category for low-literacy books aimed at tweens and teenagers. But everyone reads these books, parents, children, and grandparents. YA means easy to read, with lots of adventure worked in. You could just as easily slap on any bumper sticker: dystopia science fiction, gothic horror, steampunk, or whatever, just be certain that it, and the writing, match the focus of the book's market.

Translation (8¢ to 35¢ per word) – Editor Randall Radic translates screenplays. He gets them from an Italian producer who is a big shot in Italy but a small fry in Hollywood. He converts the Italian's English into American English in an attempt to sell it to some big production companies. Six screenplays in and no green lights. No casting calls. No mention in Variety. No lounging on the beaches of Maui. Randall Radic gets paid, none the less, because translation is a clever hustle, though tedious.

Screenplay ($200 to $15,000 per project) – It's my job to tell you, emphatically, that yes, you can sell a screenplay. Unfortunately, my experience points in the negative direction again and again and again. To get paid as a screenwriter, you have two options. First, work as a freelancer: turning clients' ideas into scripts for $5 to $100 a page (don't make them any promises). Also, pay annual dues and soak up workshops, contests, and seminars provided by writers' organizations like the American Screenwriters Association (asc@goasa.com) or the National Writers Union (nwu@nwu.org). Second, relocate. Being physically closer to agents and filmmakers will improve your odds of developing personal contacts.

If you live in a big city, become part of the scene where the influential people hang out. Chat up exhibitors at trade shows, and swap business cards along "media row" at conventions. Even small towns have media hubs. Kelly Roberson makes the most of it in person, when visiting one editor at the Meredith Publications office in Iowa, she'll pop in and meet another. She says, "Sometimes it's as simple as walking into someone's office and introducing myself."

Stack the odds in your favor. Work with an agent, an editor, a typist, or a ghostwriter, anything that gets you inside the industry. Once there, you can maneuver like a pro by understanding what sells and for how much.

✏ **Writers Manifesto No. 11 – All the jobs you bid high will be easy, all the jobs you bid low will be difficult.**

Chapter Thirteen

"Those who do not want to imitate anything, produce nothing." – Salvador Dali

EXPLOIT MARKETS
We all wonder about what our path might be. It is possible to write what comes naturally and stumble into venues where your style fits. But play to the ear of readers, and a paycheck may come with more frequency. Try out all sorts of markets. Here are some of the most lucrative.

1. *Niche Markets* – It's not what you know, it's who you know. That saying crossed my mind as I was reading an email thread between my friend, bestselling author Michael Collins, and his editor. His first book was a slow mover, but editors liked this guy. He just had some sort of way with them. Their letters really sang. And the email thread? It seemed like it was from a long-lost friend.

They just talked about business and about life. They connected. And despite him being in a prison Khaki uniform beside me, he was achieving success and getting paid while I was figuring it out the hard way. The connection was right in front of me. They'd all gone to college.

They wrote and published for educated readers. Collins, like the editors he connected with, viewed themselves as artists. Success was defined as steady sales, not bestsellers. His latest novel, *Graded Expectations*, was baited with protester sentiments and riffed on the Occupy Wall Street phenomenon. His editor was predisposed to think it was perfect for their readers.

The more I read of his work and his publishers' backlists, the more I realized. I couldn't relate to what they were talking about, not immediately. It was well written and interesting, but it was outside of my experiences, which is probably why I click with a different type of publisher. That's why you will too. Remember that the first sale is to the editor, so find the editor you relate to.

If Collins was highbrow, then Nikki Turner is the opposite. Her publishing company fit a very unique market. It started when baggy pants and large chains were the rage. She worked at a travel agency by day and studied at North Carolina University at night, but she was still "street." She had recently been persuaded by local authors to write about street life beyond the glitz and glamour portrayed on Black Entertainment Television (BET).

She had a way with words that led to self-publishing two books. Being imperfect made it real. That always resonates with people in ways that blow through barriers like the idea of a "correct" narrative style or a "classy" family saga. Some readers just want stories involving crack whores and dough boys in turf wars.

Her two books were *A Hustler's Wife* and *A Project Chick*, which were sold in barber shops and from the guts of Turner's purse. It caught the attention of *Trendsetters Magazine*, which dubbed her the Queen of Hip Hop Lit. It was the Clarian call for an underserved market. Major publishers began to take notice, making deals with Turner to re-print books that sold over 150,000 copies each.

Turner started publishing other authors with her newly founded company, Nikki Turner Presents. What surprised her were the manuscripts coming from prison. Nikki Turner's books had proliferated in cell blocks, stimulating letters, proposals, and hand-written life-stories. They were perfect; all of them were hardcore street life stories that would only appeal to the black communities that produced such writers.

She developed the practice of buying the copyright to each book for $5,000 to $10,000 and then running off 10,000 copies at printers for about $1.50 a book. The retail was $14.99, and she used the back of each book to advertise her growing selection. Each book sold more copies. She was a multi-millionaire in a few years. The glitz and glamour had become reality.

In a five-year period, Turner lost ground to competitors who were doing the same thing. Washida Clark, Vikki Stringer, and other writers got picked up by major publishing companies because their original books appealed to women. Then they started their own "street" publishing companies.

    2. *Bundling Services* – These are really hard to mess up. The idea is to package your slickest insights (like in this book) and offer them up in every possible way. The immediate impulse is to bundle a book itself: eBook, print-on-demand, audio, and PDF. But it can be more. Workshops, seminars, public speaking, and consulting services tie in with a book's valuable insight.

Notoriety helps; it lends a certain glamour to spokesmanship. That's how Robert Schifreen cashed in. He's a real hacker and the author of *Defeating the Hacker: A Non-Technical Guide to IT Security*. A commentator and IT security consultant, he's accumulated thousands of articles and blogs and maintains an expensive e-newsletter in the United Kingdom. He serves the highest bidders in both private and corporate settings.

In the early 80s, he exploited information on the British Telecom Prestel Computer system and managed to steal passwords for 50,000 customers, including his Royal Highness Prince Philip, Duke of Edinburgh. When he went to trial, he was acquitted because there were no laws on the books for hacking. So he helped them make one, the Computer Misuse Act of 1990.

Schifreen is a constant salesman with a charming story. But you don't have to make history to follow his lead. Schifreen's strategy isn't anything new; bundling is good business. That's why he gets away with charging $100 an hour consulting fees, $5,000 honorariums for seminars, and $29.95 for hardcover editions of his book.

    3. *Reports* – Every industry has a need for expert information, but that doesn't mean people need a book about it. Small presses deliver a range of short materials that offer busy readers only what they need. You'll find them online and in catalogs, available as reports, as inexpensive booklets, downloadable PDFs, or short eBooks.

Shotgun News started 30 years ago as an annual classified advertising newspaper. It's matured into a glossy monthly on Wal-Mart's shelves. Far from what its name implies, SGN is a modern, online magazine with a massive advertising base (it serves a $1 billion market composed of law enforcement, hunting enthusiasts, and militia crackpots). Where else can you find companies selling cheat guides ($80 plus s/h) for the Federal Firearms License (FFL).

Shotgun News is just one of the many companies selling reports. It's the arterial highway in its market. It serves a group of niche publishers like Paladin Press, NIC Law Enforcement Supply, and Brownells Inc.

These are some top sellers:

- *CIA Lock Picking Manual* (65 pages) $4.95
- *Improvised Munitions Guide #1* (12 pages) $2.50
- *Military Survival Manual* (115 pages) $11.95

Reports can be written for any subject, interest, or genre. There are a couple of ways to get started selling them yourself. The best way is to subdivide your information.

If you're good at educating people, you could flex your expertise by selling reports about the law, craft, or business of writing itself. The National Writers Union does a great job making extra cash by selling mini reports to its members (nwu.com). Select *Mystery* and you'll find them for Crime Scene Investigation and Forensic Analysis. Only a few pages each, available in print or PDF, for about $1.50.

Or take a page from the earliest writing scams: classified ads that promise cheap results for a dollar. Stuff like:

- Advertisement reads: Everything you need to know to make meth. Send $1.00
- Customer receives: (One page) Don't make meth. It's illegal. You'll go to prison.

Another profitable market for reports is "Universities" or correspondence programs. Many companies offer a wide variety of subjects. The most outrageous is the Progressive Universal Life Church (PULC). PULC sells Ph. D.s based on life experience, not actual college credits, for about $375. Their greatest hits include:

- MS Reiki Healing
- PhD Astral Projection
- BS Theological Science
- MS Theological Philosophy
- Ph. D Acupuncture

My favorite is the PhD in Water Dowsing. Talk about a party pleaser! Grab a coat hanger, slur loudly at everyone, "Watch this! I'm a Doctor!" Then, stagger through the hot bodies and cannonball into the pool.

The PULC materials were developed by a committee that hired a writer to produce its sales literature, PhDs, and the 40-question write-in (impossible to fail) test. While these are questionable scams, they illustrate the demand for easily digested information. The only limit is your ingenuity.

    4. *Technical and Service Writing* – The late John Gardner, author of the controversial book *On Moral Writing*, believed that his writing workshops at SUNY-Binghamton always turned out to be exercises in developing character. Not story characters, but the writer's character. He wrote a lot of books about writing that were sold to other writers, serving the profession.

There is another benefit to service writing: people take notice of well-done work. It comes back to what Gardner said about building character, building know-how, and building an edge. It is sought after in every profession.

It worked for me. Writing about prison is 180 degrees from my ambitions as a novelist. Doing it has opened up all the doors, whereas writing fiction mostly opened up snubs. I cut my teeth with fiction but got paid doing technical writing. My original work was a 30-week evidence-based personal development course designed for prisoners leaving prison soon. It was called *Take a Load Off* (TLO).

It took a few years to develop in the classroom, but when done, it ran 400 pages divided between 5 handbooks. A program manual, a facilitator's guide, and three workbooks. It was the first book I "self-published" since distribution was just slapping it down on a Xerox machine and burning it down. I shipped copies to other prisons, organizations, and got parts of it available as a PDF for download (fairshake.net). Without TLO, I wouldn't have found my calling as a writer, but otherwise, it paid the bills and helped a lot of inmates prepare for their release from prison. I served this field with dozens of articles and even a book, *Life With A Record*. The work itself was a crossover of in-service and technical writing. Here's the difference:

    4 a. *Technical Writing* – Technical writing isn't very dramatic; its value is based on insights from training and direct experience. If you work in a factory, then manuals may be needed for machine

operators. Research and development programs need proposals written, and assembly instructions for new products are always in demand. The writing just has to be clear and concise.

Wayne T. Dowdy used to rob drug stores and zone out in dive apartments. Now he writes in a cell, trying to change his situation. A quick learner, he embraced responsibility and became an instructor in Federal Industries (UNICOR), tutoring at the Quality Assurance Apprenticeship Program.

He's written tests, curriculum, and teaches others how to write instructional documents, manuals, policies, and procedures. Since UNICOR pays him to do this, he is a professional service writer. "I literally earn pennies in comparison to what I would earn doing so as a freelance technical writer in society," Dowdy says. He's right. It pays from 35¢ to $1 a word.

   4 b. *In-Service Writing* – Service writing serves a profession. That's how Jorea Hardison used her expertise in teaching nonprofit organizations (501(c) 3) compliance. She collaborated with SJM Family Foundation to produce a program now used institutionally. Her experience with writing curriculum, lesson plans, and interpreting recovery-management information helped her go even further. She's been paid to write grants, business plans, and the National Certified Peer Recovery Professional (NCPRP) handbook.

The recovery field deals with a lot of troubled souls. Alcoholism, sex addicts, and suicidal patients are the norm. The practice is based as much on psychiatric fundamentals as it is on a positive outlook. Hardison brought plenty of both to her work. The NCPRP handbook makes money by offering a 40-question certification course for $245.

In-service writing makes money differently than charging by the word for technical manuals, but it is the same business. These types of jobs are typically done for an employer (you may work as a contractor), so weigh the value of your work before you bid on the job. Usually, any book that's intended to guide a profession is worth several thousand bucks or a royalty split.

   5. *Lotto Tickets* – Lotto Tickets, by definition, have outrageous odds. We all delight in the idea of a boatload of cash. A one-hit wonder. It almost never happens. When it does, many writers find themselves in a sticky situation because expectations are set so high for their next piece. Can they do it again? Some try, like Diablo Cody.

She was only 29 when she tapped out the screenplay for *Juno*, a film which won many awards, including Best First Screenplay and a Golden Globe. This success launched her memoir *Candy Girl*, about her time stripping in topless joints and peep shows in Minneapolis. In it, she explained that after "retiring" as a phone sex operator, she decided to test another part of her body, her mind, and wrote *Juno*.

Cody (real name Brook Busey-Maurio) was unflappable through the early attempts to place her screenplay. But it was about "girl-centric cinema," which quickened producers' interest during talks. Cody dropped some of her classic gripes about how, in most movies, girls are nothing but sexy bodies. "What does he see in her?" Things just fell into place; she hit a nerve, and pow, the lottery ticket worked.

She said that there are a lot of frustrated screenwriters who were embittered by her success. "They feel like it's entirely due to my appearance. What's so funny is that my entire life -and when I was stripping -I was always told that I wasn't pretty enough. And then, when I actually achieve something that is purely intellectual and creative, I get accused of having succeeded only because I'm pretty. To me, that's the definition of irony."

Things stalled despite the buzz, the star status, and the interviews on national media when her next screenplay, *Jennifer's Body*, bombed. It couldn't even be saved by A-list actresses like Amanda Siegfried and Megan Fox. Where is she now? It's not common knowledge, but she hasn't gone back on her word just yet. "When you succeed in L.A., you develop a bit of an entitlement complex. So now I would want the guys to grind on me. I can't imagine being in the service of a male again."

A massive payday doesn't last forever. Recently, Cody took a crack at adapting the *Sweet Valley High* novels into a big-screen project for Universal Pictures, but the script stalled. We might hear of Diablo Cody in some strip joint someday, or maybe she'll crack another code of girl-cinema or something new. Until then, she'll have to be content cashing in on her notoriety as a script doctor, working out kinks in other people's scripts.

6. *Passion Projects* – Writers who invest time sharing their passions with readers can gain awesome rewards. This happened in 1955, when Sol Stein was working as an editor and wanted to publish several experimental and controversial collections in large paperback editions. One of the authors he believed in was James Baldwin, the African American success story from Harlem.

Stein's motivations were complex; he wanted to raise awareness as well as make a buck. He pitched it, but publishers kept turning the idea down. He just kept asking people until he got what he wanted. "I kept an egg timer on my desk to monitor the length of the long-distance calls." Stein wrote about it later. He swallowed hard, stuck his finger into the rotary dial phone, and listened to the rings on the other end at the desk of Malvern Arnold, the captain of Beacon Press. "Within three minutes, Mel Arnold said he'd fly down to New York to discuss my plan."

The best passion projects overlap your desires, matching your "baby" with a strong market. Debbie Puente is a cook and an author. When her book, *Elegantly Easy Crème Brûlée and Other Custard Desserts*, was published, she went right to work promoting it by demonstrating how to make crème brûlée. Her passion for cooking was infectious, plus her crème brûlée isn't half bad. She says, "Tasting samples helps sell books. Look at Costco! Handing out samples gets conversations started, and once someone stops to talk to you, there's a good chance that they will buy your book."

She conducted these demonstrations at mostly upscale cooking stores like Williams Sonoma and Sur La Table. She loved it enough to get out of her comfort zone. People have eaten Puente's cooking in lots of independent bookstores, cooking schools, expos, fairs, and even the Fancy Food show in New Orleans. She was invited.

Whether your work is conducive to demonstrations or stimulating debate, it's best to ground yourself. Consider the market, how you'll promote it, and the best way to address readers' underlying interest. If you can pull it off, you may end up one of the happiest authors out there.

✎ Writers Manifesto No. 12 – The stuff you write on the side you should probably write full time.

DID YOU KNOW?
The top 10 special writing markets are:

1. Critique (books, films, music, games, etc.)
2. Reports
3. Resumes
4. Technical guides
5. Assembly instructions
6. Sales literature and Ad copy
7. Curriculum
8. Operation Manuals
9. Authorized translations
10. Niche book-length manuscripts

Chapter Fourteen

"No one takes better care of your money than you do." – Cliff Leonard

UTILIZE THE MERCENARY MARKETPLACE
There's money in helping other writers get published. Freelance professionals make the trains run on time. Luckily, their asking fee is negotiable. Their favor is based on how strongly they feel about each project. Then you can talk about clearing their current workload and the client's budget. You can pay or get paid. Writing-related services are easy to grow into; just select projects that typify your portfolio.

MIRACLE WORKERS
In 1864, both his wife and brother died, leaving Fyodor Dostoyevsky broke and 15,000 roubles in debt. His monthly newspaper, Vremya (Time), was shut down, and his drinking was overtaken only by his gambling. He sought refuge abroad from creditors, but trouble seemed to follow him. Mostly, his fascination with roulette wheels drew him deeper into debt with the wrong kind of people.

Desperate for a miracle worker, he hired a string of assistants to help finish his next book to make some fast money. Each assistant flaked out. Dostoevsky's first novel, Poor People (1847), had brought him fame overnight, written in an apartment paid for by his father's generous allowance of 5,000 roubles a year. Those lazy days had ended long ago. Dostoyevsky lost it all after he was arrested for circulating an insolent letter against the Orthodox Church and the government (1889). He survived his punishment, a four-year sentence in a prison fortress in Omsk, Siberia, only to claw his way back to a life as a tabloid celebrity.

All that seemed unimportant as he ran from his creditors. His only hope was for a good stenographer to answer his ads. In dramatic fashion, one did. She became more than the stenographer for his new novel. Young and beautiful (and working for cheap), she pushed him away from drinking and gambling. Subsequently, The Gambler (1897) was published, and they were married. All in all, not a bad "third act" in the life of a writer, and all thanks to an inexperienced secretary.

PLACING AND ANSWERING ADS
You can't just write any ad asking for help. It's a good idea to test people's ability to follow directions and see whether they can communicate. There are all sorts of advertising guides and tutorials online, but try something like this:

Professional Assistant Needed
Writer seeks best assistant. Media or publishing background helpful. Work from home. Skills needed: editing, computer, and bookkeeping required. References required. Do not email your resume to lifewitharecord@gmail.com. Instead call 1-800-BUY-LWAR.

How would you respond to this ad? If you do anything other than call us, you're not going to make money. This test occurs when you respond to ads. You've got to prove you can adapt to the job and function as a contractor.

BACKGROUND CHECK

As a professional, I must warn you about rampant scammers. One estimate from the Science Fiction Writers of America puts the tally at 10,000 victims who shell out as much as $50 million each year to bogus agents, publishers, book doctors, and other scam artists. If anyone starts to nickel and dime you, ask for extravagant fees, or profit splitting, don't ignore the red flags. Act on it immediately. End it. Tell them not to call you.

Look up your prospective helpers on *Writers Beware* (sfwa.org/for-authors/writers-beware) and *Predators and Editors* (pred-ed.com). Do a general online search and ask around writers' forums and your writing community. Sometimes, the Better Business Bureau (bbb.org) database will turn up a star rating of freelancers' practices. Whatever you do, don't go in blind and don't be in a rush. You can't force chemistry (think what Dostoyevsky would've missed if he had).

> **Writers Manifesto No. 13 – Your contract was made by the lowest-bidding attorney.**

REVIEW THE CONTRACT

Whether you're selling or buying services, make sure your contract has an exact description of the work to be completed. Don't sign anything until there are concrete payment terms for each service. Also, it is wise to add an explicit statement about who "owns" the copyright to all resulting works, including editorial suggestions, and book cover illustrations.

If you're hiring a freelancer, then fill out a copyright form (copyrightoffice.gov, *Form TX*) with the contractor's name listed. Work is considered made for hire when the "author" is not the individual who actually created it. Instead, the party that hired the individual is officially the author and the copyright owner.

There are two situations where this applies: if the work is created by an employee as part of their duties, or if the individual and the hiring party enter into a written agreement that their work is specifically ordered or commissioned. In either case, label what they produce "Work Made for Hire" on the copyright form and add a statement that they have transferred all rights to you. Have them sign it. With the copyright registered in your name, any ownership disputes will die on the operating table.

MERCENARIES IN THE PUBLISHING BUSINESS

1. *Agents* – How do you get an agent? There's an old joke that you can't get a publisher without an agent, but you can't get an agent without already having been published. I've had nothing but rejection from agents since the beginning. Nowadays, I'd rather do the work myself and keep the royalties. But, at some point, life becomes too hectic, and we need someone with some flesh in the game to back us up. An Agent can be a great ally in advancing your career.

As hard as getting the first agent can be, trading up to a different one isn't uncommon. A *New York Times* bestseller with 40 books under her belt, Lisa Rogak did just that. "My previous agent was perfectly fine, but she didn't take charge of – or help steer – my career like my current agent." He made her focus and pick book topics with an eye toward building a career. Rogak advises, "Be ready to switch if it ceases to work for you."

> **Writers Manifesto No. 14 – Agents are 95% hope and 15% commission.**

Some agents are members of the Association of Authors' Representatives (AAR), which means they signed an ethics agreement. You can act as an agent without the membership, but it's worth the $150 annual fee to add their credential to your website. What matters is that you avoid agents who ask for evaluation fees, submission fees, or editing costs. A great source of information about hot agents is available on WritersDigest.com (the "Get Published" page).

The best way to get an agent is to submit your work yourself until an editor makes you an offer. While you are jumping up and down with joy, STOP, don't sign anything, tell the editor that you want your agent to look at the contract first. Then get in contact with an agent. Most of them will sign you on since you already did their job and have an editor on the hook.

An agent who takes you on agrees to work for a percentage, on commission. The average is 15% and will probably rise in the future (it's gone up from 10% over the last decade). What does 15% get you? Ideally, a salesperson with connections and negotiation skills who gives you editorial suggestions, business advice, and psychological boosts. Your agent runs interference for you with publishers, makes sure payments arrive on schedule, and generally looks after your literary welfare while you're busy writing.

    2. *Editors* – You can't buy software to evaluate and guide you in revising a manuscript. Qualified editors can be found all over, from online searches and writers forums, or by asking for recommendations from a writing community, or following up on ads. One of the best sources is the Editorial Freelancers Association (the-efa.org).

The idea is you'll meet editors with every submission and, in brief glimpses, every rejection. Regardless of how you interact with editors, there are some truths you must accept. Editors tend to fit into two categories.

    2 a. *Big-Picture* – They see manuscripts in general terms, whether the story is interesting, whether it's marketable, and so on. The pesky details, like clumsy sentences and scenes, are left further along in the production process.

    2 b. *Line Editor* – For the line editor, no detail in the manuscript is too small. This is somebody with eagle eyes who takes time to catch every problematic detail in your writing. Logic suggests you want the latter.

Now, pros and cons: both can get on your nerves and they can save your ass. The big-picture guy can seem over-optimistic and shallow. The latter guy can get on your nerves, nitpicking stuff that is acceptable but doesn't fit his taste. They can also encourage you to take risks that matter, and work on problems you're trying to sneak past.

The National Writers Union (NWU) estimates that editors get paid better than most writers:

- Copyediting $1.00 to $6.00 per page
- Content editing up to $3.75 to $20 per page (requires significant contribution)
- Typing 0.95 to $3.00 per page

Before you hire an editor, you want to have some chemistry with them. You may need a big picture person, a nitpicker, or a bit of both. If you ask the right questions, you can figure out what type of editor you're dealing with. All editors will make suggestions. The key to success is remaining objective, considering their point(s), and being grateful for the goodwill. If, and this is a big if, editors make a stupid suggestion, don't take it personally. Sometimes we are all flat wrong, and that is normal.

    3. *Designers and Illustrators* – Word processors and image libraries are no replacement for book designers and illustrators. A book's appearance (interior and covers) is the biggest factor in creating a first-class product. It plays a role in self-publishing as well as creating websites and sales literature.

    3 a. *Book Designers* – At the most basic level, Book Designers fix margins, use interesting fonts and graphics, and adjust the spacing between words (called kerning). No matter how little work they do,

readers can always tell a difference. Of course, for a dollar a page, it might pay for you to learn how to do it yourself. Two great guides are *Book Design and Production* by Pete Masterson and *InDesign Type* by Nigel French.

Writing community recommendations and web searches are the only way to find designers. Most have online portfolios with samples of their work. You should review all credentials and referrals from clients to match the designer best suited to your project.

      3 b. *Illustrators* – When John Grisham's *The Firm* was published, it hit tons of mass market bookstores. The cover art really seized readers. It showed a businessman in a tight suit holding a briefcase, while a puppeteer's strings controlled his movement. One journalist observed the effect when business traveler after business traveler stopped in an airport bookstore and stared at the cover. They were the heroes who had sold their souls to the corporation, controlled by the strings. They couldn't resist buying it.

If you see a book cover you like, odds are the artist's contact information is listed somewhere in the book. Another good source is art books like the Spectrum series, which lists artists' emails and websites. Even if an illustrator is represented by an agent, many still do freelance work on the side. The cost ranges from $100 to $5,000; it just depends on talent, style, availability, and chemistry.

To locate cover illustrators, you can begin your search on a number of artist communities. The most interesting are Deviant Art, Etsy, and numerous Facebook profiles. For the best results, stay on sites that focus on professional illustrators (directoryofillustration.com and illustrationweb.com), which helps pinpoint prospects who actually work on deadlines

      4. *Publishers* – Who exactly is the publisher? Is the publisher out there adjusting the presses at night? Are they making sure the copies get stocked and shipped? No. They are the CEO, the one who ultimately will sign the contract, and assume responsibility as your partner. Their job isn't to do everything; it's to make sure everything gets done.

If you become a publisher yourself, you'll spend a vast amount of your time delegating work to other people. Publishers farm out work as often as they can afford to. Editors, webmasters, bloggers, publicists, and authors are all contractors or employees working for a publisher. In some companies, the editor is also the publisher (wearing many hats).

Book projects follow a chain of command. You may convince an editor, but the editor then has to convince the publisher about it. They defend it, justify it, or point out some opportunity the work presents. Publishers are shrewd about making calls about when and where to invest in authors. They hold the purse strings and are running the business. If the project doesn't help them reach those goals, then prepare for rejection. The 10-second countdown begins with a public announcement: "We wish we could publish every submission that comes our way."

If you get to know the publisher first, they can override the editors. If they like you, publishers might make some bad decisions just to add your name to their catalog. Pass down your bogus manuscript to an editor and say, "Fix this," and that's that. If it bombs later, they can call it a prestige book. Or a mistake. Or an investment. Whatever, if they still like you, it'll be okay. Publishers are often good partners, too, since they can prioritize your book, lend an advance, or answer questions.

      5. *Other Writers* – Established writers who want to increase their cash flow can do so by offering their abilities for hire. All you need is a basic website, a decent portfolio, and the wherewithal to do okay work. They may write part of a book, research the footnotes, or handle the submission process. Each service comes with a price tag and a guarantee, well, sort of. The only guarantee is that you'll get what you pay for. They generally practice under two business models.

5 a. *Book Doctors* – Writers who call themselves Book Doctors come in many flavors and quality. Sometimes they focus on getting completed manuscripts published and call themselves Book Shephard. Others narrow their services to promoting authors, and label themselves Publicists or Marketers. Since there's no definition for what one should or shouldn't be, they can be anything.

Book doctors offer an eclectic mix of services, which include:

- Co-writing
- Ghostwriting
- Book design
- Locating freelance professionals (cover illustrators, publicists, agents, publishers, etc.)

5 b. *Bundlers* – With success, many independent publishers mimic the bigger houses and begin publishing other writers. Large services like Lulu, Book locker, and Infinity tend to rule the market with book publishing packages ranging from $300 basic eBook to full-fledged precious metals exchange rates (up to $2,000 for all the whistles and bells). There are still opportunities, however, for freelancers offering their services for about the same fees. They scoop up clients who desire a more personal touch.

Bundlers typically offer these services:

- Standard eBook and POD formatting
- Uploads to major online book retailers
- Website design and maintenance
- Social media design and maintenance
- Book trailer creation and upload
- Marketing bundles (online ads, magazine ads, direct mail flyers, email marketing, etc.)

✎ Writers Manifesto No. 15 – Edit, because it's less expensive to put ink on paper than to take it off.

RESOURCES
Background Check Directories
- bbb.com
- pred-ed.com

U.S. Copyright Office
- Circular 30: *Works Made for Hire*

Agent Directories
- aar-online.org
- agentsassociation.com
- writersmarket.com/agents

Editors Directory
- the-efa.org
- SOPS.com

Designers and Illustrators Directory
- directoryofillustration.com
- illustrationweb.com

Industry Watchdogs
- authorrealm.com/predictors

- sfwa.org/for-authors/writers-beware
- todayswriting.com/poetry-slams.html
- writersweekly.com/whispers_and_warnings.php

Chapter Fifteen

"Once you find what works for you, then you enter a new phase in your life, and you have to start all over again. Being creative isn't a fixed state." – Susan Elizabeth

FOLLOW THE MARKETS

We hear formulas and secrets for engineering a bestseller, it's riveting to believe the hype, but don't take the bait. In fact, many experts preach the gospel of bestseller formulas, probably just to keep us off balance. Nicholas Sparks is one of them. He's the author of such hits as Message in A Bottle. At the Los Angeles Times Festival of Books, he spent time explaining his theory to other bestselling authors. He said that each genre tends to have two writers who dominate it, with room for a third.

For the legal thriller, there were John Grisham, Scott Turow, and the current contender. For the female private eye novel, there were Sara Paretsky, Sue Grafton, and the current contender. You get the idea. By process of elimination, Sparks fooled everyone into believing that he had concocted a magic formula. There was only one leader in the male romance genre, that is, romance written by men for a female audience: Robert James Waller (*Bridges of Madison County*). With a slot available, Sparks decided to give it a try and was vastly successful.

✎ Writers Manifesto No. 16 – The secret ingredient in magic formulas is "gift of gab."

Suppose it was that easy to sell your soul for a paycheck, a lot more people would be doing it. Sparks' formula, like so many others, doesn't work when we think about it critically. Consider the study *Newsweek* did of over 1,300 top-selling books in one market: fitness, health, and weight loss. That's 1,300 authors who did well, no triplet of authors consistently sweeping the charts. People say they want original, but what they buy is the same old thing. If you're searching for a great story, don't overlook the thousands of stories that are sitting around out there in the public domain just waiting to be re-told.

STUDY THE MARKETS

No product appeals to everyone. Companies are tasked with analyzing all sorts of data about readers to determine if their interests fit into well-defined markets. Then other companies analyze that and explain about demographics. From these charts and findings, we're supposed to get an idea of what, generally, will sell. The truth is, they aren't always right. Just look at the black eye pollsters got predicting the 2016 election, they said Trump didn't stand a chance. It all proves that nothing has changed. Hell, the Victorian aristocrat and womanizer Benjamin Disraeli said it, "There are three kinds of lies. Lies, damned lies and statistics."

It's better to analyze the historical sales of a market and base your decisions on them. For illustrative purposes, I point to facts published by the Authors Guild. According to the experts, a successful fiction book sells 5,000 copies and a successful nonfiction book sells 7,500 copies, which requires you to write the type of book that 500,000 to 700,000 people will look at. Of those, about 1 percent may actually buy a copy.

The top 10 popular markets:

1. *Fiction* – Thriller, fantasy, historical, adventure, mystery, romance, science fiction, with sub-genres like horror, techno-thriller, courtroom drama, gothic fiction, women's fiction, etc.
2. *Nonfiction* – Religious, New-Age, Philosophy, Theology, Family History, Prayer Books, etc.
3. *Crafts/Cooking* – Collecting, Photography, Hobbies, Home Improvement, etc.
4. *General Nonfiction* – Biography, True Crime, True Adventure, Humor, Military History, etc.
5. *Psychology/Recovery* – Popular psychology, Children, Relationships, Health, Exercise, etc.
6. *Technical/Science/Education* – Computers, Business and economics, medical, science, and math, social science. etc.
7. *Graphic Novels* – Comic books, illustrated novels, manga, etc.
8. *Art/Literature/Poetry* – Literary fiction, Art and architecture, Performing Arts, etc.
9. *Reference* – Study guides, dictionaries, etc.
10. *Travel/Regional* – Domestic and Foreign travel guides, etc.

Study helps coordinate the form. Focus on top sellers that relate to your work. Check out their report card on Amazon. Has it sold recently? Are the reviews good? Does it pop up on the first page when you search for it? Listen to your gut; if it looks promising, then spend a little more time digging.

Bookmark where contenders appear, ads, social media, critical reviews, and bulletin boards. These venues are the key to unlocking readers. What websites, magazines, and blogs are they viewing? What is the total traffic? Add up the numbers and formulate a market share, then strategize to carve a slice for yourself.

PREDICT SALES
The best way to predict sales for any book is to review personal sales experience in its category. Research how similar books have done that year, what the prices were, and how large the market appears to be. One source for comparative sales figures is from a book wholesaler called Ingram.

Ingram's automated stock sales system reveals how many books restocked in each of Ingram's warehouses, how many copies Ingram has sold last year, and how many they have sold so far this year. All you need is a book's ISBN. They process more than half of the books in the U.S., so they can give you a decent idea of the rate of sales for any given category.

Amazon provides sales rankings, and they also share how many books are selling against each other. It helps chart other titles closest to your project. This gives you a real-time profile of consumer activity.

RINSE AND REPEAT
The internet creates pockets of interest for specific genres and themes. When popularity dims, it usually reemerges. A proven strategy is to anchor formulaic markets with great characters. It has worked for mystery, thriller, and romance forever. Have you heard these names: Jack Reacher, Suki Stackhouse, Claire Beauchamp, Harry Potter? We call these stories "vehicles." When they lead to successful series, they may be called "tent poles" because the original concept supports an entire franchise. As a writer, you put your hero into the worlds we have seen a dozen times before, but show us something different in the way they interact with them.

One of my students got really excited about this idea. He threw up his arm, demanding to speak. I pointed my gun finger and dropped the hammer. "Boom. Fire away," I said.

"Okay, so what if I wrote about slaves on a plantation, preparing to riot, but they get busted? That next night is a full moon, and the master gets ravaged by a beast because one of the slaves is a werewolf. The whole story is about how the werewolf interacts with the environment?" He said. I shrugged. That's a questionable idea, but it's a vehicle.

We expect certain things to pop up in vehicles. The werewolf is homesick and avenging his people. The werewolf is interacting with the Underground Railroad. The werewolf volunteered to fight in the Civil War. That's three books.

Two researchers made a company called Epagogix that used supercomputing to deduce the success of Hollywood movies. Richard Copaken and Nick Meaney used "neural networking" to consider all the angles. They cared about the venue and whether it was a love story, as well as very specific aspects of the plot that they were convinced determined the outcome more than anything else. And they couldn't care less about whether the lead was Tom Cruise or Tom Jones.

So, how did they fare? Copaken approached Warner Bros and ran sixteen television pilots through the neural network and tried to guess the eventual audience size. In six cases, Epagogix guessed the number of American homes that would tune in within .06 percent. They estimated the earnings for nine films, all of which turned out to be within a few million dollars of actual ticket sales. This amazing feat caught a lot of attention. Some film critics thought the whole idea was crazy, believing that Copaken and his associates were scam artists. Yet their accuracy rating was 99.94 percent.

What was their secret? There were thousands of factors. But regarding storytelling, it was simple. Are there clear bad guys? How much empathy is there for the protagonist? Is there a sidekick? Their neural network was simply based on repetitive plots, stories, and archetypes. In other words, stories we've heard before are just using different characters, settings, and conflicts.

Rely on wisdom to make your writing decisions. Sniff for trends wherever readers are gathering, whatever they are talking about. Find your tribe. It's helpful to cruise sites like *Reddit* and *Goodreads*, searching for whatever is trending. "Oh, a Marine operating base gets magically teleported to the outskirts of the Roman Empire. Who will survive?" If readers are *buying* regularly, then it may be worth exploring the concept with your own twists. The ideas aren't a problem; will your time be worth it? If there aren't similar books in the market, you might want to shelve it and keep searching for a better fit.

STAY AHEAD OF TRENDS
Gathering information year-round helps you spot what's hot. This is especially true for the entertainment industry. In 2013, the premier Hollywood magazine, *Variety*, quoted a big executive, "Zombies and vampires are played out, the new lineup will include witches." This was a tip-off to what films would focus on in the coming years.

If you timed it right, then your witch novel was available before trailers hit cable TV. That gave you a chance of "sale by association" since people were Googling "witches" like crazy. This trend stormed into our lives in FX's *American Horror Story: Coven*, *The Last Witch Hunter* (with Vin Diesel), another *Blair Witch* movie, and Marvel's graphic novel adaptation of Laura K. Hamilton's *Sorceress P.I.* series. It came and went.

You can find tip-offs in various places. Several great directories are available. More than 56,000 magazines, newsletters, and more are listed in the Standard Periodical Directory (oxbridge.com). Each listing is accompanied by a brief description and full contact information. *Gebbie All-In-One Media Directory* (gebbieinc.com) and the National Trade and Professional Associations' annual directories are worthwhile resources for writers who have multiple books to promote. Another source for hot tips is *Publishers Weekly*. Read widely and read between the lines.

CONDUCT MARKET RESEARCH
Research doesn't guarantee you will follow opportunities to success, but if you build a book proposal, it can help convince a publisher to work with you. Or you may decide to use the information and self-publish like graphic novelist Greg McKinney. Here are a few highlights from the proposal he made:

- According to the *Wall Street Journal*, the graphic novel industry is worth $1 billion in the U.S., including collectors and small niche presses.

- Time.com quoted a Borders official as saying that graphic novels have had the largest growth percentage of any book market in the last four years. One graphic novel, Neil Gaiman's The Sandman: Endless Nights, made it onto the *New York Times* bestseller list with 10,000 pre-publication orders. Alan Moore's *The Watchmen* made it to the *Time* 100 best books list.

- Amazon bought Comixology, a company that has released 2,000 independent comic books through its "submit" feature. Self-publishers can place single issues of their comics and graphic novels for sale and get 50% of the net, after standard mobile distribution fees are deducted.

Does this mean you can slap together a graphic novel or comic and make bank because you are following the industry? If you jump in at that Goldilocks moment with a really great piece, maybe. Be as certain as possible before you act. Usable research covers the whole market. Missing pieces make it hard to do the work that comes after you publish. In Greg's situation, Barbarretta, his second graphic novel, didn't catch a lot of readers' attention.

CRAZES

Trends have a lifecycle, and they move fast. The 24-hour news cycle speeds up their decay (killing the novelty by exhausting it). It used to take 50 years for a literary trend to really develop and drop off. But with the internet and desktop publishing, you might see the rise and fall of billion-dollar trends in a matter of years.

The tracks of a craze become overburdened and disintegrate as more opportunity seekers jump on. Consider what it was like hearing about Lindsey Lohan's first DUI in 2008. Not everyone touched the story. Maybe she was sick. She proved to be a reliable mess, and the public wanted to see more. The tabloids scooped up every exclusive photo paparazzi could muster and slapped together op-eds about Lohan's downward spiral.

At the same time, seemingly, the Gods provided a feast of grown-up ex-Disney Mouseketeers self-destructing with arrest, stints in rehab, and shaved heads. Every drunken counter hop, any public embarrassment, all the attention-seeking stupidity got covered and fed a growing national obsession for the next couple of years. Then what happened? We all got tired of hearing about it. Magazines that tried to keep the flame alive went out of business due to a sharp decline in sales.

Crazes tend to flow like this:

- Introduction
- Maturation
- Saturation
- Decline

You can jump onto the hottest new craze and try your luck. The trick is to identify its progress in the market and to time your arrival for maximum profit. Since things haven't changed since a mass market came into existence, let's turn to the musty pages of history and examine the post-antebellum narrative. It sparked a national fever that spurred writers to crank out more "slave fiction."

INTRODUCTION

It all started with true stories by ex-salves, like Frederick Douglass. But it quickly reached the masses thanks to the novelist Harriet Stowe. Stowe was like the Eminem of her era. She snatched the popular black art form and paraded it around with the sanctimony of a football. Believe it or not, she was no Iggy Azalea; her writing had quality. Stowe transcended the public hunger for sentimental fiction. She served up the raw, blacks-being-whipped violence they really wanted to read.

Stowe had haters, like Eminem did, too. Nathanial Hawthorn called her a "damn scribbling woman," which back in those times was equivalent to saying, "she is a huge pain." This made her an underdog. Her writing helped advocate causes and made a lot of money. In 1851, the scribbler's novel *Uncle Tom's Cabin* was the first book in America to sell a million copies.

MATURITY
The next big hit in the slave narrative was a brilliant trend spotter, (another Harriet) Harriet Wilson. She published this long title *Our Nig: Or, Sketches from the Life of a Black in A Two-Story White House, Showing That Slavery's Shadow Falls Even There*. Its publication in 1859 marked the first novel by an African American woman. It also marked the publication of the book with the longest title ever. The book capitalized on the human sensibilities of white northern women and unified the craze.

SATURATION
What kept the trend thriving was Frederick Douglass, who spoke to legislators and foreign dignitaries about the plight of man. It canvassed the exploitative aspirations of writers who were taking notice of the profits being made from writing about slavery. Some even posed as survivors. Manuscripts were being prepared at a record rate, and they began to fill up space in magazines and newspapers.

DECLINE
The last smash hit of the slave narrative was dropped by (understand, Harriet was a popular girl's name in the late 1800s) Harriet Ann Jacobs in 1901. Incident of A Slave Girl reads like Ann Frank in the antebellum South. Jacob's story was vivid as she survived her enslavement by hiding in the crawl space of an attic on her owner's property for several years. She used sentimental conventions to describe the plight of a black woman intent on keeping her virtue in an immensely cruel and dehumanizing system. A Northern woman rallied to buy it. But it marked the end of the line as societal change and other popular literature overtook the trend.

With unlimited searchable access to whatever we want, technology has given us an all-you-can-eat buffet. When something cool comes along, it sparks a revolution, swells with millions of fans, and then creators begin tweaking fundamental parts of the story to keep people interested. After a while, these changes become too convoluted and begin hemorrhaging post-obsessive fans.

Consider the inevitable progressions of these modern trendsetters:

- Robert Kirkman's *The Walking Dead*
- Stephenie Meyer's *Twilight Series*
- FOX's *Empire*
- George R.R. Martin's *Game of Thrones*
- AMC's *Breaking Bad*

BEFORE MARKETS CHANGE
When trends are exhausted, their market shrinks. If you aren't aware of the market's history, you may detect a false opportunity to write something that these readers enjoy, but your profit margin will be smaller than expected. Readers' tastes become less focused on the original elements. They crave variety and experimentation within plot, theme, and characterization.

Once genres and themes reach saturation, some creators decide to stop while they're ahead, to "quit at the top." For consumers, familiarity is absorbing. But when an idea, for example, "supernatural romance," nears decline (movies, books, comics, we're talking about it as a common example), then table it until you detect an interest.

Be ready to spring into action. Even exhausted markets can come back with time, as space allows novelty to return. It may take a year or decades or just one cunning writer, provided you focus tightly on a single aspect of the market. It's a matter of letting the giants bleed out, then being the first writer to re-imagine the elements that made readers fall in love in the first place.

RESOURCES

Comparative Sales Data
- ingram.com
- amazon.com

Industry Directories
- oxbridge.com
- gebbieinc.com

Industry News
- publishersweekly.com
- variety.com

Write & Get Paid

PART 4
STYLE

Chapter Sixteen

"When we study human language, we are approaching what some might call the 'human essence.'" – Noam Chomsky

READ WITH PURPOSE
What you write is the product of all the reading you've done in your life. We've been influenced by all the writers we admire, and we all want to write great stuff at a fast pace, but the imagination has its limits. In order to write more masterfully, we must do the thing we expect others to do: writers read.

Authors have a source of energy that drives them, sometimes that manifests in abstraction. Reading helps nail down abstract thoughts. For example, Philip K. Dick did not meet cyborgs struggling with human emotions (*Blade Runner*). Kafka never witnessed an office drone turn into a cockroach (*Metamorphosis*). Kurt Vonnegut didn't come 'unstuck in time' and become an alien zoological attraction (*Slaughterhouse 5*). These were abstract ways of authors removing themselves from the parts of life that hurt, and in some weird way, told us something about life in general.

Reading also provides invaluable examples of structure. Amy Holden Jones can remember the first time she had to write a horror movie, when she first had to write a comedy, and when she first had to write an action film. "I would get myself down to the Writers Guild library or the Academy Library, and I would sit down and read some of the best in the genre." It helped her the most in her career, and it'll do the same for you.

FOCUS YOUR READING
Some writers, like Ray Bradbury, like to read poems before they begin the day's work. As Bradbury said in *Zen in the Art of Writing*, "Poetry is good because it flexes muscles you don't use often enough. Poetry expands the senses and keeps them in prime condition." For other writers, it's humor that gets them going, whatever it is that allows you to enjoy yourself, read that. "In enjoying myself," said Miranda July, "just as hopefully the audience will, you kind of open up and then other stuff can come out, maybe deeper stuff." Odds are in your favor; whatever it is, the results will be better than you expected.

Narrow your focus to tone, instead of genre. Read broadly to see executions in as many venues as possible (poetry, screenplays, novels, etc.). Each manuscript has a completely different form, tone, and quality. It gives authors a variety of viewpoints to draw upon, which is the lifeblood of developing good craft. It helps to avoid predictable treatment of a subject, keep tone consistent from start to finish, and learn to recognize built-in problems.

High-quality reading can lead to good results, as John Lukas once said, "Style begins the way fashion begins, somebody admires how the other man dresses and adopts it for himself." There's nothing wrong with drawing ideas from or even emulating your favorite writers, so long as you don't try to copy them. By focusing, you can get more immediate benefits, insights, and control over your writing.

Four major types of tone:

1. *Comic*: an absurd motive, exaggeration, wildly dissimilar elements placed close together.

2. *Romantic*: an emotional motive, sensory details, metaphors, or other heightened language.

3. *Factual*: a plausible and ordinary motive, everyday dialogue, mundane details.

4. *Cynical*: a sarcastic motive, gritty details, weary emotions.

When I'm reading, it's normal to stop and mark passages I like, ones that really stand out. It may be a line of dialogue or a tense scene. If I look at my manuscript and find parts of it to be lacking in a certain area, I might reread relevant passages and let the style of the author wash over me. This clicks my head into a different mode, returning to my work with heightened awareness. Your own collection of passages could go in your Daily Planner or a separate file. Go through them periodically and see if a bit of magic prose makes a difference.

A PLACE TO TURN

If you don't feed your head with good examples, it's easy to flounder. When your ideas aren't making it to the page, it's a sign you should read more. Then write some more, repeat. If you have any doubts about the outcome, just study. There are many aspiring writers who do nothing but talk about writing. It rarely leads to any actual writing, but reading can.

I'll never forget a novice writer who ambushed me, nudging my arm with a manuscript, emphatically telling me his work was 'better than college level.' I smiled, "Sophomore or senior?" He didn't notice my joke. He had dark circles under his eyes and dreamy gestures. He smelled bad. He looked like someone who's burned the candle at both ends and is permanently singed. I sighed, took a look at a couple of pages, and waved him to follow me over to a bookshelf.

"This is what you need." I plucked one at random, *The Whiskey Priest* by Graham Greene.

"What am I supposed to do with that?" He asked.

"Read."

I read the first few pages aloud, then the first pages of his manuscript. There was no mistaking the difference. Greene's masterful flow blends descriptions and characterization in a way that grabbed our interest. I clapped the book shut and held it out for him to take, along with some advice about studying as well as reading. A few months later, he approached me with a very different attitude, with a deeper understanding and a little more command in his writing.

A few habits that boost your study:

- Keep a dictionary nearby. Words you don't know the meaning of, look them up, maybe keep a list, and copy down their definitions.

- Keep a list of eloquent lines (even whole paragraphs and pages). Read them from time to time and imitate their style. Pay attention to how authors articulate their ideas, switch focus, dialect, and other cool techniques.

- Write summaries about every book that leaves an impression, but be sure to explain what that impression was and what makes it so special. Consider not only the content of the message, but the thinking underlying it, so when you reread your notes, it'll cut to the central concept.

Imitation is the most effective way to build what Cicero and Aristotle called "rhetoric," the ability to compose thoughts in a pleasing manner. Not only does a reader appreciate high-quality writing, but writers also undergo a metamorphosis once they find the perfect word for the occasion. It can distinguish your perspective and style and get you closer to trafficking in your own ideas.

Kyle Bluelegs, a Lakota Sioux, embarked on his first book fueled by the excitement we all feel after reading great books. He sought out specific authors who write about the topics he wanted to write about. To his surprise, their style began to surface in his own writing. "I keep getting confused," he said, "The focus keeps changing depending on what I read." His concern, however, was that his voice kept changing. It's nothing to worry about. I told him that artists, athletes, writers, and many other trades rely on imitation as a learning tool.

"I've had this very question come up in writers' conferences and panels," novelist Linda Hall says, "and my best advice is to always read, and never be afraid of losing your voice, and never stop reading." A voice that you could lose would not be your voice to begin with. It will be something else, like when people fake an accent. Words come as they are, while easily expanded by learning from other writers, it's simply training for the voice you already have.

PUT ON YOUR CEO HAT
Reading the perfect thing can give you the tools to open the door to new venues. Gather inspiration from similar manuscripts. Read your publisher's catalog, and the authors they've chosen tell you everything you need to know about what styles and themes are already covered. Work in changes with each rewrite until your work is as expressive and marketable as it can be.

Don't overlook the potential of combining examples from various styles. Jennie Jarvis is one of the many authors who views hybridization as the name of the game. She took from all forms of writing in order to make herself better. She says, "I wanted to write movies and nothing else. But in this digital age, being one kind of writer doesn't really work anymore." Doing so led to published novels and teaching workshops on screenwriting versus fiction. Jarvis's success demonstrates why there is no better habit for writers than to read with professional intent.

Pay attention to the history of a genre, and you'll grasp the influences that have led other writers, as well as their audiences, to form their expectations. The path of least resistance is paved by reading with purpose. Read to answer questions, especially when opportunities pop up to write for new markets, or if you're thinking about doing a crossover, or even writing under a pen name for a different audience. Reading is still the best way to maneuver those changes successfully.

William Faulkner had a unique voice. So does Dean Koontz, in fact, Koontz's voice has consciously changed over the years as he has tried new things in his writing. Changing your style to match your taste gives you room to grow and time to process new ideas. J.K. Rowling has a voice recognized by millions of readers, but she successfully switched not only genres, but genders, using the pen name Robert Galbraith.

Mastering language goes beyond rote memorization. It's not as simple as remembering the schoolhouse ditty "I before E, unless sounding in A, like neighbor and weigh." A writer needs a different set of skills. You're like a chef who needs to know the difference between cooking with butter and margarine, depending on the recipe. Language is, in fact, always changing; the only way to stay ahead of what sounds natural is to write and read constantly.

LIFETIMES OF GUIDANCE
No matter how outrageous, absurd, or fantastical stories are, they force us to consider the human side of others, their time, and culture. By reading, you'll discover ways to show your own reality, and maybe some abstract thoughts. The interchange of ideas is never-ending.

Let's say you wanted to write an epic and had never done so before. Could you find stuff to read that will help? Yes, in fact, you could even read more than a few 'masterpieces' which were written it the same way. It took Frank Herbert over ten years to read enough, write, and rewrite Dune, the bestselling science fiction book of all time. Regarded as a masterpiece today, it all started with Herbert simply wanting to create an epic. He read and blended themes from Greek tragedies, religious, occult, military, and other histories.

The layers of mythology are unmistakable. It's no surprise that Dune evokes such feelings from readers. Its influences, from *Lawrence of Arabia*, *Oedipus Rex*, the Bible, and the Koran, grip readers with no less immediacy than the original sources. Herbert said, "I can read every page and see all the layers, each story I added, and remember what it was before." Ironically, all that blending allowed Herbert to share his original ideas. In turn, his ideas inspired a generation of other writers. Herbert's synthetic humans inspired android characters in the Alien and Star Trek franchises. His sandworms have reappeared in other people's games, movies, and graphic novels.

Some people say that everything has been thought of before, but that's not entirely true. The ability to articulate ideas more clearly or to imitate the style your editors prefer is a priceless skill. They unify the art and the business of writing under one skill: storytelling. Tobias Wolf said, "We are storytelling animals. It is how we organize the past, try to make sense of it, to see patterns our actions create, to see how these patterns break or repeat them, even in the stories of others, we begin to recognize ourselves." With consistent reading, you'll find motivation, and creativity really sets in.

Writers Manifesto No. 17 – The path of least reluctance is paved by reading with purpose.

RESOURCES
- time.com/100-list-of-best-books
- librarything.com
- goodreads.com

Chapter Seventeen

"The true writer knows that feeling must give way to form." – Jeanette Winterson

WRITE BETTER

For every rule that someone throws at you – never use narration, never use a flashback or a flashforward, never set your story in only one room, never write a period piece, never get involved in a land war in the Middle East – you'll find a successful manuscript that shatters that rule into a million pieces. Worry less about rules and more about the passion you need to bring to your manuscript.

Readers travel across the landscape of possible material; they'll know a false note when they hear it. But if there is something about it, that same thing that got the author up each morning to tell it, then a bright spot can form. Write your very best. Write your most authentic tales and characters. Passion translates to the page.

LISTEN TO YOUR GUT

It's not just about you. You may put a lot into a character, but do it to find a way to make it more objective, more universal, something that other people can relate to. Tap into something personal for yourself (anger, joy, grief, celebration) and then make a creative leap from there. Writer and director Tom DiCillo once said, "If it ain't personal, it ain't no good." There's something to be said for that.

If you care, then readers might feel the same way. Barbara O'Neal, author of 40 novels, regular blogger, and teacher of workshops around the world, said it best: "We go to the theatre to worry, it's been said. The same is true of a book. We want to be emotionally invested in a tale, and that means we need someone to worry about. To worry, we first must care."

A literature professor at the time, Tom Cole, reviewed a student's first manuscript and lectured, "This is very personal; it has your own stamp on it. Don't ever let people, with their advice, sand it down and make it smooth and turn it into something that could have been written by a lot of different people." Writing from the heart is different than writing what you know. Write to the gut.

If it feels guttural, it feels like it's coming from a very true place. You may develop plot twists. Your dialogue may become heated. Your narrative may run off instinct, in the moment, and there's nothing "writerly" about it. If you just write to the human moments – those scenes of human drama – that will pay off, because people connect to it.

It's easy to forget to write to the heart of your manuscript, but the better writer you become, the more you want to show that you're a good writer. But it's easy to switch back into that. You can access that no matter what the situation. If its heart is intact, then we can, as human beings, relate to it. That's why we download music, go to the movies, or buy a book.

MEET EXPECTATIONS

Readers are a fussy lot. They may suspend their disbelief while reading, but that runs down a narrow highway. Stray too far from that road and you'll lose the readers, perhaps for good. If you've given them a romantic story, keep it romantic. Turning it into a cynical downer halfway through will only annoy the reader. If it's a drama, don't turn it into a farce in act three. If it's a thriller at the beginning, it's better to be a thriller at the end.

Genres are well defined: romance, horror, sci-fi, thriller, action, but with their popularity comes responsibility. That includes how you fill the chain: beginning, middle, end. The norm runs like so: initiation – separation – return. That covers the totality of sagas from *Pride and Prejudice* to *Toy Story*. There are rules in every market, and you break those rules at your peril. However, give that cliché a twist and you can set your story apart, while also helping it connect with readers.

MAKE IT CHARACTER-DRIVEN

For a story to come alive, the people in it must come alive. The narrative should always be about behavior, character behavior. A lot of poorly written manuscripts make it about movement – moving left, moving right, moving towards the window, moving away from the window – and sometimes that's important. But it's not as important as behavior.

Which of these sounds more interesting: "She looked around the lounge" *or* "Perched in an office chair, she snuck a peek at the clock"? Really interesting, fresh, unique behavior makes a character somebody we want to see more of.

All you have to do is look around at real people. Draw inspiration from real people, and it's easier to work with the motives you understand for your characters. Some characters may still elude you to the very end, but there are several techniques you can use that help develop their uniqueness:

- *Physical Description* – Include their mannerisms. Joe wears a Tigers baseball cap, always.
- *Name and Nicknames* – Her name was Lucille, she called herself Lill, but her friends knew her as Nancy.
- *The Physical Context of the Character* – What they own, their lifestyle, character props. Old Gracie slept in a rundown farmhouse and stashed her government checks in a Maxwell House coffee can.
- *Dialogue* – What they say and how, including favorite expressions, repeated throughout a story.
- *The Person's Statements* – If they confide they're "worried about their son," "euphoric about the promotion," "feeling nostalgic for Kansas," it grants access to an interior life.
- *The Person's Written Words* – A letter, diaries, memoirs, reports, depositions, police statements, and recordings. These serve as a window into the character's imagination and thought process.
- *Any Item that Reflects the Character's Essential Qualities* – a painting they've done, a schooner they've built, a nonprofit organization they've created.
- *Anecdotes that Illustrate Character Traits* – When the Army failed to provide adequate food for his men in Cuba, Teddy Roosevelt bought provisions for them out of his own pocket.
- *How Others React in the Person's Presence* – The old convicts grudgingly made room for Alex at the cafeteria table.

Schools teach you about single intention, and certainly, if an actor can't play two intentions at once, it can become tricky for a writer as well. But you don't want to shortchange your entire story by writing dumbed-down characters. Characters with one goal may be simpler, but are they more interesting? The most important thing to remember while decorating your characters is that real people are multidimensional. Characters that have genuine, deep-rooted intentions, that are plural, are great. They're fun characters to read about and drive a story.

TIMELESS STORYTELLING

Many literature teachers say a story is all about tension and conflict. And, in some ways, that is absolutely true. But if that tension and conflict doesn't arouse enough interest to have people really want to know what's going to happen next, then you're screwed. You need the equivalent of a cart rolling down a hill; once it's going, you can't stop it. In *Life of Pi*, by Yann Martel, the shipwrecked hero will surely die if he doesn't eventually reach land. We care because everything Pi loves went down with the ship. And in the meantime, there is the matter of a man-eating tiger sharing his raft.

The magic that distinguishes would-be writers from the real thing is the ability to present conflict and motive in a fresh way. There is only one story: a person, group, or entity wants something. Perhaps it's to survive a blizzard, to get married, to dominate the world, or to save a child trapped in a fire. Another person, group, or entity throws up every barrier imaginable to stop that from being achieved. Classically speaking, only six themes keep popping up in that plotline:

1. Innocence vs. Experience
2. Conformity vs. Rebellion
3. Culture vs. Identity
4. Love vs. Hate
5. Justice vs. Tyranny
6. The Presence of Death

The limited selection won't hold you back. Painters use only primary colors – blue, yellow, red, black, and white – and look at the variety they produce. When scenes feel cliché, you can still surprise yourself. Ask, "Okay, what would be the conventional, expected way to do something about it?" Stop and think. What if you just took a detour? How would you get out of the situation? It can be really exciting. It prompts you to stir up unexpected elements.

When you write, consider the root of a strong plot. Carl Jung's theories of archetype and the collective subconscious give us universal structures that we find inherently intriguing. Like our passage from birth, through age to death represented metaphorically by the passage of the sun and moon, the progress of the seasons, or a heroes' journey. Dish out hidden motivations, past events, and deeper reasoning. It'll give your story substance. Readers will stay glued to a high standard.

HOW PEOPLE REALLY SPEAK

Understand that people don't often say exactly what's on their minds. There's nothing more tiresome than dialogue where people are unfiltered all the time. It's just not the way people talk.

As a writer, you need subtext and intention; you know what the character wants from each scene. Think of them as if they were real people talking in your ear. Writers like Georgette Heyer recreate the world of upper-class Londoners in *Regency England*, using formal words like "naiveté," "trivialities," "indulge," "resolve," and "continence." Ian Rankin writes about an alcoholic police detective using ordinary words like "late," "looks," and "tired." In every case, authors choose words appropriate to their purpose.

Some dialogue is so fake it feels like you're chewing on plastic fruit. Consider *Family Guy* and its puns. The obscene cultural references often make little sense, but are delivered with a wind-up, a pitch, and a punch line. It sounds like a joke, and the punch line is in the right place. So, what if we don't comprehend the humor of C-3PO hitting a Sprite vending machine for his change?

Only one method of crafting good dialogue exists: give your characters something interesting to say. Mark Twain had a distinctive voice. It came with a twinkle in the eye and a satirical bent towards the human condition. Also, the ability to string words together that makes us laugh, sometimes uncomfortably at ourselves. His ear for dialogue was apparent in the journalism he wrote early in his career. It became iconic for its slang and things left unsaid. Twain, like many masters, also used a handful of techniques to find the essence of heartfelt dialogue:

- *Cut Repetition*

    "Jill. I'm going downtown to the library," Jack said.

    "Okay, Jack, I'll see you later," Jill said.

Read it aloud. Sounds phony, doesn't it? If you cut it down, it sounds much better.

    "Babe, I'm going downtown."

    "Okay. See you later."

- *Chop Guttural Expressions*

    "Don't let me catch you cheating!" Jill hissed.

You can't hiss if you don't use sibilants. Jill growled? It won't work either. Jill spat? How about bark, rasp, or rumble? At best, expressions are inaccurate. You tend to get more effect by chopping them altogether or using them sparingly.

Stick with simple speech tags, "said" and "asked" work well. In extreme situations, "demanded" or "insisted" may be right, and "shouted" or "screamed," although that's why exclamation marks were invented. Maybe "whispered" or "murmured." Keep asking yourself, "Does this give my dialogue interesting consequences?"

- *Use Action and Description*

    "I'll track you down!" The Sheriff's cheeks were as scarlet as her hair.

Okay, it tells us something, but it's uneventful. Now look at it with some action added:

    "I'll guard you in your sleep." The Sheriff's eyes filled with tears as the knife dropped to the floor.

- *Create Interesting Effects and Subtle Pauses*

When carefully placed, speech tags can produce a pause and lend even dull dialogue a pace and rhythm that sings.

    "I know he doesn't believe I'll throw him a birthday party," Jill said. "Big mistake."

Take out the "Jill said" and you lose something.

- *Add Emphasis*

    "What am I going to do?" Jill exclaimed as one of the party balloons popped on the door spring.

It would be more eventful if Jill would stop exclaiming, and not "shout" or "shriek" or "wail" either. Like this:

    Jill stared at the deflated balloon. "What am I going to do?"

- *Careful with Colloquialisms*

"Hum" and "Ha" and "yeah" and "well" and "you know" and "okay" are overused to create the illusion of reality. Less is better. Furthermore, slang, and intentional misspelling also water down otherwise good writing.

> "Didja hear the Sheriffs gonna getcha?"

Try it out with straight spelling and it's stronger:

> "Didn't you hear the Sheriffs going to get you?"

If you want to dramatize illiteracy try just one misspelled word.

> "Didja hear the Sherriff's going to get you?"

IT'S WHAT YOU LEAVE OUT

One of the great things H.P. Lovecraft said was, "Never explain anything." It works especially well for horror. Look at a movie like *The Ring*, and then look at the Japanese version of it, *Ringu*. *Ringu* is really spare and simple, and they never explain anything. In comparison, the American version explains everything, to the point that it takes away all the magic.

Lovecraft's precept is a pretty good one to follow. At some point, usually near the end of a story, you end up only answering five questions: who, what, when, where, and why. Masters don't leap to answer all the questions instantly, if at all. They answer them without bombarding the reader. Masters strikes a balance where they only give out enough information to keep people interested in the story. It's mostly instinct, moving from one scene to the next. More accurately, it's rewriting, moving from one draft to the next.

Avoid an "explanation scene." *Psycho* takes us through the laborious and completely unnecessary dissertation on what Norman's problem is and why Norman did what he did. Not only is it a waste of time, it also sucks the energy out of the end of the movie. A bit of the energy comes back in the final shot, thanks to the brilliance of the actor, Anthony Perkins, refusing to crush a fly in his palm.

Some genres require explanation, but even they benefit from a little restraint. In a mystery, you want the reader to finally understand what happened, but you don't have to hit them over the head with it. *The Usual Suspects* does a brilliant job of putting all the pieces together in the last two minutes, without making the audience feel stupid. The suspect is chauffeured away by an accomplice who died in his alibi. It leaves "how" and "where" unanswered. Strive to take the details down to their essence, without losing the magic of the unknown. A little bit of mystery is very satisfying.

ACTIVE VS. PASSIVE

The tone of a story has a lot to do with how it's received. Masters have made their focus on widely different things, like the weight of combat gear in a jungle or the smells of a European city. This is what makes the work uniquely yours. Tone, however, is something where all the advice says to write in an active voice. Ali Selim didn't think it made a difference, but his manuscript kept getting nowhere. In desperation, he went through every line, switching passive sentences to active ones. It amounted to changing "Olaf is sitting" to "Olaf sits" and "Olaf is harvesting" to "Olaf harvests."

Editors said, "I have to publish this." Prior to that, they called it "soft." When he made it active, they called it "lean and athletic." No scene changes, no new behavior, no sex scenes or car chases. "Just dropping 'ing' and adding 's.' Go figure," Selim said. "In doing so, it went from 'distant, over there, who are they?' to an immediate and present emotion."

Masters will break all the rules they can and bend the rest. Where most advice tells us to use an active voice when writing, in which the subject of the sentence performs an action, some writers don't listen. They use the passive voice to emphasize something other than the performer of the action, to avoid identifying the protagonist or assigning blame, or to facilitate coherence by linking the thoughts in one sentence to another in a different way.

Sometimes they just break the rules because it sounds better. Consider these lyrics from "I Dreamed a Dream" from Les Misérables. The first two sentences are active, the rest are not.

> I dreamed that love would never die.
> I dreamed that God would be forgiving.
> Then I was young and unafraid
> and dreams were made and used and wasted.
> There was no ransom to be paid
> no song unsung, no wine untasted.

Whether the technique was used for nuance, a literary effect, or simply for the sake of rhyme, people the world over love it. Until you have a good reason to shut out a certain style, free yourself from the rules. Do whatever it takes to emphasize precisely, make points, and flow naturally. The important thing, after all, is getting the feeling across.

If you've got a different idea, a new approach, or a radical vision, give it a shot. My personal reminder is a quote from Tom DiCillo, a successful scribe of the bizarre, "Things don't have to be instantaneously perfect or whatever." Writing better is a matter of pushing your comfort zone until the feeling in your writing takes its strongest form; all a reader notices is that they keep turning pages.

✎ Writers Manifesto No. 18 – If the feeling doesn't fit, try a new form.

RESOURCES
Writers' Advice
- deareditor.com

Writers Lab
- mobap.edu/success
- wju.edu/arc/handouts

Chapter Eighteen

"The last thing one discovers in writing a book is what to put first." – Blaise Pascal

WRITE FASTER

I didn't start as somebody who could get up and put in a nine-to-five writing day. At first, I just couldn't do it. At the very end, when I was racing to the finish, I did. Up until that point, if I'd put in three to four hours, that was a good day. I had to write dozens of pieces, and sometimes they took more time to research or brew than I had until the deadline. What I found out was a way to move past hang-ups and get the right words on paper on time.

When I sit down to write, the first three days are the hardest. Literally, going into the room, or turning on the computer, and starting. If you spend the first two weeks of a project staring at a page, you learn to forgive yourself. That's just part of the process. The beginning is the hardest part, but I have an almost religious faith, based on the stuff I've written, that there is a point where you break through.

The first stages are a lot of non-writing: thinking, obsessing, tweaking the outline, thinking this is a disaster that is never going to happen. Then something clicks, you start to write, and you realize that all the worrying was really part of the process. Sometimes you struggle with things, and you have to literally take a day or two off. When you do that, wow, the ideas hit you and you can't wait to get back in there and get to work.

THE BREAKTHROUGH MOMENT

The breakthrough moment is a point where there's just enough stuff, you establish problems, and at that point, you start solving problems. It's not a big idea; it's something physical or, quite often, something visual. For example, a little peephole that a girl can open in the door.

Miranda July had a breakthrough moment just like that. "Sometimes I'll write a scene and I won't know until later why that little door will be opened. It seems very magical to me." But she wanted to know why it would be opened. She wrote a version with a girl opening a peephole without any clear objective. She started jumping around, senses flooding in, and eventually returned. "Oh, Robert knocks on the door because he's looking for his son!"

She started with that irrelevant detail, seemingly out of left field (the peephole) instead of "She needs to connect to this man." There's something about the irrelevancies and the physicality. At some point, you start to connect these disparate scenes. Pretty quickly, there are characters. And characters have intentions, whether you're conscious of it or not, and pretty quickly, there's a larger set of problems to feed them. "Like, how can the reader be reminded that she's thinking of him? And that becomes the 'Me' and 'You' shoes," July says. But by then, you're already moving into the next step of the writing process.

To speed up the breakthrough moment, you've got to reach a point where the problems are coming together. I usually compile a notebook, sometimes for months, sometimes for years, in advance. It's similar to a jigsaw puzzle set; it's a bunch of quotes, notes, and scenes that can be plugged in and set the problem-solving into high gear. There's always a moment where pieces begin to fit, and a story begins to develop.

THE SUBCONSCIOUS WRITER
Many honest writers confess that the first draft is what their subconscious is really trying to tell them. Look at how beautifully dreams are economically formed to express something. The same part of the brain is probably trying to write. Writing is not a science; it's an art. As such, you can really only apply so much theory to the process. After that, it's often better to let your gut take over and see where it leads you. That won't work on every draft or rewrite, but it's a good way to approach the first draft that pours out of you.

When I'm super-producing, there are more ideas popping into my head than I can keep up with, so I'll take notes of scenes, dialogue, and questions and return to them later. Try to get a bit of a skeleton in place for the events, and then try not to think too much. Prolific writers find that throughout their whole life, they've tried to get closer to switching off their conscious mind. The senses that are most alive are the ones that you think about the least; they just come out as if someone's talking to you and you're just writing it down. If you're Stephen King, that happens all the time, and if you're the rest of us, it happens sometimes, and sometimes you have to slog through some pages.

Dylan Kidd spoke about letting it flow, "For me it's important to follow your bliss in that first draft, even if it ends up (overlapping at points) or you hate everything but ten percent of it. At least you've gotten ten percent more than a lot of people have." Don't saddle your muse with too many restrictions right out of the gate. Rigidity kills creativity. Later drafts are when the craft kicks in and you start to edit and hone and tighten and improve.

You'll find that the best material is always from the part of you that doesn't think and doesn't really know what's going on. My technique, if I have one, has always been to try to get better at accessing whatever part of me knows how to write the story. I really don't mean that in any mystical, groovy, artsy way. Your subconscious mind has something it's trying to say. I'm astonished by how many elements that you would think a person has strung together on purpose just pop up by accident.

Writer and director Kenneth Lonergan believes in the power of subconscious stories. In his script *You Can Count On Me* the two lovers in the story, Terry and Sammy, bond as they deal with pregnancy and "fucked up relationships" with their families. He said, "There are all kinds of little parallels that keep coming up, and you would think that I had very cleverly laid them in because I was thematically threading them in, but they honestly just appear."

When you just let it flow, you may write about a lot of different things and put a lot of themes into your manuscript. A lot of themes can exist in a piece, in a subterranean way, but that doesn't mean that your story can't be simple. When it happens that way, people will say the story is trying to tell them what it wants to do. It feels like there's one right version. Try to let that part of your mind do as much of the writing as possible; it makes the job go much faster.

DEADLINE MENTALITY
George Romero re-invented the zombie film, indeed re-invented the horror film, when he created *Night of the Living Dead*. Before editing his own films, he edited commercials and sports shows. He got used to that deadline mentality. "You've got to sit down and have it ready for air by next Monday." Like most writers, however, he does as much thinking and stewing and trying to pull ideas together, and then just lets it flow.

"I'm weird, man. I keep a notebook and I use a little tape recorder sometimes, to do dialogue. But I don't actually start writing until I know exactly where the story's going. Once that jells, I sit down and just write it, sometimes in thirty-six hours straight. That's just me. I'm weird that way," he says.

Don't stop the flow. It usually comes in way too long, but once it's all on paper it's a lot easier to apply the craft work. During this stage, Romero usually hits the beach for a week and then comes back and reads it. He says, "If I don't need this, I don't need that, and then I just do the great big blue pencil on it." To make it across the finish line, you have to be thinking, "Do I like this? Do I believe it? Is it interesting to me?"

When you get stuck, frustrated, or even bored, sometimes by the tedium, stop and take a break. The clock is always ticking. I try to give myself goals, definitely. You have to have discipline, but at the same time, you have to keep yourself excited. If you're not excited, you can feel it. What I do is stop and say, "You have to get to a place, Tinsman, where you are re-excited about what you're doing." And when I am, the day goes by in about twenty seconds.

Once I actually sit down and get through the first draft, I just can't wait to get into the next phase. What I do is I get up early in the morning, lay everything out, make sure nothing crazy is going on, and work solidly from about 9:30 until about three in the afternoon. I just love it. Even sometimes, when it's not working, you just take a ten-minute break and come back recharged.

RELAX, SERIOUSLY
Some of the most productive people are the most relaxed. Billy Simms, writing as Cordess Sims, is an indie author who, after writing six books in a detective series, was put to task by fans who wanted a book starring one of his characters. Remember, speed is determined by how quickly you get to the problems and come up with answers. Simms found his next book to be easy. He jumped back into the world he'd created, where Simms found all that he needed was waiting.

Simms didn't need to punish himself for the answers. How does Echo get the next job? What makes this one personal? He went through his notes looking for ideas he hadn't tried yet. He went from there and wrote a short book, *The Weight of Echo*, in one week.

Once you have the pieces and the problems coming, you can just relax and "what if" a story to death.

> "So, the problems are absolutely insolvable?"
>
> "Yep. Worst problem ever. I'm screwed."
>
> "Can't be solved?"
>
> "Like I said."
>
> "Well, if you could solve it, what would the answer be?"
>
> "If I knew how to solve it?"
>
> "Yes, if you did, how would you solve it?"
>
> "Oh, well, I'd just..."

I know, I know, writing a novel in one week is pretty fast! But it's not rare. Ray Bradbury said he did it on the first draft of *Fahrenheit 451*. Hell, even I've done it once. That was after I'd written a dozen books, though. I developed my own method, which, as you can see, isn't a big secret.

Draw inspiration from everything you do each day, skim a book, paintings, music, or try something recreational. Think to yourself, "Ideas, I need you." Try all sorts of approaches, especially relaxation. Count the things in your life that matter, do yoga, or collect scenes from the day. It's amazing, really, the less you worry about what you're not doing (writing, figuring things out), the faster it happens, and unexpectedly, on its own. It exhibits a high level of skill in the major parts of creative writing:

1. *Process* (finding inspiration, getting ideas on the page)

2. *Craft* (specific techniques like characterization)

3. *Anthology* (learning by reading the masters of the form)

Despite thousands of words in a book, they are only answering five questions: who, what, when, where, and why. Fast writing isn't us leaping to answer all 5 Ws instantly. In two sentences, the character is driving a car on a road in the summer and thinking about his divorce. If the details are loaded on too fast, it feels compressed. You can always come back later and add things if needed. Get to the end and then go back over it, slow down.

WRITE, DON'T RIP OFF

We've all thought of ways to write faster. Some writers take it too far and actually rip off other manuscripts, replacing names and a few details, and then calling it their own. Perhaps you've heard about the authors who ripped off *Female YA* books? I mean entirely, word for word, only changing the names. The *Babysitters Club* has rip-offs like *Babysitters Inc.* and *Sitter for Hire*. Sell enough of these, and you pop up on the radar as competition for the original book. Fans will read it, and fans aren't stupid. Someone will tell everyone else. The publisher (yours and theirs) will be shocked.

Using a novel as a book-length fill-in-the-blank form is not a legally sound idea. I don't care how fast it is. You could get sued heavily. Pay damages. Lose your reputation. Craftier thieves ladder their way up from "Put Your Name Here" and forge ahead to make a "synthesis" of several related books, but using their own words. Stealing ideas, not words, basically. This is a questionable practice, but you'd be surprised how many authors admit to it.

Asking yourself, "Did I write a book, or didn't I?" doesn't sit right with most people. Do shady practices work? Sometimes. But they asked the same thing in *Jurassic Park* – "can we" instead of "should we" – and we know how that ended. Write your own book, don't rip it off.

MAKE AN APPOINTMENT

To write faster, you must find the right schedule that works for you. I started writing back when I could slip off the job site at about 10:30 in the morning. I'd usually go through bursts of writing. I may have taken notes when ideas hit me, and this could go on for months. Then it all built up into a solid project, and I worked every possible second on it.

This is how most writers function. Mom bloggers have to fit it in where they can. Journalists are harried by fragments of notes when they have a chance to record the facts. That's why setting aside some time to defragment your stuff is so relaxing and productive.

No matter what stage you are at with your writing, it can do some good to stop and start again with a simple regimen. The chaos of daily life is more predictable than you think. Waiting in lines, children demanding attention, and bills that have been arriving in your mailbox, this is life. Carve out some time to deal with these things so you can be more effective at managing the ordeals, the stress, and the annoyances.

Sometimes being annoyed can be good fuel for writing, but you still need time and a space to do it. For example, you could set a goal to type 1,000 words every day. Of course, this won't happen all the time. Don't punish yourself or try to catch up. Just try to get 1,000 words the next day. Mark your calendar, adjust your planner, set your word diet, and pretty soon, people will call you a "writing machine."

When I entered prison, I collected my bedroll, put on a new khaki uniform, and realized I'd been given all the time I'd need to write. Not all prisons are chaotic, but that one was. In between earning respect among the cliques, gangs, and rabbles of inmates, a routine sort of developed. But as I settled in, over the years, a loose, general approach took over. It was enough to say, "I'm going to write something today" and accept whatever was produced, whether it was on a napkin or pages saved on a word processor. Just do your best, and push it incrementally; the rest will come.

UNBLOCK YOUR WAY FORWARD

At its core, writer's block is a poor excuse for not putting ideas on the page. Motivation comes from many positive sources; you don't have to wait until your utilities are shut off, or the old lady to have a "headache," or the prospect of sitting through training at McDonald's to assist your income. Instead, use one of these techniques to give you a boost.

1. *Comfort Reading* – Jerry Gillies learned how to write ahead of a deadline working as a journalist (NBC-New York) and author of six books on personal development and relationships, including *Money Love*, which he wrote in prison. What's amazing is that if you'd asked him when he first got to prison, "Hey, are you going to keep writing?" He'd have glared at you and said, "No." He'd lost everything; it was just too depressing.

For over twenty years, Gillies conducted seminars and gave lectures across the U.S. It is no surprise that he rediscovered the power of inspiration. "Any book can lift me out of my confined existence. The best ones are those where I vanish in the pages, moved by the author's language and imagination." Comfort reading helped him overcome his "block" and relit his writing.

2. *Spark Ideas* – The hero had escaped capture, yet again. He was tasked (morally) with saving everyone, again. I thought it over and realized I'd grown bored with a predictable hero. My hero was not supposed to be predictable! I was stuck. After an hour of staring at the page, I set it aside. I reviewed notes, chatted with a friend, listened to the radio, and reread parts of the book. Everything I did was in the hope of finding a spark, to get the idea, and get back to writing. But as time stretched on into the evening, I was getting desperate.

I read whatever was lying around, and ended up reading an interview with Robert Downey Jr. It took about 15 minutes, and in the middle of reading – *pow* – the idea hit me. We call this the spark. He was talking about being a parent and explaining to his son that if he, the man of the house, takes a knee to his mother every once in a while, then it is okay, as a man, to take a knee every once in a while, in life.

I stopped reading immediately and figured out how to make my hero less predictable. The answer was, "What if my hero doesn't go back and save everyone? What if he takes a knee to all the danger and says, 'Forget that. I'm not doing it anymore?'" That's what I wrote, and it's exactly what the story needed. Of course, it was a "reversal." The scene left the reader on a cliffhanger, and the hero returned to save everyone later.

3. *Meditation* – When I'm really stuck, I lie down and take a gentleman's nap and usually wake up with the creative juices flowing again. Let the subconscious do the work. Take a shower. Walk a few miles. If my mind won't clear itself, then I meditate:

Imagine a china cup on a table. The cup is brilliant white and filled with black tea. The cup is my capacity for thought, the tea is my thoughts. Then I tip it over. The tea rushes out across the table. The cup is empty, and suddenly I am thoughtless.

If you go looking for crazy techniques to jump-start your creativity, guess what? You'll find a bunch. We are all a little nuts, so keep an open mind about it, and through deliberate experimentation, you'll find a little china cup of your own.

4. *Foster the "I Do Nots"* – *To be a writer,* you must feel comfortable being alone. Apart from being a monk, a lighthouse keeper, or a forest-fire spotter, I can't think of a more solitary profession than being a writer. If you need companionship or social reinforcement, after ten minutes of writing, you could have a fatal flaw.

Eventually, you'll stop caring about meaningless annoyances and say Forget it. With time, it gets easier to avoid anything that gets between you and your writing. It's simple, the faster route to get paid is to write at an economical pace.

✎ Writers Manifesto No. 19 – Your 10,000-word manuscript will probably read better at 2,000.

RESOURCES
Writers' Advice
- writerunboxed.com

Write & Get Paid

PART 5

HUSTLE

Chapter Nineteen

"No matter what else you do, do at least five things to market each and every one of your important books each and every day." – John Kremer

BASIC PLATFORM

You may not start out with an award-winning blog, strong media connections, or a tribe of admirers waiting breathlessly for your book's release, but you can make it happen. What you want is the basic equipment, a simple website, and obvious social media accounts, all it takes to put yourself on common ground with even the most advanced pros. Then all you have to do is out-tweet, out-hustle, and out-market the other guy. For a graphomaniac like you, it's easy to do.

Make yourself easy to find. Work at it in little chunks. Start with a good name (a domain name). The easy route is a "dot com" attached to your book title, but the best choice depends on your business model. Your name makes sense for high-volume fiction releases; stephenking.com grants access to his backlist more than a dot com for every book. Nonfiction covers a lot of ground. Writeandgetpaid.com may be adequate, but if I intend to add services, it would be wise to also buy *Publishing Revolution* or *Constant Readers Forum*.

Search engines will toss a site into the "found results" more often if its domain relates to search words (and phrases) that distinguish its market. Ask around, do research, eventually, a good one will surface. Create social media accounts with it once you have decided. Then it's time to build a website.

WEBSITE OPTIONS

Make your website enjoyable. Don't try to be too flashy. Use no more than one or two links to major areas, never leave visitors at a dead end, and don't make them backtrack three or four links to get from one area to another. It's easy to set one up with services like 1and1.com (1&1), Wix, and dozens of others. The quality and features offered don't change that much.

- GoDaddy.com Website Tonight plan is an all-in-one package, and costs $4.99-$12.99 per month, depending on the features.

- Author Guild charges $90 for the first year "dues," then $3-$9 per month. Many of its features are basic, but it's a great networking tool for authors.

- Square.com websites are known for their easy-to-make graphics and may be worth it to you for $120.00-$400.00 a year.

All of them are adequate, the only difference being the amount of pop and sizzle. With all this control over your site's layout and appearance, don't forget that your goal is to tweak it to suit your viewers. At a minimum, your site should have these pages:

- "All About You" (include your resume or bio and a picture)

- "Contact Information" (use a PO Box, new email, and free phone number for your "office" from Google's grandcentral.com)

- "Press Page" (for news releases, some biographical info about yourself, picture, and sample review for any books you are selling.)
- "Testimonials"
- "Blog" (samples of your work)
- "Buying Information" (links to your books page with online book retailers, like Amazon)

If, for some reason, you need to show off your programming skills (perhaps you write about high-tech applications), then you can use free building tools from Nvu (nvudev.com) and KompoZer (kompozer.net). Both are complete authoring systems for Linux, Windows, and Macintosh computers. If learning code is too much, professional website builders can set up your site for a fee.

Reese Spykerman, who has designed writers' websites, says, "A lot of writers, as long as their content isn't too involved, can get a site for $2,000." Sites for less are typically done by amateurs. "I'm a big fan of word of mouth," Spykerman advises. "I'd be hesitant to hire someone I hadn't heard about from someone else."

SELL EBOOKS, AUDIO BOOKS, COURSES, OR OTHER DIGITAL FILES FROM YOUR WEBSITE

You can sell MOBI, Kindle, EPUBs, and PDFs right from your site. It's a great strategy if you are publishing your own serials or recurring content. It's as simple as adding a shopping cart through PayPal or features offered by a number of services that allow you to set up sales options. You can just add a PayPal button on your site, but today there are options that include email and social integration as well as analytics. Before you decide which way you want to go, consider your options:

1. *Gumroad* – Gumroad has an intuitive and attractive customer interface and is used in 40 countries. It's quick to integrate into your website, sell on Twitter, Facebook, YouTube, SoundCloud, and through your email newsletter. Gumroad routinely gets high rankings from professionals.

PROS
- 5% plus 25 cents per transaction, no hosting or set-up fees.
- Consideration for sales tax.
- Can be used for physical items and digital downloads.
- You can set up discount codes.
- Detailed analytics and customer support.

CONS
- Does not accept PayPal

2. *Pay Hip* – Pay Hip has everything you need to promote and sell your eBooks on your social network. It's specifically aimed at being easily shareable. It also has a customizable sales page to match your site's theme.

PROS
- 5% transaction fee after PayPal fees.
- Google Analytics integration.

CONS
- eBooks only.
- Pay what you want pricing.
- PayPal only.

3. *Selz* – Selz is easy to set up, versatile, and friendly to multimedia. It has a pop-up design within your website, so customers don't leave the site. It has easy social integration, which includes sales on mobile devices.

PROS
- Integrates with most email list services.
- 5% plus 25 cents per transaction.
- PayPal, bank card, or credit card.
- Individual product pages.
- eBook and audiobook sales pages with previews.

CONS
- So far, none.

Selling physical products is a decision you should make carefully. Whether it's coffee mugs, pillowcases, or whatever products tie into your writing, you'll have to deliver the goods to customers. There are a few ways to do it. The most convenient is to use print-on-demand and drop-shipping, where the product is made and delivered straight to the customer without you having to hold stock. Sites like zazzle.com or ideacafe.com drop ship hundreds of customized products. They pay through a fully negotiable royalty split.

If you have sufficient customers and maybe an assistant, you could consider buying products and shipping them yourself. That means paying for stock up front, holding or warehousing, as well as dealing with shipping and customer service. A third option is to sell digital services on your site and sell physical products in person, like during a tour.

PRODUCE CONTENT
Once you've got a website, you can begin building a platform. It helps me to think of it like building a patio. It needs concrete pillars and a frame (blog and website and social media presence), then a plank (a blog post or article), then another and another (your press kit, a book club reading guide, media contact page, etc.). Your efforts give you something solid to base all your promotions on – a launching pad. A link to send to editors is like your business card and your backlist.

First, you'll need to generate fresh content. Try making a checklist with your content goals for each week. It helps if you focus and set a date and time for writing, editing, and publishing the work. Here are some solid goals to aim for:

Weekly
- Website, exclusive 200-word minimum post.
- Blog, exclusive 250 to 500-word minimum post.
- Video, exclusive 2-5 minute stream.

Daily
- Social Media, exclusive 50 to 200-word post.
- Twitter up to three exclusive posts.

Mix it up. A social post can be done in a few minutes, but reuse or repurpose old content, like photos, or if a topic lends itself to video, make a quick one. Some variety helps. You can also curate content from other sites relevant to your market; it saves you from producing 100 percent of everything.

After you hit your stride, organize the process by using scheduling apps. Twitter has a great app called Hootsuite, which allows you to enter up to one month's worth of tweets. Other services come with a monthly fee to use, but they streamline your updates so much that it's worth it. The site Ping.fm allows you to schedule content across multiple social media accounts. This makes all your updates possible with one click of the mouse and gives you more time to spend composing personal responses to readers.

Pros get a strong start each day by sharing a conversation piece. They scan drudgereport.com for a news feed or pull clips from the national news dump on whitehouse.gov. Authors who have become familiar with their audience's taste develop a type of radar for what piece will click. Alanna Nash regularly taps into her social network of fellow writers but is cautious to not allow it to suck up her time or most salable ideas. She pools together a variety of content and then just chats with readers. "I do that in the morning," she says, "before I start writing."

ESTABLISH A SCHEDULE

Producing regular content is exciting when you see it energize readers. Start by creating a hyperlink to your previous publications, mentions, or collaborations. If you don't have any, then just follow a schedule and produce your library a little at a time. Build your backlist in any way possible.

If you approach it by thinking that this vast assortment of content is really just a daily exercise, then it becomes less like a chore and more of a pleasant activity. To make things even easier, try recycling a 10-item list that gives you a framework for each week.

Here's the list I recycle the most:

> *Week 1*: Tour of your office (or someone else's).
> *Week 2*: Show you (and your staff) having fun.
> *Week 3*: Start a meme (like directing readers to review a new book on Amazon).
> *Week 4*: Share a link (always something cool).
> *Week 5*: Top ten list.
> *Week 6*: History about the industry (I write about several, the U.S. Correctional System and the Book Trade).
> *Week 7*: Interview (a celebrity when possible, use *Who Represents* to locate a celebrity's agents).
> *Week 8*: Company news (news releases, updates, and the like).
> *Week 9*: Professional tips.
> *Week 10*: Trends, innovations, technology, or techniques (in your field).

It was easy once I got things organized. I'd sit down each Friday and write a rough draft, then polish it up and type it over the weekend. Usually, my editor received the email on Sunday night and would post it on Tuesday morning. It took off like a proverbial snowball down a mountain, getting harder to ignore as it went. This method works because you always have a starting point for your next piece, even when you're burnt out from working on major projects.

DO NOT DUPLICATE YOUR PUBLICATIONS

I learned this the hard way because I used to do this all the time. It was lazy. It worked, and I didn't know any better. They were called "blast." When an article was finished, I'd just select "All Contacts" on my email, title the subject "For Immediate Release: Please share with your readers," and send it to everyone. They'd run it as a News Release, and I'd get results from readers.

All that mattered was that the chances were slim that readers might see the same post, because they got published on a variety of sites – from gambling advice columns to foodie websites to self-publishing company blogs. The logic was sound. But the problem was that web crawlers (Google, Amazon, Bing) penalize authors for doing this.

It's called "Author Authority," and it doesn't matter how many e-newsletters you piggyback; it's not worth getting penalized for being popular. The trick is you have to write exclusive content for each site (which is a lot of work), so the better option is to grant permission for an excerpt to appear on each site with a link back to the complete article on your own site. It only took about three months of that, and my penalties were a distant memory.

MAKE ACHIEVEMENTS VISIBLE

Write a short biography. Readers like to see who the author is and learn something about them. A good bio highlights previous publications, notable details, and nods to firsthand experience. If you can, it doesn't hurt to mention the impact you've had on other people. Standard bios run about 100 words, so they're easy to update, which you should do frequently.

Your website can contain a more detailed biography (expand on pieces of it over your social media accounts so you can give everyone something unique). Bios reassure people that authors have the right attitude, know-how, or cool factor to make a first-class product. Spend some time considering what you can add to make the best impression.

Here are a few strategies:

1. *Literary Recognition* – Winning a contest or publishing a short story in a literary journal, online magazine, or anthology is always noteworthy. Post photos of any plaques, hard copies, or trophies you get. Credentials are impressive for any writer, but literary success can open doors in your life. It's like joining a secret club, you'll be surprised how many editors and publishers have earned similar recognition.

2. *Memberships* – Professional writers' organizations help build a stronger foundation for a writing career. It's ironic because a membership is the easiest thing to obtain. Groups like the National Writers Association (NWA) have a basic application and a $75 annual membership fee, which includes being listed on their site (more visibility). There are dozens of organizations with nominal annual fees that come with various perks; join them, when you do, be sure to cut and paste their logo onto your About Me webpage and create a link to their site.

3. *Personal Interests* – Not all memberships need to focus on writing. Joining a social or cultural organization relevant to your personal interests can advance the value of what you write. If you're a leftist, perhaps the $20 minimum for the National Association for the Advancement of Colored People (NAACP) would be your cup of tea? If you want to demonstrate right-wing flair, try the National Rifle Association (NRA), and if you're libertarian, it's hard to go wrong with the American Civil Liberties Union (ACLU). If you hate politics, join the National Geographic Society (everybody loves animals), or you could announce you're working with Sex Addicts Anonymous. It's as legitimate as you make it.

When authors have some qualifications outside their book's topics, like a degree in Business Administration, then they become more interesting. Titles, degrees, honorable mentions, collaborations, research, it all makes a good curriculum vitae. Since a writer's bio is always a work in progress, target the achievements that make you more "reliable sounding" to editors, clients, and readers. It'll get you paid.

BUILD A SEARCH ENGINE OPTIMIZED SITE

You are so lucky. It used to be you needed to understand how search engines (crawlers) actually worked. Things like mirroring your web page URLs to search words (Google AdWords helped, so did Keyword Planner) and blended search results (video, text, and hyperlinks all sharing the URLs) were the bread and butter of freelance programmers who would hook you up for a few thousand dollars. Or you could do it yourself by reading Google's droll manual "Search Engine Optimization Starter Guide" on static.googleusercontent.com. Well, all that crap is in your rear-view mirror. Things are much simpler now.

There is mixed advice about when to make these investments. Some people do it all up front, a few months before their book's release. The logic is that it takes time to get all these tweaks made to your site. This makes sense, but I've always done it incrementally. There are a couple of good reasons why you should build slowly. First, it limits the financial risk in case your books fail to take off. Second, you can't convince readers that your books are good, regardless of how much money you spend on your site (widgets, games, and graphics).

When you start your website or blog, like on GoDaddy.com, you can begin with a nuts-and-bolts model for about twenty bucks a year. If your platform takes off, you can just click and purchase SEO packages. Add a shopping cart. Sign up for an Affiliate program. Host a few advertisements. It scales up quickly and cleanly.

WORK YOUR EMAIL
Equip your email with a signature so every message you send has the buying information for your book. It only takes a few minutes to set up. Your signature will appear at the end of each email. Here's the one I use for lifewitharecord@gmail.com.

A New Self-Help Reentry Book

Life With A Record
INSIDE COMPLETE REENTRY RESOURCE LISTINGS
Hundreds of complete, up-to-date entries at your fingertips.
Softcover, 8" x 10", B&W Interior, 360+ Pages

Order Today $25.99 plus s/h : www.FreebirdPublishers.com, Amazon, Barnes & Noble

Add an email "signup" link to all your sites. When you ask people for their email, tell them it's so you can contact them about their order and special offers in the future. This is called "opt in" because viewers volunteer to receive it. Once you have a decent list, say a few thousand "subscribers," then utilize an email marketing service like MailChimp, which organizes your messages, so you don't have to manage the list yourself.

You can get sales from certain markets by blasting out announcements or offers via email. But it's limited. There are many "sales leads" services that deal in emails. Sales Genie and Buzz Sumo are some of the biggest, but the problem is that if you pay $100 for 50,000 emails, that doesn't mean 50,000 people will read your press release. Less than 500 will even open the email. And spam filters are really good at trashing your clever e-newsletter. The real power of collecting emails is that it's good for bartering with other platforms. I've used it as an entry-level networking tool, essentially swapping news releases. We compare numbers, host each other's promotional content, and pick up new readers. The cycle then repeats itself.

Writers Manifesto No. 20 – A sucked in bank account is nature's way of telling you to engage some readers.

RESOURCES
The following are the top 15 sites to help you build, manage, and accelerate the growth of your platform:

Blog Programs
- blosxom.com
- movabletype.org
- nucleuscms.org
- wordpress.org

Really Simple Syndication (RSS)
- blip.tv
- blogpulse.com
- blogtalkradio.com
- digg.com
- feedburner.com
- stumbleupon.com

Multiple Account Management
- gizapage.com
- pingfm.com

Mass E-mailing Companies
- amailsender.com
- constantcontact.com
- massamailingnews.com
- mailchimp.com
- sandblaster.com

Merchandise
- idaecafe.com
- lulu.com
- Zazzle.com

Website designers
- americanauthor.com
- bookmasters.com
- lightbourne.com

Chapter Twenty

"The real story is not authors making multi-six-figure sums but the sheer number of authors making enough to pay even a small number of bills." – Hugh Howey, author of *Wool*

PENETRATE YOUR MARKET

You can probably recall the excitement when you first discovered other books by your favorite author. That's called a backlist. That same thrill makes fans worldwide. As writers, we sometimes forget how simple that is. We sin by writing stuff for "everyone" or making it up as we see fit, a novel here, a how-to there. I used to be guilty of it, too. Little do authors realize that expanding into more segments in their market runs counter to the reality of penetrating that market. It makes an author's image, and backlist, weak.

Authors who want to get more income must get clear on what they deliver to readers. To build a powerful name in the mind of readers, you need to contract, not expand. There comes a tipping point where authors realize they can no longer write on impulse; to make the big bucks, they must take the business side seriously. Market penetration is based on the concept of singularity.

Readers who pick up John Grisham know what they are looking for. Name recognition is a misnomer; it is more name association, and successful writers tend to serve one market really well. Alanna Nash, a veteran music writer and author, attributes her success to specializing. "I established myself as an expert in one field – or in music, one genre – so that editors thought of me whenever the subject comes up." The objective is to create a perception that there is no author in the market quite like you, even if there are dozens.

CREATE A DISTINCTION

Readers like authors who stay in a narrow scope and are distinguishable. When authors don't think about how their name is perceived, then confusion can happen, and you could lose readers, maybe for good. If you spread your name thin, you hurt your overall income over a career. Marketers make the same mistake all the time. Look at these real-world name-brand failures:

- Vaseline Intensive Care Suntan lotion
- Kleenex Super Dry baby diapers
- Fruit of the Loom laundry detergent
- Heinz all-natural cleaning vinegar

To turn your water into Evian, or yourself into the next Stephen King, aim high, but above all else, focus on doing one thing really well. Most authors agree it was a mistake to diversify into multiple genres over their career. Their audience helped initial growth, and they want more of what they like, not always something new. Pros like Bob Mayer and Collin Falconer have authored over 100 books between them, and they admit they should have focused on penetrating the market more effectively. It's easy to work this advice into your writing goals.

The money is in creating a backlist. Writers who build a sense for their market and how much they can produce are on the right path. The result will be plain as your income increases from new readers who discover your backlist. Whether you produce fiction or nonfiction, you can balance the creative distractions and choose which projects are the best for your market. It takes, what, a year on average to think up, write, and field a new book? Make it worth the effort. The readers in your market are certainly expecting something like the last one. Write to their interests, and your name will become associated with it.

WHAT'S OLD IS NEW AGAIN

The hallmark of market penetration began in the 19th century and matured into the Dime novel and Pulp magazine. From around 1830 in the U.S., the reading public began to look beyond the family bible for entertainment. Publishers responded with gripping tales (western outlaws, romances, tales for children) produced inexpensively for the cash-strapped lower classes. They served markets directly, titles like *Women's Journal*, Adventure, and *Tales for Boys*. Printed by Bead and Adams, priced between 5 and 25 cents, these small, approximately 100-page, paper-covered volumes appeared in regular intervals in numbered sequence.

"Books for the millions" set the standard for market penetration, and authors began to take advantage of it. Those who focused on serving single markets became household names. Irresistibility and affordability made them huge successes. For example, Dashiell Hammett, Donald E. Westlake, and Mickey Spillane were synonymous with detective stories. To hear their names to this day evokes an immediate association with more than their yarns, but the market itself.

MAXIMIZE YOUR DISTINCTION

The internet and worldwide distribution, along with cheap downloads, make the market-association phenomenon accessible to every writer. Authors have opened their eyes to the potential. If you have 10 books in a similar genre or a series, the chances of catching readers with various publicity techniques can do wonders. If they become fans, not only do you get the income, but each sale becomes easier since they trust the author to deliver what they like.

Readers get hooked by series, world-building epics, and market-defining stories like these:

- Frank Herbert, the *Dune* series
- Robin Cook, *Jack Stapleton* medical mysteries
- Jack Canfield, the *Chicken Soup for the Soul* series
- J. K. Rawlings, the *Harry Potter* series
- Robert Greene, the *48 Laws of Power* series
- Dan Brown, treasure hunts starring *Robert Langdon*
- Treasure Hernandez, the *Flint* series

For every one of these, there are dozens of authors doing the same thing. But authors who have more ideas than they can execute or whose content fits dissimilar markets must strategize. Valuable work should be maximized, not sacrificed. Sometimes it takes more than fine-tuning production, but actually delegating work to other writers. If you need help capitalizing on your ideas, there are three options. Collaborate with another writer like James Patterson, Tom Clancy, or the estate of Robert Ludlum. Use a pen name to distinguish your ideas under separate names. Or hire a ghostwriter to do the heavy lifting, while you continue working.

COLLABORATION

One of the best advantages of working with a writing partner is that you force each other to write. Deadlines are important; that's why we function well with deadlines. There's an old saying, 'If you want to get something done, give the task to a busy person.' When you're busy, you get more done, and a writing partner keeps you busy, because you write some pages and you bounce them over to them. And then they bounce it back, and it's in your court, and it forces you to address it.

You brainstorm with each other, you feed off each other. Sean Platt writes with several partners; he takes a light-hearted approach: "We try to make each other laugh. I'll put stuff in a manuscript that's never going to make it to the final draft just to get a rise out of him." He writes with David Wright and separately with Johnny B. Truant to produce books under the Sterling and Stone brand. They produce a variety of series and a lot of income.

Sometimes, creative partners can come from your core audience. Readers have had a direct influence on a series before. In 1997, Tom Lagana attended a public seminar, Jack Canfield's eight-day Facilitator Skills Seminar, in Santa Barbara. When he got the chance, he asked Canfield what he thought about a book concept. Canfield, co-creator of the Chicken Soup for the Soul series, liked it a lot. Within days, they were partners in their project, but Lagana was expected to do the work. Canfield told him, "You own the project."

Over the next three years, submissions filled a box under his kitchen table. Every morning before breakfast, Lagana and his wife, Laura, spent an hour at the table reading. Then each submission was read by a group of test readers, and each was rated. The rough compellation was sent to forty international reviewers and finally to Canfield himself. In 2000, Lagana's hard work paid off with Chicken Soup for the Prisoner's Soul, something that meant a lot to him and to readers of the series.

PEN NAME

Pen names have a mystique that's very appealing. If you can avoid it, however, do so. You must promote your writing under all the names you use. Is increasing your workload to cover several names necessary? If you need to easily distinguish your work, it may be worth managing the additional social media, website, and even writing small pieces under a pen name.

It helps to reach different types of audiences, but takes experimentation (time), and you'll have to justify. Joann Penn did just that when she decided to simplify her brand, The Creative Penn, a site for professional authors to gain advice, because it didn't align with her objectives as well as she'd hoped. Instead, she began using affiliate marketing and direct sales to make that site more profitable, and addressed her other writing focus, thrillers, using a pen name.

As J.F. Penn, she has penetrated a separate market and increased her income. Her style is masculine, with tough female lead characters. Penn thought it was easier to use initials in her name, so readers would stop "double-taking" that a woman wrote it. Her brands look like this.

1. The Creative Penn.com
   - Aimed at authors and writers.
   - Income from courses, nonfiction books, speaking, affiliate programs, and sponsors of her podcast.
   - Blogs every week and makes video content for podcasts/YouTube.
   - Smiling author photo, bright color scheme.

2. J.F. Penn.com
   - Aimed at readers looking for "Thrillers on the Edge," which includes thrillers, supernatural suspense, and cultural reference.
   - Income partly from fiction sales, her backlist (5 books), and new releases.
   - Links to interviews with other standouts, book blog, social media, and video with other thriller writers.
   - Brooding author photo, dark color schemes.

"I gave up trying to tweet under two handles," Penn says, "So I use the @thecreativepenn for everything. I don't podcast on J.F. Penn altogether, but I do record some of my short stories in audio. I have a separate Facebook page, but I'm not terribly active there. I have Pinterest boards for J.F. Penn and not

The Creative Penn, but I am on Google Plus as Joanna Penn. I have two sets of business cards, two email addresses, two different author photos (one smiling, one brooding) ... it's complicated."

Ask yourself, can I get away with just one name? Consider who your audience is. Will you be writing more books like the ones you've written? How will people perceive your name (and your pen name) in that genre or theme? Analyze your performance and adjust as needed. If you find yourself writing wildly desperate stuff, it may work out. Names keep audiences separated.

My first book was for children, which didn't lead to the success I was looking for. Then I wrote and published self-help books, which did better, so I stopped writing for children, kept my name, and focused on nonfiction. Now I'm writing fiction under a pen name, Sterling Enfield. Any inventor or artist learns that attempting things that don't work often represents the best way to discover things that do. From trial and error, writers get a chance to view things from a vantage point they can't acquire through theorizing alone.

GHOSTWRITERS

Hiring a writer to flesh out your ideas is a great way to expand into new markets. Since I often write for hire, I'm used to signing an NDA (Non-Disclosure Agreement), so there's no complications when the work is done and published under the "author" name. It's a creative collaboration; payment is sometimes a royalty split or for a lump sum, though the latter is most common.

Looking at it from the perspective of a ghostwriter, this arrangement has a lot of benefits for everyone. The "author" can spend time on their day-to-day business while their backlist grows. And the ghostwriter gets paid, though not potentially as much as if they'd received royalties from their own expanded backlist!

From the perspective of a writer, like many partnerships, there must be clear terms on the timeframe, feedback, and good chemistry for the back-and-forth required to match the author's tone. Readers won't know the difference. When you find a ghostwriter who works, you'll probably work with them on more books. It's worth the $5-$17 a page, or up to $5,000 per project, if it multiplies your offerings to a market eager for more.

MANAGE PERCEPTION

When a reader approaches me, they often have a copy of the book or magazine. There's no better affirmation that your words have broken some barrier than a reader shaking your hand. My work shares a philosophy that carries over through multiple markets, self-help, memoir, and career guides like this one. It's made my writing life simple, but also demands that my fiction gets published under a separate name.

Managing your name is important when you want to pitch new products. Say I need to refresh my platform to refocus on a new self-help series. Or to tighten the focus of the fiction I write. It'll go into a personal plan, then the Daily Planner, and finally into work orders. Throughout the preparation, work, and publicizing of new books, I'm working to do one thing really well: make sure that my name matches the perception I'm creating in the market I'm writing to.

It's easy to only focus on what you can hold in your hands. When you think big picture, you'll see how all your work creates a perception, which goes one step beyond the "Also by" list of books in your backlist. Do the themes match up? Or do some books need to be revised, or dropped, or should you start using a pen name? Review your backlist occasionally to make sure you're matching the perception readers already have. It will make it easier to thrill them with each new book.

RESOURCES
Other Authors
- authorearnings.com (details on which genres sell the most copies)

Anthony TInsman

Chapter Twenty-One

"Writing ranks among the top 10 percent of professions in terms of prestige." – Jean Strauss

BRAND YOURSELF
As a writer, you have to get published. As an author, you have to run a platform. As a household name, you have to keep readers focused on what you're doing. Let's assume you want a million fans; everyone seems to like that number. Committed writers have surpassed that number time and again. "How?" you ask. By "Martha Stewarting" themselves.

Julie Powell set herself the task of making every recipe in Julia Child's *Mastering the Art of French Cooking* in one year. Since the form lent itself to dramatization, her blog focused on her trials and tribulations. The blog gained a large following that got her noticed by agents and publishers. Next thing you know, a book and movie were on the way, Julie and Julia starring Amy Adams and Meryl Streep. She was writing a book to begin with, and blogged to raise interest. Everything led back to the book as popularity grew. It is a classic strategy.

Something as simple and steady as a decent blog can put your platform on people's radar, like Molly Wizenberg's *A Homemade Life*, which earned her a writing column with Bon Appétit magazine and eventually a book deal. Or Shreve Stockton, who started posting daily pictures of orphaned coyotes in Wyoming. His book *The Daily Coyote: A Story of Love, Survival and Trust in the Wilds of Wyoming* had an eager audience.

Whether it's about food, romance, punk rock, or whatever, quality work becomes talked about. You know it's working when each piece attracts more readers. Then you are well on your way to an exciting development.

BECOME #1 IN SOMETHING
The ultimate goal of a brand is to dominate a category, or at least appear to. It's very similar to branding on the ranch. A brand should differentiate your writing from all the other cattle on the range … even if all the cattle on the ranch look pretty much alike. What should you advertise? Leadership. It's the single most important motivating factor in consumer behavior.

The perception of leadership comes in many forms: the purest, the first, or the best. Look at how these popular products do it: Heinz – America's favorite ketchup, Coca-Cola – The real thing, Good Year – #1 in tires. Authors do it the same way.

- Master of Suspense – James Patterson
- Historical fictions unmatched talent – Conn Iggulden
- Queen of urban literature – Ashley Jaquavis
- Spells mystery and suspense – Sue Grafton

The crucial ingredient of the success of any brand is to demonstrate core values. A brand should own a word in the mind of the reader; obviously, that word should express your market. It's just that the writer's focus is structured around engaging readers.

Focus on how to become #1 with a separate, unique identity. There are examples of brands distinguishing themselves in similar markets everywhere you look. When General Mills launched Red Lobster, it became a big success, and when it decided to launch a chain featuring Italian food, it did so with a totally different brand, Olive Garden. Even if you write for a market that's already full of authors claiming to be #1, remember that you can still stake your claim. Competition broadens a category, but top brands stay focused.

Bob Hoffman runs the Hoffman Press. He had a background in marketing and established outstanding distribution relationships. He also focused on a well-defined niche, which he felt passionate about. The core of his success is that he and his wife wanted a hobby during their retirement years. They decided to self-publish a book about cooking with wine.

The Hoffman Press was successful, partially due to Hoffman's vast consumption of wine. They partnered up with the wineries mentioned in the book, who added the book to their gift shops. It's genius, really. Imagine all those tourists tasting merlot, what would be more natural than picking up a book about cooking with the stuff? Bingo. It sold.

The internet was unfamiliar to them, but it was easy to arrange a website with pictures of wine and gourmet meals. With all the free advertising in wineries and bookstores, the site accumulated traffic quickly. It led to spin-offs of the original cookbook, calendars, and all kinds of other merchandise being sold on the site. Better yet, wineries contacted the Hoffmans, who were interested in being mentioned in their new series. They decided to start ranking restaurants and wineries.

This was the tipping point; it raised their status to number one. They became the go-to people, the experts. They negotiated with a fulfillment company to pack and ship their books. Nowadays, the Hoffman Press sells over 100,000 cookbooks a year. Plus, they have all the wine a horny retired couple could stand. It's like a fairy tale ending for what a good platform can do, and the power of branding.

The Hoffman's finished product had three vital components necessary to create a memorable brand:

1. *A Back Story*: Retirement hobby turns into business.
2. *A Catchphrase*: "The best recipes for great wine."
3. *A Concrete Image Anchoring Their Message*: Wine and gourmet food.

You might think, "I can come up with my own story and slogans," but you'd be missing the most important element in Hoffman's success. There's no get-rich-quick formula that replaces the discoveries of an imperfect approach. All successful brands fit into a market they are passionate about and are willing to pivot to meet demands. They get into position to take advantage of it, and they execute. Glenn O'Brien said it best: "You start out a phony and become real."

✎ Writers Manifesto No. 21 – When in doubt, repeat what readers say is working.

LET READERS GUIDE YOU
The research that guided my first brand led me to believe that it could be preassembled using seven primitive branding techniques or sticky marketing. In 2010, my friends and I started a novelty t-shirt company, Meanbone, whose "core value proposition" was stress relief through laughter. Its mascot was a cartoon, easily reproducible by silk screeners. The image itself made "the abstract emotionally tangible." It was a cute cracked bone with a frowning face.

Our online storefront popped up overnight with all the pieces of a brand in place: "creation story," "sacred image," "leader," "outcasts," and 30 signature designs. Despite aggressive promotion, the sales were anemic. All we could do was scratch our heads and wonder what had gone wrong.

Brands require a lot of input. I learned this while searching for ideas to relaunch Meanbone. Did anyone suggest we create a design? I made it. Were there elements people liked? They thought some of the drawings were interesting. I expanded it into an archive of comic strips. By listening to browsers, we changed the focus of the humor towards "Destroying the annoying" and away from cultural and nostalgic landmarks (designs like the Statue of Liberty lofting a Meanbone, and Meanbone morphed into Che Guevara). It was hard work, but the brand began to gain traction.

Publishers don't typically succeed when they try to make books look more popular than they really are. Many a book reads "Over 200,000 copies sold!" with a gold star. The popular *For Dummies* series of books proclaims, "Over 24 million *For Dummies Books* in print." You never see the full truth, 200,000 copies sold (worldwide). One million copies in print, 990,000 still in the warehouse! Awards and records only validate products. Readers like to feel a little more involved.

My column, Dear Tinny, was a reaction to the letters I received each week. Readers were encouraged to use the street address and email attached to articles in online magazines. Accessibility drove sharing; my books are better for it. This back-and-forth even led some readers to ask, "Can I get an advance copy?" It's the same principle when pitching your brand to Constant Readers. You don't need a catchy pitch to hit on all the things you think they want to hear. You just have to show them you are a reliable source for interesting content.

Do you write fiction? Okay, examine characters like yours, what they are trying to do, and what obstacles stand in their way. You write nonfiction? Easy, focus on what you're promising the reader, would they like those results? Subdivide all those points into blog posts and encourage people to talk about them. When they hit on an idea that you can execute, then go and do it. Film it, write about it, take photos, and show it to your readers. All your efforts make your name and your brand stand out.

STEER YOUR TRIBE

Your passion should take center stage. What you're doing fascinates people. Regardless of good days or bad days, a personal touch helps when it's time to cash in on your cred. Concentrate on what makes your work unique and continue producing what comes naturally. Whether it's cooking, art, fashion, sports, or just speculating about stuff your audience can't resist. Give them a portion, and the tribe will pay for the rest.

Sophia Amoroso is a household name; she's appeared on Shark Tank and Forbes Female CEO Top Ranking, as well as modeling online, and has been called a role model for young women. That's a big leap for a former teenage vagabond and shoplifter. She got started selling used clothing because she was too lazy to leave her rental and hired her friends to show them off (hot models with doe eyes and pouty lips, who accepted payment in the form of a hamburger and milkshake after each shoot). Amoroso's dust bin fashion line was called Nasty Gal, which she promoted through Myspace almost exclusively.

When Nasty Gal went bankrupt in 2017, Amoroso pivoted to her book *Girl Boss*, seminars, and coaching services. She refocused her brand, and the bestselling author was featured in *Money* as an "amazing" comeback story. But by her own account, she knew success came from being pals with customers. She used a simple strategy when taking care of people:

1. Listen, don't just talk.
2. Ask, don't tell.
3. Be real, have a story.
4. Be interested and respond.
5. Have something to offer.

There's no trick, she said, "When I was in school, I ran with a red string until everyone was convinced I was flying a kite. I've always had the ability to make people believe they can fly a kite by running with a red string of their own." People who look like they're having fun attract attention, because who doesn't want to have fun too?

WARTS AND ALL

To turn writing into a fun thing, Austin Kleon turned his blog into a multimedia extension of his art. He photographed what were essentially tags. One of his earliest was a sign by a Lost and Found, painted over strategically to make a halting statement:

> ATTENTION: Do not leave your longings unattended.

An impulsive talent, Kleon began blogging as a way to give advice to a "previous version of himself." When readers asked, "Where do you get your ideas?" He said, "I steal them." He was being honest, and people just loved him more. Plus, he kept the conversation going; he shared anecdotes about his art's core and what difference he hoped it would make in the world. This led them to start buying his poetry, which they would never have read before.

His poetry was created by covering up newspaper print. His first collection was called Newspaper Blackout, with hundreds of simple phrases peeking through extreme 'government document style' redactions. Some of them shared the tone from his blogs and photos. One poem read "Creativity/is/subtraction," another "You would like to think that/Bohemia/is/a kind of/work."

With a torrent of creative displays, his site became a hotbed of reader activity. His brand exploded when the book hit bestseller lists and editors from NPR to the Wall Street Journal took his inquiries for interviews seriously. By then, Kleon's platform had surpassed his wildest dreams. He got there because, whether he intended to or not, he kept the tribe focused on what he was doing. The raw nature of it created an icon.

No matter what you write, there is potential for creating a brand. Grow something memorable. After a while, it won't feel so strange to hear these epithets used to describe you: hero, guide, and role model. Maybe "showboat" will be attached as well, but you can shrug that off if the money is right.

RESOURCES

Here are some tools to turn your adventures into an amazing brand:

Affiliate Program Directories
- 100bestaffiliate-programs.com
- affiliatescout.com
- linkshare.com

Syndicators
- bussle.com
- ezinelocator.com
- ideamarketers.com

Keyword Tracking/Alerts
- checkrankings.com
- disqus.com
- freekeywords.wordtracker.com
- googlealerts.com/alerts
- intensedebate.com
- tweetdeck (twitter)
- woopra.com

Discussion Groups
- Forum software

- groups.google.com
- groups.yahoo.com
- ninjaspost.com
- thinkofit.com/webconf/forumsoft.htm
- wallphone.com
- zoho.com/forumssoftware

Chapter Twenty-Two

"While publicity misused can be nothing but an ego trip for the author, well used, it can be a powerful sales tool." – Ali Lind

PUBLICITY

Every author is a potential celebrity. Whether it's through public speaking, guest appearances, book tours, backroom sales, or a little Q&A over the air, everything you do makes your writing more noticeable. It is easier to coordinate than you might think. The most successful promoters are masters of getting free coverage; they understand that each venue just needs the right content. Oscar Wilde said that everyone gets fifteen minutes of fame. But you can get much more than that by casting a net like a fisherman, again and again.

The hype is that some readers are active, that they'll comment and share it with their friends like the Faberge' Organic Shampoo commercial, "And she told two friends, and so on, and so on, and so on." The viral loop is a fairy tale. Publicity is all about one thing: out-hustling the other guy.

DOING IT YOURSELF

It's probably a bad sign when authors and publishers take a tip from Hollywood, because nowadays it's expected that you create a "trailer" and air it online. The quality of these things ranges from quirky DIY videos (the author acts out a scene from their book) to full-blown productions with blockbuster glitz (the original trailer for *Orange Is the New Black*). This counts as publicity in most people's minds. When it doesn't get them results, they toss in bonus content, circulate a press release, and wonder why they aren't a bestseller yet.

The internet, especially YouTube, has fogged over the idea of what counts as publicity. It is true that social media can work; it's false that your content will grow into a YouTube associate cash cow, streaming ads overnight. The power of content marketing is that with each mention, like, and share, your ranking on various web crawlers increases (Google, Bing, and Yahoo). That makes your stuff pop up more often. It is actually a basic piece of your platform.

Let's clarify what publicity really is. Diane Schindelwig has owned numerous businesses, from freight fleets to tax consultants. A lifelong entrepreneur, she founded Freebird Publishers after experiencing hardship with the law. Her background in marketing has carved out a considerable influence in a niche market serving millions of target customers.

With titles like *Cellpreneur*, *The Best 500+ Non Profit Organizations*, and *The Cell Chef*, they utilize print advertising, direct mail, email, and an annual catalog called *Inmate Shopper*. But the majority of their customers are reached with a top-notch website, online promoters, and any interviews Schindelwig can get into the mainstream media.

Piece by piece, Freebird has gone from glued together and underground into a primetime TV attraction. Schindelwig scored a local report on NBC channel 10 in Rhode Island (Winter 2017) that created a steady climb in publicity for the small company. Did one interview change everything? No. But each appearance can hook potential readers, draw their interest to the content on your platform, and drive sales.

Going from one stunt to the next is certainly how publicity reaches an audience. Setting some goals and taking time to prepare will pay off as one opportunity leads to another. It's not unusual for an author who gets featured in a local newspaper to get a call from a radio producer who spotted the article or for a writer who gives an entertaining talk on a popular podcast to be invited to appear on TV. The trick is to keep the ball rolling.

SHOULD I LOOK FOR HELP?

Most of the authors who have appeared on the *New York Times* bestseller list have hired a publicist. They know that their publishers will do little to promote their titles. They don't want to deal with arranging interviews, taking calls from pals wanting a book review, or any other distractions. It frees them up to collect royalties, sip beverages with an outstretched pinky, and work on a spectacular tan on the beach.

Book publicists primarily write and place news releases, organize autograph parties, and place authors on TV and radio. They usually work on a retainer basis, some on a per-placement basis, but rarely do they work by the hour. The average monthly retainer is between $2,000 and $4,000. Publicity takes time, so you must hire a publicist for several months to see any results. Most recommend six months, but then again, they are getting paid whether or not it does you any good.

You might not feel comfortable with those prices. If you lack a strong platform, sales record, and photogenic charisma, then it is a gamble. You could spend the money yourself on services like Cision with a list of more than 1.5 million editors, journalists, and other contacts in traditional news outlets. Cision charges $3,000 a year. But access to an editor's name and email address doesn't mean you understand how that editor should be pitched.

Publicists are effective at marketing books within a market in which they have developed contacts. They know how to approach editors, producers, and promoters because they've worked with them in the past. Many have an expertise in certain markets, like pets, cooking, or whatever. If you have a Spanish language book, or a Christian book, or genre fiction, try to match it to a publicist who's dealt with that before.

If you've developed some good media contacts, then you can do this on your own. If not, it may pay off to hire a professional. Just negotiate until you get a deal (and risk level) you can live with. Most publicists understand this and will work on a "pay to play" basis, meaning they only get paid upon arranging certain interviews and appearances.

SHOULD I INVEST IN PUBLIC RELATIONS (PR)?

If your books and writing are marketable to lucrative clients (like corporations, glossy magazine venues, or affluent individuals), you'll want to super-size your publicity. More and more frequently, authors who have enough income are hiring their own PR firm. When it's practical and affordable, consider hiring a marketing service or attending courses about marketing and sales. It will level the playing field among writers who recognize that publishing is a business and that marketing is essential.

    1. *PR Firms* – There's some confusion about the differences between PR firms and publicists. Publicists primarily write and place news releases, organize autograph parties, and place authors on TV and radio. A PR firm takes things to the next level. They create promotional material, online advertising, manage SEO, and interactive customer referral systems (like bazaarvoice.com), which maintain contact with customers. There are many firms that will assist you, so shop around until one feels right. Firms usually work on a retainer basis, some on a per-placement basis, and occasionally by the hour. The average monthly retainer for Public Relations firms is between $2,000 and $10,000.

2. *Book Marketers* – Marketing services specialize in distributing, promoting to libraries and special sales sources, sending galleys and review copies, organizing cooperative advertising and exhibits. Services like Integrated Book Marketing (ibmarket@oponline.net) offer expertise in certain markets: cookbooks, fiction, Christian books, etc. They have contacts with editors who can place reviews, interviews, or freelance articles by or about you. As always, find the right fit for your books and your budget.

MAKE A PRESS KIT

Media professionals want to see a press kit. It doesn't have to be complicated; in fact, one or two pages is all it takes to get the job done. It has all your information and sales literature already inside it. This makes things easier when it's time to cover your story, publish a news release, or make an announcement. Make this info easy to locate, spend some time arranging a media page on your website, and make it downloadable as a PDF.

- State who you are (author, hobbyist, profession, etc.)
- List your exploits (degrees and skills)
- Explain why you should be contacted (testimonials that verify you are an expert)

You can add to this page by creating a biography with author photos (headshots or action shots) and any promotional literature you use for your books. Make sure everything is available in PDF and hard copy. You can use vistaprint.com to design fancy press kits with customized folders, business cards, and color coordination. You never know when the opportunity to hand one to a media personality or important client may arise, so keep one handy.

Use your press kit any time you issue a press release or pitch radio and television editors to set up an interview. All you need is an interesting reason for them to cover you. It doesn't need to be front-page material; simple stuff works, like your book's release, an important stop in your tour, or your expertise on a specific subject that's being talked about in the news. It's no different than the process of matching your manuscript with a publisher.

NEWS RELEASES

A little mention here and there in local newspapers, magazines, newsletters, and journals can sometimes get you some sales. It's not hard to do, just tie in current news, commentary, or politics. Make it a story. Make your books the subject of the theme of the story, and then quote yourself, as "author of" blah blah blah, saying blah blah blah about the current news. Submit it under a pen name to avoid any conflict of interest, or have a famous friend send it in. If that sounds too difficult, don't worry, there are companies that will do it for you.

Hire a press release service to send your news release to thousands of journalists. It may get picked up and run in major publications. You'll get a leap, a spike, or an uptick in sales. There are companies that target specific demographics to get better results, for example, Black PR. They've cultivated contacts inside black focused publications, distributing releases to 40,000 journalists, bloggers, and nearly 1,000 media outlets for $150. It can pay off with good timing and a well-written release.

If you want to cherry-pick media outlets and make your news release stop traffic like a dumpster fire, then Press-ReleaseWriting.com offers targeted releases for $249 per "channel." Many channels reach over 100,000 journalists, bloggers, and probably a few trolls. News release services are usually your best bet for getting cheap national publicity.

One or two journalists will follow through and run your release. If it's to work, you'll need a catchy news release. In my experience, you'll want to develop your skills first and start by sending news releases to smaller venues, like bloggers and small companies. Ask them to share the information with their viewers in their next newsletter or in a special post. It worked for me again and again, and it builds the chops.

The following is a template for creating a publishable news release.

replace with LOGO

Contact **ABC Pvt**
Telephone [Company Phone]
Cell [Cell Phone]
Email [Company E-mail]
Website [Website]

FOR IMMEDIATE RELEASE
[Date]

[MAIN TITLE OF PRESS RELEASE IN ALL CAPS]

[Subtitle of Press Release]

[City], [ST], [Date]– [Insert your announcement here and then briefly describe the benefits.]

> [Insert a quote from a company executive about what the announcement means.]

[Add additional paragraph(s) as necessary to describe your announcement and the benefits it provides.]

> [Insert a customer quote or news about partnering with another company, if appropriate.]

[Insert your company's boilerplate message.]

#

If you would like more information about this topic, please contact ABC Pvt at [Company Phone] or email at [Company E-mail].

TV, RADIO, AND NEWSPAPERS

Most people think that authors are experts or celebrities. Radio and television talk shows prove this every day. More than 10,200 guests appear on television stations each day (local interviews and talk shows across the country). Just flip through the channels, and the majority of guest authors are people you've never heard of before. They either got their press kit in front of the show's editor or hired a publicist to set it up. The rest is up to them; if the show goes well, it gets easier to book more.

It's not hard to get publicity in the media, so long as you are willing to work the small venues, the late-night programs, and with the up-and-comers trying to make a name for themselves. The first radio program I got involved with was an eye-opening experience because it was relatively easy. *Incarcerated Voices* was a volunteer program operated from a small office in Saint Francois University. I needed to promote my children's book, and they were the first program to take me on, while I waited for responses from niche programs like *Pacifica Radio* and *Prisonworld Radio Hour*.

I contributed essays and call-ins to IV, which resulted in a permanent profile on their site, letters, and most importantly, downloads of my book. Here's what I learned: rehearse. Talk to the editor about what you will speak about and then rehearse. Send them a list of questions you'd like them to ask you and rehearse. When the time comes to do your call in or sit down, take a shot of something strong and loosen up a little. Your first radio experience will be the most stressful, but after that, it gets as easy as pie.

You can interest local TV programs, radio jockeys, podcasters, and the media by timing your appearances with something newsworthy. These are all solid pitches to get their attention:

- Hometown author gets involved with literacy program
- Club or association event where the author will make an appearance
- Expert in (fill in the blank, tie-in with current affairs or general interest)
- Author raising awareness about (fill in the blank)

Update your website by adding links to your best performances so editors will see you as an entertaining guest. Before you know it, you will actually be a celebrity. Worst case, you can prowl the late-night programs (cable or AM radio) until you find one that needs a "talking head" to drop commentary in their next segment.

TOURING AND SELLING PHYSICAL PRODUCTS IN PERSON

Autographing, mini-seminars, workshops, and speaking engagements bring attention to a book. It's also a great way to meet clients and find freelance work. There are all sorts of tours, but what's essential is how you alert readers to your appearances. Your first step is to post a schedule on all your sites. Be thorough, with dates, times, and even little maps with clear directions.

It's a good idea to utilize *Publishers Weekly's Authors on the Highway* (publishersweekly.com), which allows authors to post a tour schedule. Then post it on the American Booksellers Association's *This Week* page. If you really want to go the extra mile, have a printer make a thousand copies of your new book so when you travel, you'll have something to sell. Traditionally, you'd complete the application process for a seller permit in each state, but tools today, like Intuit's GoPayment, factor it in. Some folks still collect cash under the table; it's questionable, but who's going to know?

The indie movement has cut across many industries and produced a renaissance in craft fairs, local markets, and people interested in buying directly from the creators. Authors can improve their odds by taking some products that tie into their book, as well as the books themselves. If your market targets a corporate audience, you'll notice many public speakers waiting to sell books and spin off products at the back of the room. Whether you sell in person or establish other distribution channels (retail stores, etc.) it is a good use of your subsidy rights, specifically merchandising.

It's easy to set up for sales:

- *PayPal Here* – A separate card reader that works with your mobile devices. Charges a one-time fee for the reader and then 2.75% for chip and pin cards or PayPal.

- *Intuit's Go Payment* – Plug in a swipe device with a signature that works with your Apple or Android mobile and all major credit cards. Works with QuickBooks accounting software. Has a pay-as-you-go or monthly rate charging with swipe rates of 1.75%-2.40%
- *Android Local Register* – Card readers and app. Charges 1.57% per swipe. Income can be used on Amazon or deposited directly into your bank account.

Once people know who you are, they'll be eager to buy. All of these sales options require traffic to your website, and you need an email list or some other means so you can tell people about books, products, and appearances. Get the platform built, and the rest is easy. It's never been better to sell in person, since most swipe device services account for easily forgotten nuisances like sales tax or customer service. These options make your brand more valuable, since you can sell one book and several products to the same customer.

If you are a gifted speaker, then consider public speaking and joining a speaker's bureau. It's an excellent touring strategy. Many bestselling authors are speakers. Speaking generates substantial income on its own through paid speaking engagements. After a Bureau has you booked solid, you can break off and do your own thing using the contacts you've gathered.

List yourself on Guestfinder.com, which makes public speakers available to the media, promoters, and small venues (clubs, churches, and convention halls). They may consider paying you a $500-$2,000 per diem to speak. The trick is you need to be fun, credible, and, oh yeah, smile a lot.

If you have a publicist, have them contact local TV editors to set up appearances. Interviewing with print media is a good way to kill time between delivering books to bookstores and small organizations along your route. Look for opportunities to make a video and post it on YouTube. If you have a poor turnout at events, then roam around with a book in hand, introducing yourself as "Today's Author." Chat up staff; booksellers in particular are a fount of information. Ask questions. "What books are getting your customers excited these days?" "Do you see any trends in the (fill-in-the-blank) genre?" Your next stop can only get better.

TOURS AT BOOKSTORES

✎ Writers Manifesto No. 22 – If bookstores were a good business, they might be able to pay their bills.

The most physical thing any writer can do is go on a book tour. There are some pretty disappointing stories out there about bookstores. If your book is on the shelves at the Wymyn's Radical Book Collective, you did well. You might sell a copy or two a month. That's realistic, and not a lot of work. What's unrealistic is expecting major success with book tours, unless your name is easily mistaken for Cornwell, Grisham, Patterson, or those other folks.

A successful book tour requires your full attention. Suzanne Thomas, author of the bestselling book *Rental House for the Successful Small Investor*, has been very successful in getting into bookstores. This was no accident; she did a lot of footwork.

"Model" is the term Barnes and Noble uses, so she used it too. They model a book to be carried by a store. When the book sells, the computer automatically orders another copy. A store could be modeled to carry one or more copies per store, although not necessarily for all stores (some topics sell better in different regions).

She would go directly to the store manager, sweet-talk them into ordering just one of her books, to try it out. If it sells (mom buys it), she would ask the manager to buy another (BFF scoops it up). It was time-consuming, but once she proved that the book would sell, she figured it might be possible to convince B&N to "model" the book in her entire region.

Thomas kept her CEO hat on at all times. She would organize her book signings. She notified certain organizations about her appearance dates and times. She did 13 book signings at B&Ns, selling about 25-30 books a month. With the book selling in other stores and online, she moved about 500 copies the first year. She purposely did signings in stores that hadn't yet "modeled" her book.

Two years later, instead of being modeled in 50 B&Ns, she's in almost all of them. They have kept it modeled with as few as 4 to 6 copies selling per year, per store. The automatic stocking system is easier to leave as is than it is to delete slow-moving books.

It's plain and simple, there are books that are ideal for bookstore selling, and there are books that don't sell in bookstores. It's not impossible for the same author to have both types of book. Filipino immigrant Veltisezar Bautista, owner of a small publishing company, bookhaus.com, sold his first book in bookstores. Check out the title, *The Book of U.S. Postal Exams: How to Score 95-100%*. It won the 1998 No. 1 Bestselling Title Award (in study guides) from Amazon.

That's swell. But his next book bombed. It was titled: *The Filipino Americans (1763-Present): Their History, Culture, and Traditions*. It was sold to some public and school libraries and online. We're not talking mega-sellers here. The royalties from bookstore sales will keep the lights on and maybe enough to buy lunch afterwards.

TOURS AT WORKSHOPS AND CONFERENCES

There are more options. Writers' workshops are paid learning experiences that draw small groups. They focus on actual skills, and the appeal of learning more about the hobby draws in many aspiring attendees. But you may end up teaching other professionals. They prefer to learn from an "expert." Many of them also pursue the offerings at the tables at Book Exhibits and Book fairs. These events are organized by colleges and writers' groups across the country. Simply visit their website and send a media kit along with a request to speak at or rent a booth at the next one.

These are often exciting events and will recharge your batteries. Take advantage of the situation by always having a few copies of your book ready to sell and autograph. There are people there who can teach you about the book industry: distributors, wholesalers, reviewers, and readers. Make the most of it by taking lots of photos, if you meet any celebrities, ask them to conduct an exclusive interview.

TOURS AT EXHIBITS

Exhibit services will put your books on display with those of other publishers. Some of the largest co-op exhibit services are: Combined Book Exhibit (CBE) and PMAAS for library and book trade events, Association Book Exhibits (ABE) for professional conferences, and Academic Book Exhibit and Scholars Choice for academic meetings. Check out several of them and compare prices. Try it out and ask for package deals for a whole season if it works.

Of course, you'll always do better if you go in person. You can become familiar with how they operate and take advantage of opportunities that pop up. This also works with Exhibits that have something to do with your book's theme. Or it can have nothing to do at all with your book. It's not unheard of for authors to hook up with nonprofit 501c3 organizations and offer them a carton of books at a steep discount. There are churches, gardening clubs, and after-school centers that put on bake sales and other fundraisers. Set it up so the organization keeps the difference from any book sales towards a donation. In the meantime, you get some FaceTime and possibly new readers.

PUBLIC SPEAKING TOURS

Authors are interesting people. Maybe that's why author appearances can pay $100 an hour or $5,000 per event. You can make more if you are well-known and guaranteed to draw a crowd. There are tons of venues for speaking tours; approximately 40,000 seminars are given each year in America, generating $110-$160 million. As long as you have fresh content, the bookings will keep coming. It's a great way to tour and can bring in stunning income. Also, it's more impressive to post clips of you speaking to a packed convention hall than a clip of you interacting with five people at a bookstore signing.

It's no mystery why authors can make so much for showing up and delivering a speech. Public appearances force people to see you and your products. By joining a Speakers Bureau, you can negotiate payments just for showing up on time and having something interesting to say. Many authors use speaking tours to boost their income, and that's why you should consider it. When you toss in workshops, consultations, and merchandise, you can make six figures a year.

When you put it all together it is not hard to see why publicity maximizes income. Jeff Henderson has shared his journey from a nineteen-year-old major crack dealer to the first black Executive Chef at the Bellagio hotel. He originally got bookings after Random House published his memoir *Cooked*, appearing on TV and radio. He bundled his speech to include business and financial advice, which opened up all sorts of bookings from high schools to corporate seminars. The bookings were managed by a Speakers' Bureau that worked to schedule him as much as he wanted, and the visibility from speaking helped draw in crowds to his restaurants as well as bookstores.

You can do the same thing if you're sociable and have a charismatic personality (or can fake it for a few hours in public). Bureaus are easy to join. They require you to submit materials, define an audience, and set your prices. Since you promote yourself, most of the materials are already on your website.

Most of what a Speakers Bureau needs, you'll develop out of necessity while touring:

- Speech outline
- Sample speech
- Press Kit
- Video (of you speaking)
- Action shots (of you speaking)
- Products you intend to sell (books, DVDs, framed photos, posters, etc.)

The National Speakers Association (NSA) has nearly 5,000 professional speakers in its database, with tips on how to hire them. Clients can set up the details with your bureau, and you can still work as a free agent. The bookings come from all sorts of groups: service organizations, adult education programs, church groups, PTAs, and on and on. The fact is, people will listen to your success story; you are, after all, an author who knows how to get out the message.

RESOURCES
Publicist Directory
- Public Relations Society of America (prsa.org)

Publicists
- atlasbooks.com
- book-publicity.com
- cypresshouse.com
- freepublicity.com/tv13
- kbookpromotions.com
- lovelife.com
- prpr.net
- readersradionetwork.com
- smarketing.com

Newspaper Directories

- 50states.com/news
- newspatch.com
- onlinenewspapers.com
- thepaperboy.com

Press Release Sites
- free-press-release.com
- prbuzz.com
- prfree.com
- prleap.com
- prweb.com

Reporter Referrals
- helpareporter.com
- pitchrate.com
- reporterconnection.com/press

Newsletter Directories
- ezinehub.com
- ezinelocater.com
- newsletteraccess.com

Book Trailer Designers
- authorbytes.com
- cosproductions.com
- movingseries.tv
- squidoo.com/booktrailers

Podcast Hosting Sites
- libsyn.com
- podbera.com
- wisegeek.com

Locating Conferences
- allconferences.com
- shawguides.com
- smarketing.com

Display/Promotional Products
- choicepromotionalproducts.com
- empirepromo.com
- gopromo.com
- qualitylogoproducts.com
- superioerpromos.com
- vistaprint.com

Teleseminar Services
- conferencecall.cm
- easycall.com
- xiosoft.com

Scammer Detection
- EZ.com

Speakers Bureaus
- speakersdirect.com
- americanspeakersbureau.com

PART 6

BOOKS

Chapter Twenty-Three

"Writing is a quiet life. Publishing is an active life." – Linda Meyer

GOING WITH A PUBLISHER

She took a breath and tapped the mic with her pinky. Deep booms echoed from the speakers. Someone coughed. No one saw how she trembled behind the lectern. Then she spoke: "I don't publish blacks, gays, convicts, or people who are right-handed." Colleagues stared at her up and down the aisles of the sci-fi decorated auditorium. Who would say such a thing?

Her name was Grace Campbell, and she was an editor for Alban Lake Press. "I publish stories, poetry, articles, and art. If I think it's publishable, I don't care who wrote it." Any of their shock melted away and poured into the roar made by clapping hands. The common opinion of most editors is that good writing is really all that matters.

Feel no concern about locating professionals to work with you. Don't worry about an MFA or some big award or even a residence in some community college. I have seen this play out again and again for some of the most "undesirable" writers you can imagine. Namely, they are impoverished, do not use the internet, and hang everything on their talent. Eventually, someone takes an interest and helps out. The only difference is whether they work at a small or a large press.

BOOK PUBLISHING VENUES

Book publishers come in a variety of venues. There are the large, mostly New York-based houses that would include W.W. Norton and Company, Knopf Doubleday, Penguin, Random House, Harper-Collins, and other imprints. These are the publishers that pay top dollar in advances and have access to the best publicity machines in the business, the kind that can get valuable TV and radio spots and take out prestigious and visible advertising.

Ironically, many authors say that it's made no difference. The logic goes: "No one ever asked me who my publisher was; they asked what the book was about." No one ever decides to purchase a book because Tor, Bean, or Ace publishes it. And authors get less royalties from each sale through big presses, like 15%, and when you factor in other costs (like an agent's 15% of your 15%), authors don't have many incentives to jump through all the flaming hoops to get published by a big press.

    1. *Big Presses* – Big Presses, also called Large Houses, are the hardest to get interested in a project. They are a business. If your work makes money, they stay interested. They don't play favorites. In this competitive arena, they pick the authors – those with a good track record of sales and lucrative new books to publish. You can browse any bookshelf and find these companies' imprints (little logos on the spines of the book). Most large publishers are owned by large conglomerates, so you'll find that many imprints are operated under the same roof as Viking, Penguin, Putnam, and TarcherPerigee.

The challenge with all this is that when you try your manuscript with one editor, most of the time you can't go back and try another, their decisions are final. Agents are almost always required for submissions. Without a representative, your submissions won't even be returned. They go straight into the dumpster.

You must work your way up to attract an agent (who is qualified to approach a big press) while simultaneously establishing a reputation as a writer who attracts readers.

That's why the advice for big presses is the same for getting an agent. Get a profitable book first, and then approach a big press with it. Since you've established your customers and have a track record, they'll be more apt to sign you up. In fact, they will call first.

    2. *Small Presses* – Small, independent presses are the mainstay of authors everywhere. These are university presses that publish books that win major awards and reach important audiences. They are small Mom and Pop operations put together by business-savvy professionals that promote their books to a tight niche. These presses may not offer advances, but they are less likely to jinx your work by over-editing and making title changes.

There used to be a dust-up over small presses' ability to distribute books, like actually getting them into bookstores. But with the eBook revolution and the domestication of print-on-demand services, the market is no more dominated by bookstores than the video rental industry is dominated by Blockbuster or the music industry ruled by record shops. In fact, many small presses choose books that will appeal to their readers, so you don't have to be an established author to get in. Their marketing is usually more effective than the big presses, since they target a list of existing buyers.

There are many presses in the field, but to cite a few: the University of Georgia and the University of Nebraska are publishing good books of creative nonfiction. Among independent presses, Graywolf Press and Sarabande Books are effective. On the flip side, you'll find Sunbury Press churning out eBooks on a trial basis. With a little persistence and a new Writers Market, you can hunt up a nice little press and get published.

A JOURNEY WITH PUBLISHERS

Award-winning author Michael Collins shares something in common with nearly half of all federal prisoners who are serving sentences for drugs: he has little to no criminal record. Collins' literary work has followed a trajectory uncommon for most imprisoned writers. Literary heavy hitters like Fyodor Dostoyevsky, Edward Bunker, and Damien Wayne Echols all built careers around their experiences in the criminal justice system of the era. What makes Collins unique is that his novels aim outside the themes of prison and addiction.

One editor commented, "At least you have the courage to write about something different than most people in your situation." His work had commercial value because Collins is well-read. He began serving his seven-year sentence in 2010, after eluding authorities for several months. He had been supplementing his college tuition and his personal habits by selling drugs on campus. When the ordeal was over, he inherited a prison cell and a 2006 edition of *Writers Market* from another convict.

He decided to try his luck with freelance writing. The quickest thing he could write was poetry. Collins submitted his verse to several contests, one of which he actually won. Now he could call himself an award-winning writer. Wow, he thought, this is really coming together.

His first autobiographical novel, *Hamster Wheel Manifesto*, was released in 2012 by Rio Norte Press. It explores the events leading up to his arrest "without the fluttering 'I's found in most memoirs" and provides "a glimpse into the dark world of heroin addiction on campus within a leisurely afternoon read."

Collins did all this from a United States Penitentiary using a computer in the factory where he worked to save and edit his book. It was marginally illegal. When he'd smuggled the finished product out, he began submitting it to publishers. The first 6 letters he'd sent to publishers were stamped Return to Sender (RTS). He simply bought a 2011 *Writers Market* and wrote some more until Rio Norte responded.

The letter Rio Norte sent simply read, "We can publish it. But eBook only?" Collins wanted to be able to touch his own book, but printed books, according to Rio Norte, were "a black hole for money." It was either an eBook or no deal. Collins didn't care. He valued himself as a literary artist who had a future as a novelist. This deal, his first book, would certainly lead to more opportunities. He said, "Yes!"

Because he kept current with the news and technology, he saw the opportunity to get anything published as a great achievement. If the world were turning to eBooks, then he wanted to ride the wave also. Since the 2007 introduction of Amazon's Kindle, e-readers have exploded with competition from Barnes and Noble, Kobo, Pocketbook, Sony Reader, and many others, including the iPhone and smart tablets. Collins was pleased to hike up his glasses and get on the forefront of a trend. He signed a contract, and work began.

After almost 3 months of "issues" with formatting the book (the pages were OCR scanned and had to be "reconstructed" line by line), it was finally available. Unfortunately, Rio Norte refused to offer the book in print. The editor told Collins, "eBooks are inexpensive and test sales. Print on Demand (POD) is only an option if a book sells a considerable number of copies." Rio Norte's chief editor told Collins that the number was 300 downloads. "Then we'll look into POD."

Feeling like a stepchild, Collins moved on and shopped his second book with a small publisher called Lady Bug Press. Due to the owner's health problems (Georgia Jones died of cancer in 2014) the deal fell through. But Collins motored through it, and his third book, *Graded Expectations*, was published by Walker Publishing. His childhood friend, indie director Harmony Korine, helped by getting his publicist to write a review and sent the book to Paul Constant, editor and reviewer for *The Stranger*. A well-earned smirk became one of Collins's permanent features.

From the forty-foot-tall concrete walls and gang violence of Maximum-Security Prison to the open fields and driver's license of a Federal Prison Camp, Collins's career was finally established. Small presses made it happen. He has settled down in Seattle. Prosciutto and a laptop await his next novel in some tucked-away boutique, probably some bigger publishers too, if that is what he wants.

SHARING CONTROL

Nothing moves fast when it comes to getting work published through big or small presses. The glacial pace of publishing has many explanations. Editors decide what writing gets used and what doesn't. If the author has been lazy and sends a poorly written manuscript, it gets trashed. In my experience, a little patience pays off. Publishers are focused on the bottom line; they don't want to rush into anything. In comparison, writers can get overtaken by the excitement of getting published and make rash decisions that lower the quality of their overall work. Just hold on and funnel all your energy into another book.

My friend John Lee Brook said it best: "I'll give them a couple more weeks, then I'll send them a polite message: 'Just wanted to make sure you got it, blah, blah, blah.' Which is code for 'WTF is taking so long?!' And they'll wait a few days and send back a polite response: 'Yes, we received it and it's next on our to-do list, blah, blah, blah.' That is code for 'Leave us alone and maybe we could get to it!'"

Feel free to follow up, but don't expect it to speed up the process. In between agreeing on book size, format, design, and cover art, the next big hang-up is agreeing on the book title. It's usually a case of overthinking it. Some authors choose titles that aren't descriptive of their books, yet they do well. Look at *Who Moved My Cheese?* It's a bestseller that has nothing to do with cheese; it's about corporate leadership. Publishers have gone to great lengths to come up with titles they think will attract people, and sometimes they are right, but there are no guarantees.

✒ **Writers Manifesto No. 23 – All book titles are come-ons.**

Carried to its logical extreme, we could test everything in a book. Do readers like the title? Do they like the story? Do they like the ending? Do they care about finishing this survey? It's possible to cut everything Constant Readers don't like, but at the end of the day, it's your book; compromise at your discretion. The thing is, you'll have to play a game of give and take with publishers, very much like a marriage. That is why people tend to love and hate publishers at the same time.

OUTGROWING A PUBLISHER

Educate yourself about the industry, your market, and ways to exploit both. If you detect opportunities that your publisher is missing, consider working with them to get paid. One of the biggest issues with publishers is what they do (and don't do) with books after the initial release and big marketing push showcasing it to readers. Big presses don't keep books around that aren't selling, because of this, several opportunities arise for authors who know how the industry works.

One company, Cool Gus, made a business out of negotiating to get authors' backlist books, books that have gone out of print. These books received new cover art, introductions from the authors, and tweaks to the page design. Then they are promoted as eBooks. They've freed up over 400 books and breathed life into their author platforms and bank accounts.

Hugh Howey made industry news when he got Simon and Schuster to agree to his terms to republish his self-published novel *Wool*. He'd already built a large following of readers and didn't feel pressured to take their first offer, which included a hefty advance. He insisted that he retain the electronic rights to his books, allowing him to simultaneously publish eBooks while Simon and Schuster produced print editions. Also, he wanted the full rights to his book to revert back to him if Simon & Schuster didn't print new editions for three years. It took several rounds of negotiation, but Howey got what he wanted.

Publishers are focused on selling a book and then moving on to the next one. It's a little short-sighted and usually costs the author sales in the future, especially if their contract binds up the right to use the work with that publishing company. That's why savvy authors are standing up to publishing companies. They negotiate the most favorable deals possible with an eye on what happens to their books after the initial publication. Consider working these terms into your contract before signing with a publisher; you'll thank yourself when the time comes.

RESOURCES

For a list of publishers, their preferences, and which editor to contact, refer to these directories:

Publisher Directories
- thewriter.com
- writersdigest.com
- writersmarket.com

Publishing Organization Directories
- obpa-online.org
- spannet.org
- spawn.org

Chapter Twenty-Four

"I believe in benevolent dictatorships, provided I am the dictator." – Richard Branson"

INDEPENDENT PUBLISHING

The chief benefit of self-publishing is control. With the click of a mouse (or swipe of a finger), your book can be distributed worldwide for the price of a slice of pizza, but the potential for well-done work is nearly limitless. Brittany Geragotelis got started by sharing excerpts of her novel through Wattpad, an online community where readers and writers connect. "I was constantly getting requests from fans who wanted to purchase their own copy of the book, which was really what ended up fueling my reasoning to publish." She self-published *Life's a Witch* and, in one year, had 18 million readers. That landed Geragotelis a three-book deal with Simon & Schuster.

There are plenty of authors, however, who self-publish to control the creation and get all the profit. That's why authors like James Altucher switched teams. "I've published eight books in the last seven years, five with traditional publishers (Wiley, Penguin, Harper Collins), one comic book, and the last two I've self-published. I can tell you those two have already sold more than my first five books with traditional publishers, combined." Altucher wrote that on his award-winning blog. It's more than a manifesto for self-publishing; it's an expression of the core value of having control over what you create.

HOW IT BEGAN

Dan Poynter worked as a Skydiving Safety Instructor in the 1960s, becoming an expert in the field, offering his time for military training and as an expert witness. He amassed tips and ideas for new equipment and complied them into a book. No one wanted to publish it; the market was too small, they said. He printed the book himself and began the work of distributing copies to bookstores.

This fateful decision, unconventional at the time, led Poynter into an entirely new adventure. Into the world of small publishing and running a company called Para Publishing, short for parachute. It was a stiff middle finger to the conventional and the birth of modern self-publishing.

The success of his skydiving book taught Poynter the ins and outs of writing, printing, and selling one. He found he loved it. Today, Poynter would be called ADD, ADHD, OCD, maybe even a superficially charming neurotic. Back then, people just called him an expert, and they respected him for it.

He scrutinized every detail about the industry. It was endless. He researched and wrote people and called them up until every answer was exhausted. Distributors, publicists, printers, you name it. When he was finished, he could tell you what paper you wanted on a book cover, all the way through to how to design a good-looking rubber stamp. It all went into a binder.

Around 1967, he decided this information was valuable in itself. He'd read books about traditional publishing houses and detected an opportunity for authors like himself. He arranged that information into his own book about publishing. Poynter used his contacts to get on TV, radio, and in newspapers, branding himself as an expert. What he did was open Pandora's Box and put it in layman's terms.

It became *The Self-Publishing Manual*. And it's been sold for over 28 years, using little gimmicks and non-stop publicity to keep it selling. The humility of the first book has been lost over 20 printings. With thousands of confirmed successes, Poynter hyped himself as the "Ombudsman for authors," as the "Father of self-publishing," and regularly got paid to speak about it as a Certified Speaking Professional (CSP).

Poynter said (before his death in 2014) that he'd authored more than 120 books. Well, technically, he'd only written six books and then revised and republished them (using the same titles) a couple of dozen times each. Because his product works, it was easy to overlook his ego. Poynter's influence had very real results, like demolishing the stigma surrounding self-publishing. Fifty years later, and it's mainstream, driving the last nail in the coffin of big publishers today.

MAKING YOUR BOOK IS EASY

The basic steps for making your book are:

1. Write, edit, revise, and finalize your manuscript.
2. If you go for a printed book, choose its size, format, and text.
3. Put together your cover image, back cover, front matter, and back matter.
4. Prepare and upload your digital files to your publisher's system.
5. Receive and review proof(s) of the book.
6. Publish and market the final product.

The top four online eBook retailers (Amazon, Apple, B&N, Kobo) each have their own unique reading devices and file specifications. If you ask their customer service for help, it's usually good enough to get you started. Most importantly, authors must understand what formats are available, which is pretty simple because there are only two:

    1. *Fixed Layout* – Children's books and graphic novels are formatted in a "fixed layout," replicating the text and images of each page in a set width.

    2. *Standard eBook* – Novels are formatted as "standard eBook" and have resizable text that automatically reflows.

Designing and formatting your text files and putting together your cover takes creative and technical skills, but you don't have to hire a professional. You can use the templates and image galleries available with your self-publishing service (they're cheesy but good enough to get the job done). Familiarity with Microsoft Word or Adobe InDesign will help you format your book, but if these programs are too time-consuming, there is help all around.

Your first stop should be Lynda.com, which has all the latest tutorials. YouTube provides some decent micro tutorials on self-publishing tools as well. Additional sources are tech sites like Mashable (mashable.com) and writers' organizations like the Society of Children's Book Writers (scbwi.org). They explain how to use new apps and software and dish out best practices.

The number one formatting tool recommended by indie authors is Scrivener; it is amazing software that only costs $49 (try it free at literatureandlatte.com). One of the practical features is its drag-and-drop functionality, so you can write out of order and then just switch things around later. It also has a Compile function, which means you can format your own Mobi files for Kindle and EPUB files for Kobo, iBookstore, and everywhere else. You don't have to pay a book formatter either, or you can update your files anytime you like. If you want to learn how to use the functionality even faster, you can get lots of mini video tutorials through Learn Scrivener fast (http://bit.ly/Z7Jou7). The best thing is its intuitive software; it is easy to get the hang of with a little practice.

The self-publishing revolution keeps making it easier and easier to make your book. Some tools like EPUB (the industry standard for eBooks) are obsolete now, thanks to tools like Book Baby and Book Creator (the #1 app for iPad, yours for $4.99). They are simple and intuitive for making fixed layout books for most e-readers. With the touch of a finger, you can drag and drop images, input text, and add background music or invisible audio buttons. With innovations like these, there's no limit to how cool your book can be.

This leads us to interior formatting for print, which is detail oriented work. It's easy to overlook even small errors because you're taking in so much detail. Things like incorrect page numbers can pass scrutiny even in bestsellers! To reduce errors, all the major book publishing platforms offer templates for interior page design. Just be prepared to run through your 'Proof Copy' with a highlighter, it makes changes faster to locate when you adjust the file. The decision whether to do it yourself, partner with a publisher, or hire a professional is based entirely on how much time you have to spend on this part of the process.

SET YOUR PRICE

Price is determined by what your readers expect. Smashwords did a survey and found that three to four dollars is the sweet spot for e-books and earns even more than books priced higher. But many first-time self-publishers think they can drop the price to pennies, and it will attract people. Readers will avoid your book if it's too cheap, like "What's wrong with it?" Constant Readers expect to pay for quality. All you'll achieve by dropping your prices is screw yourself. It takes the same amount of work to sell a cheap book as it does an expensive one.

Check Amazon and you'll find these price ranges:

- eBook (fiction) $0.99-$4.99
- eBook (nonfiction) $0.99-$6.99
- POD (fiction) $6.95-$11.95
- POD (nonfiction) $9.95-$19.95

Higher price ranges exist in some markets. Academic textbooks (or niche reference books) might be worth $24.95-$49.95. To set your prices, simply compare your book to the competition. Then price it at the maximum value. If your competition charges $39.95, then that's what you should charge.

A rare option is to charge $1,000 to $2,500 per book. This happens with investment strategy guides that "reveal the secrets" and promise to pay for themselves. Usually, the author interacts with the customer to show them the system described in the book. If you have contacts with these types of readers, then go for it. Meanwhile, the rest of the world will purchase a *For Dummies* version of it for $19.95 and probably learn the same thing.

PAYMENT

Self-published authors keep the lion's share of the profit. A quick analysis reveals just how much profit can be had. Most authors receive a 6% to 10% royalty from large publishers (a pittance). If they sell 5,000 books for a list price of $20, the gross is $100,000. However, the costs of printing, delivery, and promoting may be 70% to 80% of that. Let's say you get $1,000 when it's all finished. That's why big publishers are having a hard time competing with self-publishing.

When you self-publish, you get around 70% of the gross. When a book sells on an online retailer's site, they take a small "download fee." This fee varies from site to site but averages 30%. Sell the same 5,000 books for $20, and the gross is $70,000. You get to pay taxes on whatever's left after you round up your deductions and expenses in April.

GETTING HELP

Authors who know their market better than anyone else prefer to control their backlist from the very beginning. Roshad Carter writes alternative black history/humor. "Before I knew what direction I was going to go, I was comparing publisher info and indie publisher info." He eventually chose an Author Service Company called Crystell Publications and paid $1,400 for a turn-key package. Nine months and one round of proofs later, *Maaan, You Know That Ain't White* was in front of Carter's unique audience. He says, "Getting this first book out there was expensive, but I feel it was worth it."

Using an Author Service Company simplifies the journey. They offer a menu of services that include cover design, editing, eBook formatting, print-on-demand, ISBNs, and bar codes. Expect fixed prices for each and discount pricing for bundles. Reputable companies like Outskirts Press, BookLocker, Dog Ear Publishing, and many others have published hundreds of thousands of authors. The process is streamlined and relatively fast. Books can be completed in as little as a few weeks, compared to a 6-month average for traditional publishing.

Before you settle on a self-publishing service, investigate the customer reviews and be cautious when paying for extras (like marketing packages). A dozen companies offer identical services – just shop around until one fits your specific needs (graphic novels, magazines, novels, eBooks, customized merchandise, etc.).

Most of the sharks have been shut down, but a few "Subsidy" publishers are in business. They want you to pay for the publishing costs and then split some of the profit with them. This business practice was deemed "unethical" long ago. Don't fool with these people. Hire companies that don't play with profits; you own 100% of your creation, no one else.

Once the book is uploaded to online retailers, you have full control of the account. If that sounds like something you'd like to try, then make sure you can afford it. The costs run from $500 for a slapdash job, up to several thousand dollars for a professional treatment. Just be sure to weed out the rotten apples by reviewing their services.

Here's a breakdown of what's legit and what's a waste of time:

Legit Services

1. eBook file preparation and upload to Amazon, Barnes & Noble, and iBookstore.
2. Custom interior design and formatting (up to 120,000-word manuscripts).
3. Basic cover from the cover library and upgraded custom cover design.
4. Editing

Questionable Services

1. Partner/Subsidy publishing (you should retain 100% rights and profit from a book)
2. Registered ISBN and Library of Congress Control Number (LOC).
3. Fulfillment of orders in short-run printed books (shipping not included).
4. Worldwide distribution channels with more than 36,000 sales outlets.
5. Most promotion services.

One of the worst services I've seen is called "Book Return Insurance," sold for one year for $499, two years for $699, and subsequent years for $299. The pitch was that bookstores won't stock your book unless it's returnable. Large Houses operate this way. Since your book will be Print-On-Demand, it can't be returned. The company came up with this offer and "encouraged authors" to pay the fee. It was a way to shake down authors for more money.

"By listing your books as returnable with our wholesaler, you'll level the playing field with traditional publishers. It prevents delays in catalog updates and gets your book in bookstores."

An editor I know had this to say about such companies: "Most author service companies keep it simple. They upload a PDF to CreateSpace, owned by Amazon. CreateSpace approves it, picks an ISBN, and sends a proof copy for final approval. Within days, it will be available in paperback through POD. It costs the company time to format it, but the tools cost them nothing. The truth is, many do sloppy work."

ELECTRONIC BOOKS (EBOOKS)
With eBooks, interior design means almost nothing since the reader chooses the font and the size and most other aspects of the appearance of the text. All you need is a finished book and the covers to format. One choice (which everyone seems to make, including myself) is to limit yourself to just the two biggest players. Amazon Kindle (Kindle Direct Publishing, kdp.amazon.com) and B&N's Nook (pubit.barnesandnoble.com).

If you want to cover the whole market, Smashwords and Scrivener offer one-stop shopping. They can adapt your MS Word text to the file formats needed for compatibility with most reading devices. They also set up distribution with major vendors (smashwords.com and literatureandlatte.com). More apps are available that increase compatibility, mainly from Apple and Amazon. As the industry continues to mature, formatting will become more and more universal. Even with the tools at hand, the writers' community on *Wise Link* says 40 percent of all eBook revenue is going to indie authors.

PRINT-ON-DEMAND (POD)
Print-on-Demand is a digital printing technology and a business model. Books are made only after they are ordered, even in single copies. In the past, authors had to print several thousand copies of their book (to get the unit cost down). Most of those copies ended up in a garage, unsold. With POD, the costs are already low, and the risk of turning your garage into a stockroom (and expensive eyesore your family will complain about) is eliminated.

It's easy. Launch your book as an eBook and POD (all free to create). If actual sales indicate that it makes sense to print a thousand, switch over to press printing. The files can be downloaded by local printers, but if your order is small, it will take them a while to get around to it. It doesn't require a change of ISBN or anything. If sales really take off, you can pivot to become a real small publisher and make deals directly with distributors.

Big publishers deal directly with Lightning Source. They print virtually all POD books in America and are owned by Ingram, the largest wholesale distributor. There is an active group focused on POD publishing with LS that helps new publishers navigate the latest trends and get established (finance.groups.yahoo.com/group/pod_publishers). If it looks like you've got a hit, then this is the community you want to get involved with.

Big or small, you decide the print size of your book.

Fiction, nonfiction, technical manuals, etc.

- US Trade   6" X 9"
- US Letter   8.5" X 11"
- Pocketbook   4.25" X 6.87"
- Digest   5.5" X 8.5"

Photography, art, children's, cookbooks, etc.

- Small square 7.5" X 7.5"
- Square   8.5" X 8.5"
- Landscape   9" X 7"

POD reduces the costs of transportation and warehousing books, but you can still purchase books (in lots of three) at wholesale prices. The cost is determined by the book size and page count. My book, *Life With A Record* (360 pages, square), sells for $25.99 retail, but I buy it from CreateSpace for $7.50 per book, plus priority shipping. It doesn't matter if I order three or three hundred.

This is handy for delivering advanced review copies and other promotional giveaways. It's also less risky than printing 5,000 books (to lower the printing cost to 2.00 per book) for a nonrefundable bill of $10,000. In a nutshell, that's all the motivation you need to embrace the preferred printing method of over one million authors.

GETTING LISTED WITH THE BOOK INDUSTRY
Before the internet, self-publishing advice was pretty archaic; authors were directed to fill out a bunch of "Book Industry" applications for exclusive serial numbers and codes and other hoopla. Armed with the right registrations, you got free listings in library journals (20,000 readers) and book industry catalogs (60,000 subscribers) and on and on. But with the explosion of online self-publishing, it's no longer relevant.

If you're an independent author, then Amazon gets more done instantly. But if you decide to start a publishing company, there are some benefits to getting listed. It's the only way to be taken seriously by wholesalers and distributors. Part of the reason is that when you publish with online retailers (like CreateSpace), they issue an ISBN for free, but they are listed as the publisher, not you. The only way to change that is to buy batches (10 minimum) of ISBNs and issue them yourself.

Here are the Book Industry applications a publishing company must know how to use:

    1. *International Standard Book Number (ISBN)* – Since the 1960s, ISBNs have been the worldwide book identification system. If you want to own your ISBN (which is only practical for small publishing companies), an ISBN and barcode combo costs $295 from R.R. Bowker. You can complete the online application (isbn.org) in about five minutes. ISBNs can also be purchased in a handful of countries and from Google.

- U.K., Nielsen 10 for €132
- Australia, Thorpe Bowker 10 for AU$ 84
- Canada, CISS, free
- Google, 'ISBN plus your country', free

    2. *Library of Congress Number (LCCN)* – These numbers appear in the copyright page of your book. Registered books are listed in the National Union Catalogue; most public and private libraries subscribe to it, with nearly 20,000 in total. Complete the forms online (pcn.loc.gov/p.m.) about 6 months before your book's release, specifically "Procedures for securing Preassigned Library of Congress Control Number" and a "Request for Preassignment of LCC Number" (Form 607-70).

    3. *Advanced Book Information (ABI)* – You can apply for an online listing (bowkerlink.com), which is simply an intent to publish. You do not need an ISBN to file the announcement. After your books are published, update the form, and the listing will appear in R.R. Bowker's Books in Print, an industry catalog for publishers, libraries, and bookstores.

Just getting registered isn't enough. You have to pitch it to distributors. That means actual companies that move books in cases, with forklifts and trucks. Lawyers and union reps can't help you. You can always show up at the warehouse and try charming the dispatchers (authors have done that). Or ask for help from organizations like National Book Network (nbnbooks.com), Consortium Book Sales and Distribution (cbsd.com), and Independent Publishers Group (ipg.com). They all move books for traditional publishers, who are grandfathered in from the pre-Internet era.

If getting into bookstores is an ego trip for you, then you're unfocused. If it's based on actual sales, then it might be worth it. But it's easier to convince the book industry that you're a cash cow if you already are one. Most books never hit shelves, so don't make that a goal. Instead, use online retailers and build your backlist. That's how modern bestselling self-published authors do it.

STARTING YOUR OWN PUBLISHING COMPANY

✒ **Writers Manifesto No. 24 – The first forms of organized crime were business, government, and publishing.**

Once you master the enterprise of self-publishing, there are several new opportunities to get paid. Take it from the "Ombudsmen of self-publishing," Dan Poynter. He turned his expertise into a profitable company selling reports and publishing spin-off books. Para Publishing established relationships with an entire generation of independent reviewers, publicists, and editors that lent him free publicity. That, in turn, drove *The Self-Publishing Manual* to become an international bestseller. Not bad considering it got started with just him and his wife.

Becoming a small publisher isn't a bad idea, provided you can market books effectively. If you like that level of control and customization, you'll have to don the general contractor hat, acting like a traditional publisher by seeking out and hiring the appropriate experts for each project. If you want the upper hand as a writer, editor, or publisher, consider these educational programs:

    1. *Creative Writing Courses* – You don't have to fork over $30,000 to earn a Master of Fine Arts (MFA); there are plenty of Associate's Degree programs ($16,000). Key courses are English, Creative Writing, and Literature. If you don't want to waste time applying for grants and loans, you can just skip traditional college programs altogether by studying and testing out through a CLEP (College Level Examination Program) testing center, for about $80 a course.

The benefits of a conventional college education are twofold. First, your work gets critiqued by a professor. Second, the course will force you to read and analyze writers' styles you may never have been exposed to. Of course, you can achieve basically the same thing by following the course outline in any Creative Writing textbook, so it's your choice.

    2. *Publishing Courses* – Some of the great programs cost a hefty sum but can be worth it, mainly for the connections you'll make rubbing elbows with one percenters. The NYU Center for Publishing (scps.nyu.edu), University of Denver Publishing Institute (du.edu/pi), US Berkley Extension (unex.berkeley.edu), and Stanford Publishing courses (publishingcourses.stanford.edu) are premier programs.

With a price tag of $42,000, you'd expect some major benefits, but what you get is interaction with other publishing professionals. It is basically a big opportunity for networking. Meanwhile, these courses will educate you about all the trends and tricks that will assure your success as the leading force of a publishing company. The lectures and feedback are always good, but it's possible to get a watered-down version of the benefits by exhibiting at a publisher's conference for a few hundred dollars plus travel expenses.

Author-entrepreneurs can start at any time. When things aren't instantly perfect, they stop panicking and recognize it's another opportunity to learn on the job, pivot as necessary, and keep grinding forward. After her appearance on *Money and Work* with James Crosby, Rhonda Turpin realized she needed to write a book. "It's kind of a domino effect," she says. "My mutation into a grant writer grew into being an author." She wrestled with the chief indie stigma "not good enough for a normal publisher," but crunching the numbers of royalties and print runs convinced her it was good business. To make it more professional, Turpin created her own company, World Books. None of it was especially difficult to orchestrate, so she ended up considering other authors, as well as publishing six more of her own books.

Indie authors who are more comfortable working on other people's deadlines can turn their skills into a lucrative Author Service Company. It avoids the hustle and bustle of long-term contractual obligation and dependence upon a publisher. All you need is to catch the authors' interest and offer quality self-publishing packages. Bundle services to assist writers, fulfill them in a timely fashion, and get paid. Do quality work, and word of mouth (WOM) will take you wherever fate allows. Once you have a few success stories, get your company reviewed by the Independent Publishing Magazine (mickrooney.blogspot.com) and point clients to it for confirmation of your legitimacy.

Here's some wisdom:

1. Get a lawyer (or at least have one review your contracts).
2. Operate under Doing Business As (DBA with your state, if it takes off, then incorporate.
3. Be honest and always deliver.

RESOURCES

Book Designers and Cover Artists
- arrow1.com
- beitnow.com/publishingdesign.htm
- bookgraphic.com
- dotdesign.net
- dunn-design.com
- fostercovers.com
- freebirdpublishers.com
- kleinedit.com
- knickoutbooks.com
- macgraphics.net
- midnightexpressbooks.com

Editorial Services
- editorialdepartment.com
- penultimateword.com
- topressandbeyond.com

Author Service Companies
- abbotpress.com
- archwaypublishing.com
- authorhouse.com
- booklocker.com
- dogearpublishing.com
- freebirdpublishers.com
- infintitypublishing.com
- iuniverse.com
- kdp.amazon.com
- llumina.com
- lulu.com
- midnightexpressbooks.com
- trafford.com
- wastelandpress.net
- westbowpress.com
- winepublishing.com
- xlibris.com
- xulonpress.com

Publishing Sites
- Amazon KDP – kdp.amazon.com

- Blurb – blurb.com
- Book Baby – bookbaby.com
- CreateSpace – createspace.com
- Draft 2 Digital – draft2digital.com
- Google Play – bit.ly/1A2289D
- Ingram Spark – 1.ingramspark.com
- iTunes – itunesconnect.apple.com
- Kobo Writing Life – kobo.com/writinglife
- Nook Press for Barnes & Noble Nook – inookpress.com
- Scrivener – literatureandlatte.com
- Smashwords – smashwords.com

Chapter Twenty-Five

"Though our publishers will tell you that they are seeking 'original' writers, nothing could be farther from the truth. What they want is more of the same, only thinly disguised." – Henry Miller

EXPLOIT SUBSIDY RIGHTS

Authors only write a book once, but they can make multiple products out of it, and multiply sales. It helps to start thinking that readers are more than; they are multimedia consumers. Some want books, others prefer audiobooks, and still others need consultation for their business. Once a book gets a sales history, authors can orchestrate all of this pretty easily.

Obviously, there are plenty of multimedia products you can make out of your writing. eBooks, print, and audiobooks are relatively simple to make. By comparison, some subsidy rights are harder to exploit without expert knowledge. Film and TV rights are one of those. You can't force anything. Have a great book with a sales history, and doors will open. Hugh Howey managed to attract director Ridley Scott with *Wool*, negotiating through his agent, and James Fogle attracted independent filmmaker Gus Van Sant with *Drugstore Cowboy*, communicating through his lawyer. It's mostly a matter of right-place-right-time.

Focus on exploiting the subsidy rights you can control. Partnerships are what make subsidy rights open up to new markets. Your rights are contractually based and fully negotiable, so don't sign them over without considering the big picture. Independent authors like Howey negotiated to only grant print rights, while managing their own electronic and audiobook rights. Other indies have retained 100% control in the U.S., U.K., and Canadian markets, and they take advantage of developing international markets by partnering with foreign publishers. They spread translated versions through Europe, Asia, and the Middle East. And that's just the beginning of what can be accomplished.

THE TRIFECTA: EBOOKS, POD, & AUDIO

The highest-selling format for books is eBooks. The main file types are Mobi (for Kindle), EPUB (for most other devices), and PDF (for reading on a computer). You can do these yourself on each online retail service, or use alternative tools like Scrivener, or use conversion services. It's easy to get files on multiple devices: Kindle, Kobo, Nook, Apple device, cell phones (through apps), as well as on computers. You'll get paid from each store separately.

Though bookstores have pretty much faded from the consumer market, print books still enjoy healthy sales. Print-on-Demand technology means you don't have to pay up front or warehouse and ship physical products anymore. Authors sell on services like CreateSpace, Ingram Spark, or Lightning Source, they upload files and have books available for sale on Amazon, Barnes & Noble, and all the rest. Books are shipped directly to customers; one order equals one shipment. Better yet, you can do a short run of copies if you have a means of distribution.

While eBooks and print cover the largest parts of any market, many Constant Readers spend hours commuting every day. The ease of using digital audio files makes audiobooks a good market for certain genres. Major sales outlets include Audible, iTunes, and Brilliance. One site in particular, ACX.com, hooks authors up with audiobook narrators who work for either a royalty share or for hire. Whether authors use a service or source their own talent, if they have a series, it is wise to work with the same narrator. D. Preston and L. Child's *Pendergast* series gets the treatment from Rene Auberjonois; meanwhile, their *Eli Glinn* series is read by David W. Collins. Regardless of format, audiences enjoy consistency, and authors who deliver that tend to multiply their income.

AUDIO BOOKS

If authors have the time and are easily recognizable, their own voice may work best. Scientist Richard Dawkins does it in *Brief Candle in the* Dark, where he delves into his intellectual life. Otherwise, the process for turning your book into an audiobook begins by uploading a sample for narrators to audition with. You probably have a specific idea of what you're looking for, and services like ACX allow you to pick narrators from a list. Whether it's a true crime story or a coming-of-age story, tell narrators up front so they can determine if the project fits them. Once some auditions have been submitted, review them and pick the voice that makes your project come to life.

The right voice will make a big impression. If budget isn't an issue, a little star power can work very well. Tom Clancy (with M. Greaney) does this routinely for Jack Ryan novels like *Threat Vector*, which was read by actor Lou Diamond Phillips. No matter whom you choose, take time to find a match. It adds dimension to your words.

The ability to work with people is a necessity throughout life. Standard stuff like establishing a timeframe upfront, being respectful of others' skills, and letting small things go isn't anything new. Working with a narrator, however, brings some unique challenges. It's a creative partnership, and narrators bring their own interpretation to events. If you are frustrated by the end results, it's your own fault. Re-read your text aloud to be certain you are happy with how it flows. Make any changes before you start the narration process.

Writing strong characters is a different skill from bringing them to life with a narrator. It has an extra dimension, defined by nuances of emotion, inflection, and tone that requires a balancing act. Things like character accents, while they may be authentic, are too strong of an accent and can be hard to understand. Also, language issues arise, which require you to give the narrator feedback, like "The Nueces River is pronounced Natchus, not noose-us." Also, think about how you can make editing simple, for example, include a time stamp. "At 16:50, Nueces is mispronounced." It makes the job run smoothly and results in a product that customers will be pleased to buy.

TRANSLATION

Unlike the U.S., where most people speak one language, other countries teach a second language in school. These emerging markets are exciting because online distribution is just opening up to them. I remember the first time one of my articles was reprinted in a Turkish newspaper. My first thought was, "How the hell are they reading it?" Turks speak English and German as well. While you can expect readers in other countries to buy your book if it's in English, realize that we all prefer to read our native language.

The top 5 popular languages are:

- English (1 billion worldwide)
- Spanish (400 million worldwide)
- Mandarin (270 million)
- German (120 million)
- French (40 million)

Don't rush into anything. Make sure you're ready, use the Kobo Writing Life platform, which has a world map showing which countries people have bought your book in. Make sure it's worth it. For example, there are over 400 million people worldwide who speak Spanish, and a translator could pay off. But realize that Spanish has dozens of dialects.

Make sure you pick a translator who has some experience. If you're doing a partnership (royalty split or for hire, doesn't matter), they need professional skills (timeliness and hard work). Interview them (phone, email, Skype) or in person. Check their references. And get a sample translated so you can have L2 readers give you feedback. Focus on honest and open communication. They will have questions about what the author actually meant. Be patient, because word choice will change based on intent.

DO IT YOURSELF OR USE A FOREIGN PUBLISHER

Translation is a creative process. The challenge is trying to communicate the nuance of the author's voice in a way that works in another language. It's not as easy as using Google Translate to change line by line. The text must work as a whole, and automated or rushed translation will result in jarring vocabulary errors or omissions that pull the reader out of their experience. Requiring such skilled work means you've got to treat translators as creative partners; after all, your shared goal is to make a product the reader wants to buy.

Doing it yourself means more control, which, if you're organized, can be a good choice. If you source your own translators, you'll need to think about more than language issues. It's a "best practice" to sign a 50/50 profit-sharing deal with translators. Partners are incentivized by the promise of higher pay. You should also pay language specialists to translate promotional materials (book reviews, press releases, blogs, etc.). Distribution tools like Smashwords allow you to upload files to Amazon, Kobo, iBookstore, and Nook Press, but each country is called a "territory," and you'll have to upload them accordingly.

It's easiest to attract a foreign publisher with a book that's already selling. You'll need to put your CEO hat on and read contracts, make sure you control the "foreign rights" from any existing publishing agreements, and negotiate with the foreign publisher to be sure to take advantage of their distribution model. Foreign publishers are lumped together in several directories, including the Writer's Market online database. However, IPR License and PubMatch let you upload your book, search their database, and pitch it.

Before you stumble on it, don't say "Wait. Don't I need an agent?" Stop and realize that in countries outside the U.S, U.K., and Canada, agents are used a lot less often. Agents who specialize in foreign markets can work on your behalf, but the percentage they seek is a little more than that of domestic ones. U.S. agents usually get 15% commission; to work with foreign companies (using sub-agents), they get 20%. If your book is doing well, you'll probably get approached by someone anyway. The decision to enlist an agent is purely based on the time you have available, since all the tools to do it yourself are at your fingertips.

RE-ISSUE OLD BOOKS

It's easier to make changes to an existing book than it is to write a new one. Turn a re-issue into an opportunity to improve things. When I pitched the revised and expanded edition of this book to the publisher, many of the changes were based on reader feedback. This technique works for any book. If reviews point out errors or areas you could strengthen, then fix things and market them as if they were new. Add bonus content, re-emphasize information for a crossover market, update content to stay fresh and relevant, or simply clean up any blemishes that made it through the original. It's easy to adjust files, and with a little TLC, your backlist will always be attractive.

If you have a series, then a reissue can represent a considerable investment in time and money. The decision should be based on ROI, put it off until you see sales slowdown, or after you've finished the next book in a series and want to refresh it for your audience (better covers, maybe). If you write a book that's similar to an existing book of yours, you could reissue it, placing an excerpt of the new book in the back. Though a fully revised edition has a lot of appeal in eBooks, readers who bought it in print can also be convinced to replace worn-out or obsolete copies.

There are four areas you can focus on to make an old book feel new again:

- *Size* – hardcover's with special dust jackets or print versions with embossed designs are always attractive.
- *Cover* – a new, or touched-up cover can work, adding awards, sales ranks, and testimonials looks nice too.
- *Front Matter* – a new foreword or pictures of your other books can work wonders.
- *Interior Design* – new or touched-up illustrations, kerning, or some needed edits are all it takes to get a new look.
- *Back Matter* – a new afterword, author's note, ordering information, and an excerpt from a new book are good choices.

A new edition is a new book, basically, and it can be promoted as one, without having to actually write one. It's a proven tactic that works for just about every publisher. The reasons are simple, especially if you have several related books. Readers buy more of what they like. Popularity speaks for itself, and a re-issue communicates that your book is worth a second look, referral, or both.

SPECIAL EDITIONS
If you control your rights or can work with your publisher to unlock them, there are even more options for making your books into additional products. If a product is good, it will sell consistently over time. Even changing a few small details can be enough of a reason for readers to buy it again.

1. *Box Sets* – Making it easier for readers to jump into a series really drives sales. Authors rely on previews (the first 10% of a book file) to draw in readers, but there are more cunning options. Barbara Freetby, the bestselling KDP author of all time, made it by bundling her series. With over 35 books available, she sees an overall effect when someone discovers her books, scoops up a cheap box set, and dives into her backlist.

A single full-length novel may sell for $4.99, with novellas costing $2.99. A box set, say three books, may sell for $5.99, but separately, they cost $14.97. It's a good deal for everyone. All you need is a cover that looks like a box set, and create a file with multiple books in it. This makes it easy for readers to wet their beaks and hopefully seek out your backlist.

2. *Anniversary & Commemorative Editions* – If a book has done well, you have more to celebrate than its sales. Books make great collectibles. The 25th Anniversary edition of Fahrenheit 451 had over 50 pages of back matter about how the story developed from a play and into a novel. It bundled things that fans would see value in. This included original hand-written pages, drawings, and illustrations from the first printing. All that was tied together in a running commentary that added a new dimension to the story that fans love. So, of course, it sold.

It's possible that the new promotions undertaken for an anniversary edition could attract new readers, but it's also an effective strategy for fans who already know your name. It's especially useful when you complete a series. Exclusive things like an interlocking collage across multiple book covers (that form one image) can make an older book very desirable. Also, with the added expenses of making a collectible edition, you can set a price that's higher than normal.

3. *Gift Books* – These work best with a direct sales model. Special editions with a high price tag can take the gift of gab to sell. Also, loyal fans like to touch and admire the quality. Cory Doctorow sells hand-bound hardcover editions of his book *With a Little Help*; it's a gift, a keepsake. Of course, a nice hardcover can be mass-produced if you have the distribution set up. Scott Stigler writes a galactic football series that he runs on POD and sells directly to fans. Since he autographs them, it's something special. These are real keepsakes, giving a book added emotional value above the pulp and glue holding it all together.

MULTIMEDIA

On the extreme end of subsidy exploitation, you'll find super success stories. You've heard of Tony Robbins, the rags-to-riches motivational guru who targets professionals with a suite of products based on his books and philosophy. He's as likely to sell audio, video, and computer variations as he is to do paid speaking or consultative services. A select group of author-entrepreneurs follows the same model.

The genius of this approach is that the value offered in their books (whether it's corporate-level stuff like sales strategy or personal motivation in the form of thigh-burning aerobics) is molded into apps, memberships, and training courses. This requires extra hands, with expert skills, not to mention the personality to prop up a brand. This justifies some authors to set high prices, which, if your market supports it, could bring in a nice income. Corporate pricing has an implicit warranty, however, something like "Your investment will pay off." Be certain you're calibrated to deliver on that promise.

Most authors are a little introverted; they find the idea of becoming a guru too overwhelming. Instead, they focus on multimedia that serves their specific area of expertise. Selling book-based products to people who share your interest can be refreshing, and it doesn't demand the manic pace you'd expect of Tony Robbins. Lee Hammond is such an author; she's taken her artistic skills and written books, then filmed instructional DVDs in her studio, and also offers workshops and art kits for hobbyists. All while living a very private life. This helps Hammond sell art and take on commissioned pieces, which in turn gives her more ideas for book-based products.

To drive home a certain message takes a dash of charisma, not all of us can pull off a book like Gillian Michaels' *5 Minute Burn for a Leaner, Fitter You*. That's why authors utilize speaking tours, do direct sales as they go from group to group, and network to schedule more bookings. Still more authors rely on podcasts, blogs, and other stationary content-based marketing to take advantage of their book's full potential.

    1. *Non-Book Products* – Sold on websites and in person, non-book products that are successful embody some aspect of the focus their brand exhibits. Things like slogans, iconic lines from popular characters, and even cover designs could be worked into merchandise. T-shirts, posters, key chains, phone covers, calendars, and other merchandise can generate quite a lot of income. You'll have to make the decision if it fits your market; if it does, then you either make the designs yourself or hire an artist.

    2. *Apps* – The actual software for app development is available, but it's a wise choice to hire a programmer who can design your app and versions that are compatible with a range of other devices. Most indie developers are focused on one type of app, adding a nice product mix to books and other book-based products. The best apps work on the principle "give a little, get a little." Games and reward systems are always popular, but you'll have to be creative and innovate a way to fit your book's message into an app. It could simply enable a link to your podcast or newsletter. Meanwhile, rewards like licensed products (t-shirts, coffee mugs, etc.) are a great tool for user interaction, and so are coupons for books or attendance fees at your next appearance.

Since apps are usually "sold" as free to download, income is derived from features, functionality, or content. In-app transactions yield 91% of income across most mobile platforms. These updates should build a story. Literally, posting novellas, excerpts from your books, and other writing is a good strategy. You can promote your app on your website, social media, and through cross-platform networks like Chartboost, which can reach over 105 million unique users in 100 countries. For analytics, try Direct Deals Marketplace, and if it's successful, mine into your app's potential with monetization and distribution networks like Apple's W3i.

    3. *Instructional Products* – Tapes, MP3s, DVDs, and videos are a desirable model to showcase information-based products and the smart use of authors' subsidy rights. Authors who traffic in how-to, self-help or lifestyle advice can have success selling instructional products. They have a built-in pitch.

Elaborate skillsets, whether it is *7 Habits of Highly Effective People* or *Guitar for Dummies*, fans benefit from extra instruction.

It is possible to use Microsoft Movie Maker to produce quality videos, but the equipment and time to create these products can represent a large investment. Authors may also need to rent a studio or modify their office for filming and recording. Travel presents a new set of challenges. An assistant with a background in cinematography or sound engineering who can arrange clips from events into dynamic content would be useful. However, outsourcing the technical aspects by hiring a production company, like Digitorial Media, may be the best bet for busy authors.

Think of making a series, so fans can dive in. Make a separate backlist that will feed sales from book to video and back again. Bob Ross, the painter known for turning "happy little accidents" into masterpieces, made 24-minute episodes that ran on PBS for years. He also sold them separately. Exercise, cooking, arts and crafts lend themselves to instructional videos, but don't overlook videos of live seminars, or documentary-style videos that tie in with your book's topic. If your message only needs a narrative to make a point, audio can sell just as well.

If you have something to say, something that customers are happy to buy, there's almost no limit to what you can do. Take advantage of free tutorials like those available on YouTube for video production, app design, merchandising, and book printing. Make whatever you do really pop. What's important, throughout everything, is to remain mindful of new ways to reach your market. Every way you successfully exploit your subsidy rights, the more your income is multiplied.

RESOURCES
Audio
- audacity.sourceforge.net

Translation
- acx.com

Foreign Publisher Directories
- IPR License.com
- PubMatch.com
- WritersMarket.com

App Development
- Appcelerator.com
- appmobi.com
- konysolutions.com

Mobile Advertising Networks
- buzzdoes.com
- fisku.com
- InMobi.com
- kickanotch.com
- MillenialMedia.com

Mobile Rewards Network
- Chartboost.com
- DirectDealMarketplace.com
- Kiip.com

Product Design and Drop Shipping
- ideacafe.com

- zazzle.com

Video Making
- digitorialmedia.com
- fixmymovie.com
- seesmic.com

PART 7
BOOKSELLING

Chapter Twenty-Six

"One of the simple rules guiding my practice is this: hustle, hustle, hustle." – Ian Harvey

PRO TOOLS
Anyone who has published a book immediately discovers they need to get more people to buy it. Traditional publicity only moves the needle so far because it doesn't target exact groups of readers. The modern book promotion industry fills that gap with online book clubs, reading communities, rating services, and targeted advertising. Pay-to-play defines their business model, but authors should never ignore the number one trick in the toolbox – put on the charm. It worked for Jacqueline Susann (author of *Valley of the Dolls*) back in the 1960s. Susann wasn't much of a stylist, but torrid tales of drugs, sex, and show business spoke to America. It's a timeless theme, just like her approach to marketing.

It's not for her novels that she's remembered in the book industry. It's for her ability to promote herself. Dressed like she was going to a cocktail party, she'd show up with doughnuts at the book warehouses and so charm the staff that trucks loaded with her books would be sent to every outlet the dispatcher could think of. She learned everyone's birthday and the name of everyone's spouse, and when those birthdays rolled around, she sent personalized cards along with warm regards to the spouse. The book business had never seen a promotion like this. No one has ever equaled her inventiveness, though a lot of people have mimicked her.

The book industry has changed, of course, but not the good old-fashioned bribery. When experts say things like "social media has forced authors to become more personal in the way they interact with readers," it's a little redundant. What's changed is that you have to butter up online promoters to get a few thousand people to download one of your books instead of buttering up a few warehouse dispatchers, like Jacqueline did. It's easy to do today because there are lots of online businesses that will help you do it for a fee.

BOOK PEDDLERS
Book promotion companies reveal themselves to the public in a lot of creative ways. The best-known service, Bookbub, calls itself the largest online book club, whereas K Book Promotions labels itself as an analytics service. I liken both to the Wizard of Oz, whose misty green face was only the projection of a shrewd little man behind a curtain.

No matter how they operate, they are legitimate services; that means they won't accept every book that gets submitted for their consideration. Mike Enemigo, founder of small publishing company The Cell Block, submitted several new titles that were rejected. TCB's books are a little rough, and it's not just the graphic content, but also their appearance.

Bookbub rates books based on these standards.

- Book's appearance and quality
- Interior design and page design
- Grammar, spelling, and detectable plagiarism
- Available formats (the more the better, including phone, eBook, POD, and audio download)

- The nature of reviews and testimonials

Bookbub is responsible for presenting books to hundreds of thousands of readers. If they feel a book isn't up to commercial standards, or if its market is too niche, they'll pass. The problem with specialty publishers' books can be traced back to their overall market. They publish urban fiction and how-to books on pimpology. There isn't much wiggle room in pitching these books to a large audience, if themes like romance, mystery, science fiction, and general interest non-fiction topics rarely surface in them. They get dropped.

The trick is to focus your writing for a popular market and build a multimedia backlist. Then services like Bookbub will throw the doors open and hold their hand out for payment. Starting packages run about $600. Your book is placed in their system for one week as a free eBook. You'll get thousands of downloads. Yes, you'll be giving them away, but after a week, the book remains listed, with tons of new reviews. This helps convert Bookbub's viewers into more buyers.

Meanwhile, online book retailers take notice of the eBook activity and bump up their ranking, so it appears more frequently on their lists and affiliate programs recommendations. The cumulative effect is that you'll sell a bunch of books over the next few weeks. Then it'll peter out, and you'll want to pay the wizard behind the curtain again. But you'll have to time things appropriately.

Most book promotion services have restrictions on how often authors can use them. You can't have used any other giveaway programs (like Amazon, Goodreads, K Book Promotions, and LibraryThing) in the last 60 days. Plus, you'll have to wait another 60 days before you can use it again. This helps keep readers from getting burnt out on free giveaways, and it also keeps the book promoter high in the search engine rankings because of the exclusive content. Fortunately, there are plenty of other pro tools available to keep you busy through the downtime.

SOCIAL MEDIA PRESENCE

When you boil it all down, authors are selling the whole package: the author and their book. Call it image, branding, or popularity, but that's what you have to do. The topic of your work determines which groups you'll target. The author just has to develop a nice personality and be "present," meaning you must interact with people every day.

Once your platform is up and running, look into using fee-based social media tools, like Facebook advertising. A small press did a Facebook campaign for about $200 to target people who were active on other Alzheimer's and caregiving-related pages, and the author's Facebook page (facebook.com/caregiving101) got a few hundred "likes" from these ads.

The company's publicist encouraged the author to ask the audience questions, post pictures of her husband (whose condition inspired the book), and describe her experiences in detail. She posted several times a day, and within a year, her Facebook page had more than 14,000 "likes." Actual sales were a percentage of that number, around 3.2 percent, but it was still a wise investment.

Social media advertising works on the principle that information contained on your profile draws in customers. Setting up an ad campaign is pure simplicity; it's based on age, gender, location, interests, and in some networks, profession. You'll find tools on all the major sites. Just start cheap, be diligent, and develop a tribe.

A successful ad campaign for a spiritual meditation book targeted 2,200,000 FB users who met the following criteria:

- Resident of the U.S. or Canada
- 21 or older
- Female

- "Liked" Ashtanga Vinyasa yoga, meditation, self-improvement, compassion, self-help, or Hatha yoga.
- Not already connected to the author on Facebook
- Classified by Facebook, based on their status updates, "likes," posts, etc., to be interested in the broad categories of charity/causes or health and well-being.

Of the group, 146,979 people had the ad appear on their FB page, 529 clicked on it, and 398 "liked" the author's page. All of that for $200 or 0.50 per "like." Now, convert "likes" to sales, which was about 150, and you make a skimpy profit. But engaging those 398 followers again and again with good information will continue to pay for itself as they share.

Let's say you wanted to advertise a romance novel. Here's how you'd set that up using Twitter ad tools:

- Target is anyone tweeting about the latest Nicholas Sparks or Julia Quinn novels.
- Target people using the hashtags #romance or #romancenovel in their tweets.

The tools are at your disposal. It's not that expensive or difficult to notify your readers about your book's existence. Tinker with your targets from there. It's good practice as you build your way up to coordinate more sophisticated campaigns. It also brings focus to your platform, which is a nice bit of leverage when you deal with professionals. You'd be amazed at what kind of deals 14,000 avid followers can get you.

TRACK YOUR EFFECTIVENESS
Have you ever tried eating with chopsticks? It's clumsy, tedious, and a bit embarrassing. Those same feelings overwhelm you when attempting to track the effectiveness of promotion techniques. Sometimes, despite all the fancy "tools," you can't get a solid answer about your results. You post a blog or a book. How many readers? You can measure traffic, clicks, impressions, and dwell time. You can measure sales. But success comes from the unified effort, not a single attempt. Just like chopsticks, you must raise each grain of rice ever so carefully.

Tracking your effectiveness requires a variety of methods. Tracking browsers online is easy with "cookies," which are available from Google. Cookies do all the work. The problem is it takes time to weed out the information that will actually help you. For example, most browsers flip through websites at a fast pace, rarely clicking on banner ads or Buy Me buttons. But when they stop on a site, you may get lucky and find a new forum or group that fits your book market. Sifting through the data can be tedious, though little discoveries can lead to more effective ads and sales.

The most basic method is using codes in your ad copy. Codes are a user-friendly tool. Simply use a different code with each advertiser: Code 123, Code 456, and Code 789. Tell customers to use the code (maybe offer nothing special, like free shipping, if they include it). When you get a response, you'll immediately know which advertisers are getting you sales.

Talk to blog editors. Did a recent piece get any good comments? Follow up with an ad manager from any magazines you place ads with. Did they get many inquiries? Did sales spike during a certain publicity stunt? Who did you use? It's a lot of logic and puzzling it out. You must do it, because odds are if it worked once, it'll work again and again.

BUILD YOUR BACKLIST
The best publicity is a new book. List every single version of your book: eBook, PDF, audio, hardcover, paperback, whatever. Reissue each book, but promote it as something new: New Edition! Totally Revised Edition! Editor's Choice Edition! 14th printing! Toss in a new forward by the author and other easily mimicked ploys used by other publishers and authors. When it comes to promoting your backlist, the mantra is simple to remember: "If it sold before, it will sell again."

PUBLISHERS SHOULD WORK TOO

Publishers are in a position to offer incentives like wholesale discounts, free shipping, gift cards, and the like. They target readers on a schedule to keep these special sales offers in their faces. Here are 7 of the most effective sales techniques.

Pre-publication Sales – These are a good way to get income early on. Just don't offer a book before it's complete. If you sell in June but say "Available in April," then expect complaining from April until the day it arrives. Send out a monthly reminder letting everyone know if there are delays.

Specials (Combos, Discounts) – Nothing dramatic here. Books are sold at retail; they are marked up. Knocking off shipping or slashing 25% off the cover price isn't exactly turning loaves of bread into fish. (Labor Day blowout bonanza!) But it gets people thinking. (July 4th explosive deal!) Coveting. (Black Friday blackout special!) And eventually buying. (Valentine's love offering!) The offers can be tied in with holidays, current events, anniversaries, really any excuse to stir up customers' interest is a good one. (Groundhog Day sales slam!) Go wild. (Spring Break lay away!)

Reminders – These are a part of life. We forget things. The "Honey Do" list is a great example. It's nice to have it all spelled out as if a little buzzer comes on and asks, "Did you do everything?" When you run deals, you have to remind folks about the deadlines, the codes, and the whizz-bang special conditions. It helps more people get from just thinking about buying your book to doing it.

Announcements – Great for new books, new blogs, and new services. Anything worth letting people know about.

Monthlies – Exactly what they sound like, easily converted into a newsletter by adding an article, some filler (quotes and trivia), and wrapping it up with a listing of all available books. Tweak the arrangement and content each time you post, and this sales tool will gain value among readers.

Contests – A great way to grab people's attention. We love free stuff. Raffles and competitions are just a few of the popular contest formats. But publishers can get really inventive, such as best Book Trailers, best Book Reviews, and best book selfies. Tie it all back to your book, and contests become interactive sales experiences.

Wholesale – This is all about selling in bulk to bookstores, mail order merchants, professional organizations, whoever wants a carton. Publishers slash the prices to leave some room for these groups to resell and make a buck. Sure, you lose a little on a 20% to 30% discount, but you sell 100 copies. Some distributors want a 50% break, but if that results in hundreds, or even thousands of sales, who cares? It's sales. Congratulations!

🖉 **Writers Manifesto No. 25 – Gimmicks don't sell books, hustlers who use all the gimmicks sell books.**

ADVERTISING

Advertising is expensive, but as author Giacoma Giammatteo says, "I can point to numbers. I can say, without question, that the money I spent sold an extra 4,000 books at $0.99 and an additional 350 at $5.99. I can calculate the royalties and tell the ROI (Return on Investment)." Few alternatives offer that type of reliability.

The people selling advertising space talk about the number of "impressions" and "cumulative impact" when they try to sell you ads, but it's the cost per sale that tells you if you're winning or not. There are many factors to effective advertising. Some of it is out of your control; the rest of it is just good practices and strong ad copy.

For that reason, advertising should be put off until all free publicity has been exhausted. Testing magazines, newspapers, and sites with content marketing can show you which ones get results. Do this before you pay for advertising. It'll be money that never comes back.

When the decision to advertise is made, your ad should be crafted as carefully as any manuscript. To make an ad stick, it must be useful to the audience. Remember, there are two buyers for any book – those who find the information vital and those who find it interesting.

The guidelines for effective ads include the following:

- Pay Attention (use color, a simple design, or cool effects)
- Understand and remember it (make your ad copy as strong as possible, maybe funny if you're talented at it)
- Agree or believe it (site facts, quote experts, make it sound professional)
- Care (since you're #1 in your market, explain how it will change their life)
- Be able to act on it (click here, buy now)

Timing and other factors weigh in on buying patterns. The phenomenon of seasonal influences is easy to prepare for and is more reliable than sales trends that burn out all too quickly. Advertising is mostly time-based. A typical promotion schedule looks like this.

- January-March: Business picks up.
- April-May: Strong, springtime is a great time to promote.
- June-July: Graduations bring upticks in gift giving.
- August: Slow. People are transitioning from vacation to fall work and school.
- September-November: Business picks up after Labor Day, and early fall is a great time for promotion.
- December: Crowded with holiday ads.

There are all sorts of gimmicks in advertising. Using unexpected headlines, terminology, or buzzwords, using concrete images, quoting a review, or adding your ISBN, and offering incentives like free shipping are common. The most important strategy is to stress the benefits of your book and provide a call to action: "buy now."

Consider what makes your book unique from the competition. Test your pitch, if it's a mystery, anyone can say, "Will keep you guessing until the last page." Think, what can you stress about your book that makes it one of a kind? Something like "Was the man Detective (so-and-so) put behind bars a decade ago actually innocent? Find out in (book title)." Once you have it all together, cinch it off with the price and ordering information. Most experts agree that saving the price for last is wise; price is a turn-off (now, that'll be $19.95).

ONLINE ADVERTISING

Online ads can be the most difficult to master and expensive. Hire a professional. Not only do you need good ad copy, you also need good luck with search engines. The simplest advertising is a link, a "Buy Me" button, or a banner leading straight to Amazon, Barnes & Noble, or Kobo. But those are sketchy. Most people will ignore those ads.

Another sketchy approach is called keyword advertising. Basically, you pay Google AdWords and the Yahoo/Bing Network to serve up better placement for your site. The trick is picking your search words thoughtfully. When people search for your phrases or keywords (weight loss, writing success, back pain relief, etc.) you pop up. You'll either pay per click, meaning anytime someone selects your link, and that costs you anywhere from a few pennies up to $0.50 per click, or you'll pay per 1,000 times your ad is displayed (cost-per-thousand).

RADIO/PODCAST ADVERTISING

Popular Podcasts and some radio stations (especially AM radio) will sell "slots" for short ads. Many want to preview your stuff before pitching it to their audience. If it's a fit, you can usually get air for a month for a couple of hundred dollars. Radio and podcasts serve narrow audiences, so if you match your work to them, it can generate enough sales to be profitable.

Full-service radio/podcast advertising saves you from an embarrassing "stiff" voice (if you aren't used to being on the radio). Podcast like Dawah International will "cut" your ads for you for a fee, just send them a script and any images you want used. It's worth it, because listeners are used to hearing Rufus and Jenny Tripplett on the air, and when they talk about your book, it's like a third-party endorsement.

Pay attention to a radio program and you'll notice that most ads are voice-overs from the DJ. Do your research and locate stations that your readers listen to. If you like the way the DJ flows, consider investing in them. If it works, then keep doing it.

PRINT ADVERTISING

The benefit of advertising in magazines, newspapers, or flyers is that they can penetrate hard-to-crack niche markets. And issues tend to last, print ads get passed around "as is" for years in what marketers call "pass-along readership." You should buy a few issues first and judge if for yourself. Is it a good match? Do your readers like this? The decision to use one has to be made carefully.

There are a lot of promotional services that try to sell authors expensive packages, they talk about the "cumulative impact" of ads, and that it's normal for responses to be slow. Don't believe it, if ads don't get immediate sales, then it's not worth it. Contact the marketing representative for any publications you plan on using and inquire about their rates. They will provide metrics for their subscribers, who they are, and what they say about the magazine.

My advice stays the same. Test any venue with small ads first, then make larger investments if it works. Too many times I've seen publishers buy splashy half-page ads ($1,000-$3,000) only to get lackluster responses. Try to get something printed for free first, like a book review or article. If you get an immediate response, it may be worth purchasing a classified ad ($25-$250) to test it further.

JUNK MAIL

Beware of obsolete promotion packages. Something called Direct Mail is the biggest offender. Basically, you send sales literature (flyers, postcards, and maybe a press kit) to a list of potential buyers in an attempt to sell books individually. It's not worth it.

When I began promoting my children's book, Hungry Robot, I mailed out thousands of pieces of literature. It got some results, but at the end of the year, I broke even. Direct mail is rarely profitable. The last time I did it, I spent $375 in postage, $180 in color copies, and spent a few hundred hours stuffing envelopes. My investment yielded a $ 73 royalty check for that quarter.

Another wasteful option is to send out less expensive postcards. They don't work either. If you want additional proof of this, visit any magazine rack and consider the subscription flyers piled around people's feet. They get swept up and tossed in the trash by a stock boy making $8.50 an hour. I'm sorry, but people just don't stop to look at information that routinely gets labeled "junk mail."

A WORD ABOUT AMAZON

If you ignore Amazon, you'll need a good reason for why people don't know your book exists. Amazon has the easiest and most effective bang-for-the-buck book promotion tools out there. You will be amazed at how easy it is to use the handy stuff Amazon has created just to help you both get paid.

LISTMANIA AND AMAZON PAID PLACEMENT

Most consumers act on the suggestions made through recommended reading lists. It's more convenient to shop. Proper categorization can impact the course of book sales. "Four months after self-publishing my debut Victorian mystery, *Maids of Misfortune*, I hit a wall," says Louisa Looke. "I had a few good reviews, but my sales were dropping, and though I'd started a blog, no one was reading it." She found that her novel was not showing up in the historical mystery category, got it fixed, and because the category had only 71 books in it, became an instant best-seller. Lists are arranged in a categorical fashion, so fans see what they've already bought side-by-side with whatever is new.

Amazon ranks books in bestselling order. If you have two books, one of which is ranked 100 and the other at 980,000, the latter is basically invisible to readers. Fortunately, you can buy your way up these lists for a short period. The price depends on rank and duration.

There are dozens of lists, dividing and subdividing every category into the most minuscule genres. Amazon even lets you make your own lists, titles, and everything, using a program called Listmania. If someone searches using the right keywords, then it has a chance of being displayed. If you make one full of books that complement your own books, then this is a path to free publicity.

Amazon Paid Placement is a more aggressive promotion tool. For a small fee, about $100 a week, your book will appear on the lists people actually search. These are listings that Amazon curates and pushes on people. If that leads to enough book sales, a higher ranking is assured.

AMAZON REVIEWS

Amazon provides reviews through its Advantage program. Don't dismiss the effectiveness of book reviews and think, "Nobody reads reviews. Half of them are fake." Yes. But that's the fake reviews we (writers) set up ourselves. Like some early reviews for my children's book *Hungry Robot,* posted by Fiverr mercenaries for $5 a pop.

Like it or not, people read your reviews. They are looking for the first reason *not to* buy your book. It's true. If you pay a bunch of Fiverr experts, then you'll have a bunch of cheap reviews. 5 stars, 4 stars, basic one liner, "I stayed up all night reading," or "Orgasmic," or "I liked this one." The browser may get bored, shrug, and buy the book.

Amazon offers better fake reviews. And they make sure that their fake review is displayed where browsers can see it, right next to your book. A much superior convenience to the reader looking for a "sign" that a book is worth buying.

Amazon also helps you keep your star rating high. Just clean up the bad reader reviews. They do you no good. All you need is a good enough reason to talk to the customer service drone (toiling at a desk for minimum wage) at Amazon into removing a bad review for you. Here are some examples:

    1. *Personal Attacks* – Someone has a personal vendetta against me and is attacking my book. They are saying things like this book is bad and it sucks and took longer to delete than to download.

    2. *Mom Reviews* – Basically, it's a relative or a parent saying something. "I'm so proud of my baby" and "This is my son's book" should never appear. I speak from experience; my first book had a few of these, now I don't even tell family about a book's publication, just to prevent it from happening again.

    3. *People Who Haven't Read the Book* – If, for any reason, you disagree with the review, you can always say, "Obviously, they did not read the book." And have it removed so "It doesn't confuse other customers."

Amazon thinks of everything. Additionally, if you participate in the Amazon Advantage Program, please submit your titles to Amazon for possible review (Amazon Books Editorial, P.O. Box 81226, Seattle, WA 98108-1226). Include some flyers or whatever sales literature you have printed up. Every mention helps.

AMAZON ASSOCIATES PROGRAM

You can make money selling other people's books, especially ones that complement your market. Join Amazon Associates and you'll be well on your way. It will help you make people aware of your own book's existence and give you some extra pocket change. You won't have to sell your soul to the devil to get paid as a writer. However, you may need to strike a deal with Affiliate Marketers.

Affiliate marketers link books from retailers to their websites. If potential book buyers follow the link and buy the book, the website owner is paid a commission of 5% to 15% of the book's price. When you post a blog about anything connected to your book's subject, post a link to books related to that genre or theme. For example, if I write a blog about self-publishing, a good link would be any book about writing, self-publishing, or promoting books. Add a "Buy Now" button beside that blog and you're done.

GOODREADS

In 2013, Amazon folded Goodreads into its pantheon of services. Goodreads is a social media site just for authors to connect with each other. Users share book recommendations, review books, and use virtual bookshelves to keep track of what they've read and what they want to read.

One of the most interesting features of Goodreads is the ability to run book giveaways. Many authors report that the number or people who add their book to their "to read" list jumps after a giveaway. This can influence other browsers and generate interest in a larger audience, sometimes.

Amazon bought it for a reason. And that reason is control, because "give always" can be overdone. Amazon offers a Partners option for its eBooks, where authors agree to exclusively give away their book for 30 days. They can do it again 30 days after. However, if you've used other services like Bookbub, K Book Promotion, or Goodreads to manage a giveaway, you'll have to wait a month from the end date to use another Amazon service. The idea is to use them all as much as possible and stay in front of readers.

The effects of a little charm hold up over time; by comparison, book promotion tools simply cut through our crowded marketplace. They help fans and authors connect. Do so, and the people who work in the book industry will count you among the pros.

RESOURCES

Affiliate Programs
- amazon.com
- youtube.com

Online Book Peddlers
- bookbub.com
- goodreads.com
- librarything.com

Customer Profile Tools
- kbookpromotions.com
- facebook.com/ads
- twitter.com/ad-tools

Ad Concept Forum
- guerillamarketing.com

Online Advertising
- usfreeads.com

Book Clubs
- doubleday.com

- militarybookclub.com
- cookbookbookclub.com
- sciencefictionbookclub-sfbc.com
- mysteryguild.com
- bookofthemonthclub.com
- bookplanet.com
- crossings.com
- rhapsody.com

Chapter Twenty-Seven

"There is nothing to writing. All you have to do is sit down at the keyboard and open up a vein." – Red Smith

BOOK REVIEWS
There are two opportunities to get paid for book reviews. There are benefits of having a critical endorsement in front of Constant Readers. A scintillating one can drive sales. But even generalized reviews like "This book is great" are better than none at all. That is what makes the service reviewers so enticing.

The other opportunity is to become a book critic yourself. It pays $50-$300, depending on where you can get reviews published. Also, you'll meet many influential people wanting their books to receive some publicity. They may trade cash or favors, like sharing your book's buying information on their platform. As with most things, the benefits are limited by your creativity and negotiation skills.

My career as a book critic got started by accident. I needed inspirational success stories, so I turned to some friends who had been published. Writers like Michael Collins, Kevin Bullock, and Rhonda Turpin. It gave them some publicity, but I found that book reviews were easier to pitch to editors, so I wrote more, eventually earning a decent income. If I'd known what I know now, I'd have shifted to reviews earlier.

Good reviews sell books. Experts tell us that, along with all their book-selling advice, few seem to offer any firsthand experience. They say this: get the most book reviews you can. A better approach is to arrange for reviews to appear in the venues that appeal to Constant Readers.

THE BUSINESS OF BOOK REVIEWS
In the early 1980s, the independent publishing "Godfather" Dan Poynter was dropping off a batch of books at the loading dock in the back of the post office in Santa Barbara. He saw a young man with a cart full of packages near the dumpsters. Poynter curiously watched the man rip open the cartons, take out what appeared to be books, and place them in a large bin. Whatever didn't fit into the bin was thrown in a dumpster.

Unable to stand it any longer, Poynter approached the man and asked if those were lost-in-the-mail books. It turned out those packages were for *Los Angeles Times* book critic Robert Kirsch. The gigantic load was being received at his home address; it was only a small piece of what arrived at his office. He didn't have time to pick up the books himself, he didn't have room for the wrappers, and he didn't have time to review them all.

Poynter's shock took a while to wear off. He had self-published over ten books and had become a millionaire. For each printing he produced, he sent at least three hundred reviewers a package stuffed with reply cards, media kits, and a free book. Though his system worked, the Santa Barbara post office inspired him to send even more books to reviewers! He figured that they couldn't all be that busy.

The truth is well established: reviewers like Ruth Coughlin of the *Detroit News* don't have time to even consider each book. "I arrive at my office each Monday morning to find 200 books outside my door." She says. *Washington Post* reviewer Alice Digilio doesn't sugar-coat the business side of book reviews: "These reviewers are paid by their publisher to review books for readers." They rarely pick and choose from the mountain of books. Authors need an inside connection, or really catchy packaging, or phenomenal luck, to get a review from a major source. Fortunately, there are plenty of mercenaries, hobbyists, and freelancers who will give you a shout-out.

FREE BOOK REVIEWS

To most readers, all endorsements sound alike: "As reviewed in the *Arkansas Democrat-Gazette*" is equal to the *New York Times Book Review*. That's good, because you have a home advantage when soliciting regional venues. Caroline Pratt, editor of *Birmingham Parent*, said as much when I sent her a review package for my children's book: "We only cover authors who are currently, or have been, residents here." It's not so easy getting a free review elsewhere.

A national source like the *Midwest Book Review* gets distributed to corporate, academic, and public library systems. That's over 100,000 subscribers, folks! Let's not get ahead of ourselves. Jim Cox, publisher of *MBR* lays it out bare ass, "Of the 1500+ titles a month received, about half get assigned, and only 450+ get reviewed." That's about 1/3 of the total, and that ratio is one of the highest in the industry. Most run about 1/8 or lower. You actually *do* have better odds of breaking a Casino at the Blackjack table.

There are a handful of review sources that will, at least on paper, hook you up with a free one. Unfortunately, problems just keep popping up with this stuff. Next thing you know, Booklist rejects a review because it wasn't sent pre-publication, like three months in advance of the book's release. Okay, so you send the next book 4 months in advance, and it still doesn't get a review. Now you're mad. What you don't see is that *Booklist* receives over 30,000 titles each year. Yours just got lost in the nightmarish avalanche of writers pleading for free promotion.

CHEAP REVIEWS

S. Maria Vernon, a reviewer for the *Pacific Book Review*, has helped authors spread the word online. They offer reviews to help authors succeed for about $100. One of these reviews was for my friend and graphic artist Greg McKinney, creator of the graphic novel *Barberretta*. It was torn to pieces by readers, but Vernon did her best to see the strong points in his work.

Another source for cheap reviews can be located on fiverr.com, though you have to be careful since Amazon flags "fake reviews" and targets Fiverr regularly. The good part is that pro-reviewers advertise there, review, plus publish for between $10 and $250. You can also advertise your own book review services.

If you find a reviewer with some decent connections to editors or a large following on social media, it's well worth a pitch. That's how one author afforded 50 reviews (on Amazon) and drove his book up their algorithm. Find other authors, and there's a chance they'll do the old *quid pro quo*: "You review mine, and I'll review yours." All you have to do is download each other's books.

$300 TO $500 DOLLAR REVIEWS

Armed with the knowledge that reviews are good publicity, can sometimes cause authors to jump on what they perceive to be the best deal. Paying a professional reviewer is one thing, but paying a name-brand magazine should really do the trick, right? It's forgivable to think so, but it's wrong. A "premium" review costs $300-$500 (and sometimes much more) and doesn't always reflect the best features of your book.

Most premium reviews are in fact generic. They're crafted to read like every review you've ever seen on the back cover of every book. What you are paying for is the name: reviewed by *The New York Times Book Review*, *Kirkus Review*, or *Publishers Weekly*. The thing is, most readers don't pay attention to who reviewed it; they want to learn something about the book.

Compare that to locating a professional critic and paying them instead. You might not say "Oh, it was reviewed by Paul Constant," but the review will appear in local papers, so mention it as "appeared in the *Portland Orion*." What matters is how much the review draws attention to the elements that appeal to readers. Is it fiction? Does the review do justice to your characters and the plot you worked so hard to craft? Is it a self-help book? Is it clear how the advice can help? Shop around and read critics' work, find one that matches your needs. These are the types of reviews you should pay for.

REVIEWS WRITTEN BY HANDSHAKE

You get what you ask for. To get a variety of endorsements, instead of them all reading "this book is great," experienced authors send a sample review with each request. The sample should be boilerplate, just the pitch and highlights. Whether in person or pixel, steer the conversation so unconventional reviewers can relate their expertise or audience to your book. Be straight up, explain that your book needs a quote from a respected professional, or bait them: "I wish someone would say this about my book." It often gets good results.

A good example is the reviews found on a book called Prisoner Reentry, by Joan Petersilia, Ph.D. Reviews are tightly designed on the back cover. The experts include a distinguished professor at John Jay College of Criminal Justice, a former president of the American Correctional Association, and a chief of the Ohio Department of Rehabilitation and Corrections. All of them were easily swayed to add their endorsements, both to help their friend and to get their name on a book.

Find experts whose interests match your book's topic and ask them to write reviews. Collect reviews so you can show them to other experts when you ask them for reviews. Let opinion-molders read samples, then quote them on the cover of your next edition, your website, and sales literature. These endorsements make your work more distinguishable, which can persuade readers to buy it.

ONGOING REVIEW PROGRAM

Writers must stay on the lookout for reviews. So, most reviewers. I've sought out small publishers and offered to review their books, usually in exchange for some favor or as a preview of my abilities. I chose books that dealt with topics I had already covered. It helped my platform more than pumping out unrelated reviews. But there were more, less obvious, opportunities.

There are a variety of perks a good reviewer can get by bartering their services:

- Exclusive access to an author (such as for an interview)
- Publishing opportunities, such as blogs, books, or anthologies
- Work as an exclusive critic, publicist, or consultant for the publisher

The only problem is when companies begin sending you all their books – literally, package after package of them. I had to spread out my schedule in order to post all the reviews each week on *AndSociety*, *BlogCritics*, *Stella's Reading*, *The Grind*, *Simon & Shuster* and the *Huffington Post* so as not to overload anyone. The one thing I must stress to them, and I'll stress to you: reviews are an ongoing activity, not a one-time event.

Success isn't a fixed state; the sales graph rises, plateaus, and dips like a heartbeat. My profile of Luz Thompson, "The Hot New Act in Science Fiction," underlined her backlist with the speculative details her readers liked. It paid off. Sales leapt for all three of her books. Her ranking on Amazon jumped from one million to the top one thousand in 24 hours! "Now you have a tribe." I explained the good news, "It's perfect timing to plot the follow-up." We settled on an interview and devoted reviews for each book, spaced out to keep a rhythm.

Reviews are a product endorsement useful in all forms of publicity, which is why, when done regularly, they help manage perception. Each time a new edition of a book comes out, review it. Each time you arrange an interview, make sure that the book is thoroughly reviewed. When reviewers find faults in a book, fix them. Then get another review. Find ways to keep it going.

If you are selling reviews, try these methods:

- Follow up with updates about where the review was published and verify sales during that period.
- Send a media kit to authors, ask them to post your link on their site, "so media can verify the reviews' authenticity."
- Write articles about the craft of book critiques, getting reviews published, and hard sales data that backs it up.
- Send ideas for follow-up articles that highlight the book within current news or trends.

These strategies keep your book and your brand in front of readers. It looks good, and it looks even better when your income increases. If you freelance as a reviewer, you'll be in a good position to publicize everything you write. When review copies start to stack up, there are several things you can do with them. Use them as giveaways on your website or resell them on eBay. Remember, good books don't lose their value.

Writers Manifesto No. 26 – No one ever made a statue of a book critic.

RESOURCES
Book review directories
- acweb.org/bookrev.html
- dir.yahoo.com/arts/humanities/literature/reviews
- w.stepbystepselfpublishing.net/free-book-review.html

Book reviewers
- bookbrowse.com
- bookcrossing.com
- bookideas.com
- bookloans.com
- bookninja.com
- bookpleasures.com
- bookreporter.com
- bookreview.com
- bookslut.com
- compulsivereader.com
- jennydavidson.blogspot.com
- midwestbookreview.com
- newpages.com
- nybooks.com
- rainbowreviews.com
- rebeccasreads.com
- reviewchoice.com
- stellasreading.com
- washingtonpost.com

Chapter Twenty-Eight

"Obscurity is a greater threat to authors than piracy." – Tim O'Reilly from O'Reilly Media

CONTENT SHARING

Content sharing can be divided into three categories. First, the Share Button on Facebook captures the heart of what needs to happen. A more focused second tier exists among content marketers and gurus. The muster call for the last category is manned by pirates: malicious file sharers. All three can be useful to promote your books, and when used right, their combined powers are almost unstoppable.

Socializing on the internet can be very effective in short bursts, especially if you engage "Market Influencers," individuals who have pull over a large crowd. In 2014, I deliberated overusing Mychosia Nightingale to promote my first book. A trusted source of "Sure Pleasures," for $300, Nightingale would share your book's info on Facebook and Twitter among 120,000 followers. It worked for a certain type of book; she was, after all, married to the rapper Rick Ross (a.k.a. The Boss). But influencers vary as much as the audience they gently persuade.

Successful authors focus on delivering what their audience has come to expect. Allison Winn Scott, author of *The Department of Lost and Found*, has a blog, "Ask Allison," where she answers questions from readers and chats about all things book-related. "The blog helps me sell books in ways that I never imagined," she says. "I've also made dozens of blogger friends who are happy to promote my novels far beyond my initial audience." Journalist Debbie Abrams Kaplan points out why favoritism is so effective. "Other people can say things about your qualities that you can't say yourself." It also means more than if you were to say the same thing.

Once you figure out how to break the ice, it only takes a handful of influencers to make something happen. They may not use a lot of social media to do so, or have a high Klout score, but they are authentic thought leaders. Influencers come in a variety of experts, bloggers, reporters, and fans who might not realize their value, while others shrewdly work like a coin-operated arcade gallery.

JOIN THE PRESSGANG

You don't want to clutter up your life with a lot of social media obligations. Writing demands plenty of your energy as it is. When you do spend time using online tools, experiment a little; the services that pay off are the ones you should make time to fit into your schedule.

A great place to look for influencers is a site called Mashable (mashable.com). The Mashable community carries on with conversation threads about the latest and greatest apps, tools, and hacks for using social media for business and pleasure. These folks know what they are talking about because they are in business themselves. When they speak, people listen.

Now, before you rush to apply all their advice and go app-crazy on Facebook and Twitter, stop for a second and think about the readers you are targeting. Who would they listen to more, you, a distinguishable writer, or the voice of an expert? Many of them will belong to some kind of group. They read the same blogs. Those groups may or may not have a direct relationship to your book's topic, but when you mine the topics, you'll find some crossover. Keep digging into sites like Technorati (a blog rating site), and odds are you'll find a perfect match for your market.

When you find the right experts, use search tools like Digg, Disqus, or Technorati to confirm they have a high placement. Like everything in the world, when you want tools that mine these groups for you, it'll cost you. The good news is that free tools and a little digging can produce the same results; it takes just a few hours.

Most major sites have forums or bulletin boards. They tend to frown on blatant advertising, but a tactful author can slide in a few whitewashed plugs. If you haven't found like-minded sites yet, it's as easy as a search using keywords. For example, "forum" and "gardening" or "bulletin boards" and "cats." Poke around until you find groups talking about stuff relevant to your market. Once you locate them, a good tactic is to point people to cool links and content you have "found," which should track back to sites featuring your writing.

Basic preparation should be given to your username, which should reflect your website, blog, or book title. A questionable but effective solution is using another login, acting as a bystander pushing links – your links. "I love it [boilerplate hook about plot, character, or category], can't wait for the next one!" Experiment and repeat what seems to be working.

Each group has its own style; instead of spending valuable time to match it, just write well. Above all, you want them to respond to your message. Show confidence (even if you don't feel it, no one can see that), they are more likely to act on your info than if you matched all their jargon. They'll relate to it, and you will do much better.

The gift of gab is a boon; it's a synthesis of many good social habits. Like all "best practices," it's presumptuous to state the obvious, but it's mostly experimentation, until you identify the 'drivers' that make each group move. Make use of the parts you like. What matters is that you remain comfortable in your own skin, as Red Smith said, "All you have to do is sit down at the keyboard and open up a vein."

Here are 5 tactics that give authors a jump start:

- Build social currency. Share things that illustrate people's strengths; we all appreciate that kind of notice.
- Admit to your triggers. Acknowledge that you talk about things that are top of mind.
- Balance emotions. Develop a sense for imitating what you see others do.
- Deliver practical value. Drop news that people can use.
- Tell stories. Stories pass Info along under the guise of idle chit chat.

You'll want to plant little seeds in appropriate places before trying to win over influencers and have them begin sharing with their followers. The idea is called sharing for a good reason, for best results, each time you do so, think of it as planting a seed. Each time you schmooze influencers directly, it's like watering it. If conditions are right your own following will grow as you stand out in the minds of readers.

LEAD THE MUTINY

Nothing is sacred. We've all grown accustomed to free downloads: movies, music, and yes, even books. While many companies (and artists) wear a grim face at the prospect of being the target of blatant theft, there's an opportunity to turn it to your advantage. What could happen if you instead offered up a little of your valuable content (a chapter or two from a book) on piracy sites? People will only see that it's free. Also, earnest file-sharing pirates may see what you've done and shrug away interest. After all, what's the point in "freeing up" material that's already available? It gets the right eyeballs on your work and the wrong ones off it.

For some authors, the idea of trying to convince influencers (and readers) to sample their work and languishing until they are successful has led to innovations in content sharing. Literally, it can mean leaking an excerpt of your work on a well-known piracy website. Who knows, as part of a strategy, and if the writing is good, success can follow. Paulo Coelho, author of the worldwide hit The Alchemist, leaked eBooks in Russia on piracy networks deliberately. His sales went from 1,000 to over 1 million per year. Coelho said, "Don't be fooled by the publishers who say that piracy costs authors money."

Seeking out Russian pirates may be too much for most of us. Luckily, the alternatives are pleasantly familiar. Plain old file-sharing sites can do the trick. Tim Ferriss launched The 4-Hour Chef on BitTorrent, deliberately releasing a section of the book on their network, which drove sales on Amazon. It's not hard to understand the appeal or the effectiveness of this approach. In today's world, it's better to be pirated and get in front of readers than to be cloistered on online retailers without any sales. Just be thoughtful, once the cat's out of the bag, you'll have to live with it.

Here are a few tips to consider before leaking anything:

- Pick a chapter that won't be used (as an excerpt or in a preview) elsewhere. Put something exclusive out there.
- It's easier if you're self-publishing, since most publishers may not be cool with the idea of leaking files. Of course, if you're slick, it isn't hard to do it without them knowing.
- Use a great excerpt. You want readers to get hooked, not crinkle their nose at it.

Measure the effect on one book at a time. Coordinate the timing to take advantage of giveaways with Amazon, Bookbub, or Daily Deal offers. The simplest way to distinguish results is to start either at the beginning or end of giveaway terms (30 to 60 days, respectively). Then track sales with giveaways before leaking, and again after leaking. It'll give you hard numbers about what's really working, and where.

Leaking files isn't fundamentally any different than working writers' forums like Goodreads. Instead of reaching a narrow group, you're opening the files to anyone who downloads from networks. It's easy to see why this is catching on as a low-cost marketing strategy for authors. It puts what would otherwise be a fearsome weakness to work for you, exploiting people's temptation to take what is free, and finding unexpected success.

TAKE COMMAND

A good next step is PublicEye.com (a book publicity website), which provides suggestions for crafting pitches that bloggers like. Remember that influencers aren't in the business to help authors; they're in business to provide content that their readers want in order to grow their own platforms. Pitch your ideas to them in a way that will appeal to their readers, and you're far less likely to end up in the trash folder.

Here are some solid tips:

1. Look at the blog's review policy to understand what they're looking for.
2. Read the blog to get a feel for their style and subject preferences.
3. Open the conversation by leaving valuable comments and becoming an active member of the blogger's community.
4. Write a personal email to the actual recipient. (Nothing screams "I don't know who you are, and I don't care" like a form letter.)
5. Have something to offer the blogger, such as alerting your followers about the highlights of that blogger or offering a "giveaway" of your book on their site.

Thousands and thousands of people work every day to create better quality content, improve conversion rates, and overall content effectiveness, creating more visual content, reimagining or repurposing content, measuring ROI, and becoming better storytellers. Usually, all that manpower is brought to bear by businesses working to sell to other businesses. However, tons of bandwidth are consumed by businesses marketing to customers directly.

These efforts present numerous opportunities for writers. Not so much as in selling them your writing (unless you went to college with them), since Influencers prefer to control their content. Instead, the goal is to feed them something they need: more experts with something fresh to share.

All those in-person events, webinars, websites, videos, blogs, case studies, white papers, eBooks, research reports, newsletters, and microsites are host to more than just idle chatter. They influence hundreds of thousands of people. Look for someone willing to stick their head up and discuss the future of something.

Many of them have become experts only on their company network or among their associates. And that's fine – in fact, it's perfect. Instead of trying to break in yourself and compete with the volume of content they create, authors need only find ways to convince them to share with their followers for a week, maybe longer if you get an uptick in sales.

Here are a few evergreen topics:

1. *Sales* – If you've had blow-out sales, come up with an angle that tells your story in a sales-focused manner. There's social selling, sales management, indie sales, external sales, consulate sales, and collaborative sales. If they run the story, it could lead to more articles and fans.

2. *Security* – If you had success from sharing on piracy networks, it'd be ironic to sound the alarm or write as a watchdog. Share tips about how to spot it, stop it, or exploit it, or something new, unique, and appropriate for their audience.

3. *Stress* – Stress affects us all. Maybe that explains why one of my T-shirt designs was popular and epitomized the company slogan "Destroying the Annoying." It had the image of a snarling teddy bear with the text, "*Hug Me!*" The right stress relief tip can carry your message to any audience. If your influencer has a high pay grade, try to tie into their needs, like middle management or productivity. Regardless of profession, however, we all can use a reminder: "This too shall pass." Tailor the tip to readers, whether they are more familiar with conference tables or changing tables.

Appearances on high-ranking platforms can raise authors' status. Monica Bhide, food writer and cookbook author, believes in content sharing if for no other reason than the credibility that comes from being quoted by an Influencer. "I think editors are looking for writers who can write for multiple types of media," she says. "Let your social network know when your post goes live, making sure to appreciatively acknowledge your host." A thank you might help you get invited back. Then, it is good form to check back on your post, especially on the day of and the day after. When readers comment, try to keep the conversation going, some of it might even get shared like our ancestors did it – in person.

When an influencer impacts your sales, carve out a presence on their platform in any way possible. Pitch a related article. Send a media kit and request a guest appearance on their podcast or newsletter. Many influencers are also authors; they swap book reviews. Once you get quoted or included as a link for a given subject, there is no limit to how often your story (and your books) can be dispersed through networks.

RESOURCES

Other Authors
- Neil Gaiman speaks about how piracy helped sales of his books http://bit.ly/lw34AGE
- JA Konrath discusses piracy vs. obscurity http://bit.ly/1pIRfJm

File Sharing Networks
- BitTorrent
- Reddit

Forums and Bulletin Boards
- directory.big-boards.com

Discussion Group and Message Boards
- wallphone.com

Influencer Lead-Finding Tools
- Appinions.com
- BuzzSumo.com
- Followerwonk.com
- GoogleMarketHub.com
- GroupHigh.com
- LinkedIn.com
- LittleBird.com

Write & Get Paid

PART 8
THE LAW

Chapter Twenty-Nine

"I love being a writer. What I can't stand is the paperwork." – Peter DeVries

GET IT IN WRITING

Lawyers have created a language that only they can understand. This legalese forces the layperson to hire a lawyer just to decipher documents. It took me years as a freelance writer and a year as a small publisher to approach these documents with confidence. Despite the intimidating language in a lot of these documents, they perform a basic legal function. Once you understand general provisions, you can design your own publishing contracts, work agreements, and release forms.

EVERYDAY USE

I'd been writing for a long time when I first got in contact with Prison Law Blog (PLB). They syndicated articles from various news sources by "reprinting" them on their website. There are some interesting legal aspects to cover here: first, PLB had to get permission from each source to re-print an article (CNN, CNBC, Reuters, BBC, Breitbart, etc.). PLB's editor, Randy Radic, made requests via email, which were simple.

From: Randy Radic, Editor, Prison Law Blog

To: Editor, *Huffington Post*

Date: 8/12/14

Subject: Reprint Permission

Hi. Please grant permission for PLB to share your article at http://prisonlawblog.com and save it. Your article will be attributed "Previously published on *Huffington Post*." Thank you for your time.

Later on, I would type a similar Release Agreement (electronically) granting PLB the right to post each of my blogs. That may sound like "seat of the pants," but they were valid agreements that would hold up in court because it was used in the course of doing business and can be submitted as a "letter of record," or evidence. Most release forms are pretty skimpy. After reading Prison Law Blog for a few weeks, I shot a query to the editor explaining I'm a writer and I'd love to contribute "content" and sent him my résumé and a bunch of links.

The editor, Randy, said, "Sure, what do you have in mind?" I was just starting my career, and Randy was a well-established author; we crossed trajectories, and we clicked. I pitched a book review/article about the challenges of parenting from behind bars. Randy liked it, and that's what I wrote, tastefully plugging my children's book. In two weeks, the article was blasted on PLB. It all snowballed from there, turning into weekly blog posts. People inside and outside the prison started recognizing my name as these blogs started getting archived on more and more sites.

I pitched new articles to Randy each week, and he would suggest a new site every once in a while. We were just working together, writers helping each other. Still, we observed all the formalities, granting permission for each and every piece to be published and making sure things were clearly stated in our emails. I wrote a few reviews for his book called *Santa Muerta the Bloody History of Mexican Cartels*. The review was good enough to be selected by andsociety.org as an editor pick and appeared on their home page. Permission granted, of course. Everyone was happy.

LEARNING THE ROPES

My connections in the writing community were piling up. One of those connections was a writers group called Group at Old Pink. One of its members was a French-educated "riot grrrl" named Luz Thompson, who writes erotic science fiction and needed a little publicity. I bookmarked her info and stayed busy with my existing schedule, because I was about to begin my most ambitious project yet.

Randy had avoided being fired for 5 years, which was a feat because his boss, a fop who got $8,000 a month from his trust fund, had fired everyone he'd ever hired in less than a year. Randy said he was getting in hot water for helping me out. I told him, "Wow, if I were raking in $8,000 a month, I'd never have come to prison!" We switched to personal emails and worked on the side.

My publication wasn't going unnoticed in their camp. "I'm sure he has your name on Google Alerts and sees it's popping up everywhere," Randy explained. In the end, Randy got fired because he was having better luck helping me for free than he was charging the fop $40 an hour to manage his sites. It was the straw that broke the camel's back. Randy quoted a friend about it, "I was looking for a job when I found this one."

We bonded over the episode and collaborated daily on reviews, books, and websites. Each of us shares paying opportunities with the other and promotes each other's writing. Our motto was "Forget Em All!" During this explosion of successful freelancing rebellion, I wanted to self-publish a book, which started what would eventually become my first publishing company.

Randy would work for hire as the editor and webmaster; I was the owner and developer. We put our heads together and signed a work agreement. The company's name was FCZ Press. I designed a standard author contract and a few other documents, and work began. All of these documents (emails, release, and work agreement) would later save me and the authors at the FCZ Press stable. But we're getting ahead of ourselves. I started transferring files and money, and our website was up and running in a couple of weeks.

Anthony TInsman

Consultant's Work Agreement

1. **Parties:** This Work Agreement is made between the following parties:

   Name(s): _____

   Address(es): _____

   _____

   (hereinafter Contractor), and

   Name(s): _____

   Address(es): _____

   _____

   (hereinafter Consultant).

2. **Name of Project:** _____

   _____

   _____

3. **Work to Be Performed by Consultant:** _____

   _____

   _____

4. **Work/Payment Schedule:** _____

   _____

   _____

5. **Date:** This Agreement shall be effective as of the latter date below written.
6. **Recitals:** Contractor has one or more ideas relating to the above project and desires to have such project developed more completely, as specified in the above statement of Work. Consultant has certain skills desired by Contractor relating to performance of the above Work.
7. **Performance:** Consultant will perform the above work for Contractor, in accordance with the above-scheduled Work/Payment Schedule, and Contractor will make the above scheduled payments to Consultant. Any changes to the Work to Be Performed or the Work/Payment Schedule shall be described in a writing referring to this Agreement and signed and dated by both parties. Time is of the essence of this Agreement, and if Consultant fails to perform according to the above work schedule, contractor may (a) void this agreement and pay consultant 50% of what would otherwise be due, or (b) require that Consultant pay contractor a penalty of $_____ per day.
8. **Intellectual Property:** All intellectual property, including trademarks, writings, information, trade secrets, inventions, discoveries, or improvements, whether or not registrable or patentable, which are conceived, constructed, or written by Consultant and arise out of or are related to work and services performed under this agreement, are, or shall become and remain, the sole and exclusive property of Contractor, whether or not such intellectual property is conceived during the time such work and services are performed or billed.
9A. **Protection of Intellectual Property:** Contractor and Consultant recognize that under U.S. patent laws, all patent applications must be filed in the name of the true and actual inventor(s) of the subject matter sought to be patented. Thus if Consultant makes any patentable inventions relating to the above project, Consultant agrees to be named as an applicant in any U.S. patent application(s) filed on such invention(s). Actual ownership of such patent applications shall be governed by clause 8.
9B. **Disclosure:** Consultant shall promptly disclose to Contractor in writing all information pertaining to any intellectual property generated or conceived by Consultant under this Agreement. Consultant hereby

assigns and agrees to assign all of Consultant's rights to such intellectual property, including patent rights and foreign priority rights. Consultant hereby expressly agrees, without further charge for time, to do all things and sign all documents deemed by Contractor to be necessary or appropriate to invest in intellectual property, including obtaining for and vesting in Contractor all U.S. and foreign patents and patent applications which Contractor desires to obtain to cover such intellectual property, provided that Contractor shall bear all expenses relating thereto. All reasonable local travel time and expenses shall be borne by Consultant.

10. **Trade Secrets:** Consultant recognizes that all information relating to the above Project disclosed to Consultant by Contractor, and all information generated by Consultant in the performance of the above Work, is a valuable trade secret of Contractor and Consultant shall treat all such information as strictly confidential, during and after the performance of Work under this Agreement. Specifically Consultant shall not reveal, publish, or communicate any such information to anyone other than Contractor, and shall safeguard all such information from access to anyone other than Contractor, except upon the express written authorization of Contractor. This clause shall not apply to any information which Consultant can document in writing is presently in or enters the public domain from a bona fide source other than Consultant.

11. **Return of Property:** Consultant agrees to return all written materials and objects received from Contractor, to deliver to Contractor all objects and a copy (and all copies and originals if requested by Contractor) of all written materials resulting from or relating to work performed under this Agreement, and not to deliver to any person, organization, or publisher, or cause to be published, any such written material without prior written authorization.

12. **Conflicts of Interest:** Consultant recognizes a fiduciary obligation to Contractor arising out of the work and services performed under this agreement. Accordingly, Consultant will not offer services to or perform services for any competitor, potential or actual, of Contractor for the above Project. Consultant will not perform any other acts which may result in any conflict of interest by Consultant, during and after the term of this Agreement.

    [Check one]
    - ☐ Consultant represents to Contractor that prior to this agreement, Consultant has not made and does not own any inventions relating to the above Project.
    - ☐ Consultant has made or does own inventions relating to this Project and has provided a list of such inventions on a separate sheet incorporated in this Agreement by reference.

13. **Mediation and Arbitration:** If any dispute arises under this Agreement, the parties shall negotiate in good faith to settle such dispute. If the parties cannot resolve such dispute themselves, then either party may submit the dispute to mediation by a mediator approved by both parties. If the parties cannot agree to any mediator, or if either party does not wish to abide by any decision of the mediator, they shall submit the dispute to arbitration by any mutually acceptable arbitrator, or the American Arbitration Association (AAA). If the AAA is selected, the arbitration shall take place under the auspices of the nearest branch of such to both parties. The costs of the arbitration proceeding shall be borne according to the decision of the arbitrator, who may apportion costs equally, or in accordance with any finding of fault or lack of good faith of either party. The arbitrator's award shall be nonappealable and enforceable in any court of competent jurisdiction.

14. **Governing Law:** This Agreement shall be governed by and interpreted under and according to the laws of the State of _____.

15. **Signatures:** The parties have indicated their agreement to all of the above terms by signing this Agreement on the respective dates below indicated. Each party has received an original signed copy hereof.

Contractor: _____ Date: _____

Consultant: _____ Date: _____

We signed on a couple of authors; one was Luz Thompson, the French riot grrrl. The others trickled in. One I knew, a friend of exceptional talent. Another author also approached Randy; the problem was that he was in prison. FCZ Press needed authors who could work social media, travel locally, and when the timing was right, partner up. I signed on two prisoners in the end, Jordan Davidson and Robert George III. All in all, we had 8 titles in the pipeline. The publishing contracts were simple, based on a copy from Rio Norte Press; the difference was that I didn't have to pay a lawyer $50 an hour to make mine.

LEAVE A PAPER TRAIL
I did something very different with FCZ Press. I focused on authors who'd self-published. When I chose authors, I looked for books that appealed to distinguishable markets. I can't sell passion projects or cheap porn. At least Luz wrote stylish porn! When I found authors who met my criteria, I wanted their self-published books too. Luz and Robert had a series out already. Their deals were easy to negotiate since they owned all the rights to their work and could agree to transfer them to FCZ Press. It was done in one contract.

FCZ Press scooped up their files, edited, made commercial page designs and covers, got advance praise from recognizable critics, and worked a heavy promotion strategy for each re-release. We were all wild cards, drawn into one deck. Randy called us heathens. Luz called us sexy maniacs. It was all about to end horribly.

BE RIGHT WHEN THINGS GO WRONG
Maybe money changes people, or maybe people are all messed up and they just run with their first excuse to be stupid. FCZ Press fell apart over a few months while Randy neglected his duties and held onto my cash. Without the capital to hire another editor or access to all the files, I was looking at a real mess. He didn't respond to me or any of the authors, and they began griping to me daily.

Then it got worse. I spotted a book review written in my name, published using my account with *The Huffington Post*. The review promoted Randy's old employer, the FOP, which got $8,000 a month. Randy had betrayed us, run off with all the passwords and cash. He had to be stopped. Luckily, I held the paper trail.

What followed was a furious legal offensive that began with a Cease and Desist order, which stated in chronological order that infringement had occurred, as well as breach of contract, and that if all infringing materials weren't removed and all property returned within 30 days, I would take action. To make the deadline intimidating, I included details about the complaints that would be filed with the Federal Trade Commission (ftc.gov/idtheft), the Postmaster General, and the Social Security Administration. Charges would include ID theft, SSN misuse, and wire fraud, all of which could get someone a few years in federal prison.

I got what I wanted – money (most of it was refunded), property returned, and a semblance of normalcy returned to my life. Explaining things to the authors was heartbreaking, but I didn't have the funds or trust left to try it again immediately. I freed up the authors by dissolving their contracts in writing. It was a depressing experience, but thanks to doing things the right way, it wasn't a complete disaster.

Write & Get Paid

FCZ PRESS CONTRACT

Made this day of September, 2015, between Anthony Louis Tinsman ("PUBLISHER") and Luz Thompson ("AUTHOR")

1. AUTHOR SHALL PREPARE original manuscript, The Pauli Principle ("the WORK").

2. AUTHOR GRANTS PUBLISHER the exclusive right to print, publish, and sell the Work throughout the world during the full term of all copyrights and all reworks thereof, and to license, sell or otherwise use all subsiding rights hereunder, and the right to reproduce and disseminate the Work and portions thereof by all methods and in all media formats.

3. PUBLISHER SHALL PAY AUTHOR a 50% royalty on all net income resulting from sales of the Work. Net being defined as the revenue Publisher receives from sales after expenses.

4. PUBLISHER MAY ENTER into transactions with respect to the Work. The AUTHOR agrees that she will not enter into any transactions based on the material in the Work. PUBLISHER SHALL PAY AUTHOR a 50% royalty on all net sales PUBLISHER receives from said transactions.

5. AFTER PUBLICATION of the Work, or any TRANSACTION with respect to the Work, PUBLISHER shall render annual statements of sales under this Contract as of each December 31 and shall mail the statements and applicable payments during the following March, but no later than March 31.

6. ALL matters relating to design, appearance, production, promotion, and sales of the Work are to be determined by PUBLISHER.

7. THIS CONTRACT contains the entire understanding of the parties and cannot be changed orally. It shall be binding upon and endure to the benefit of the heirs, executors and administrators of AUTHOR and the successors and assigns of PUBLISHER.

Signed by the PARTIES OF CONTRACT on this 10TH day of September, 2015.

AUTHOR

Luz Thompson *[signature: Luz Thompson]*

PUBLISHER

Anthony Louis Tinsman *[signature: Anthony Tinsman]*

Everyone I was responsible for walked away unharmed, a good sign that deal-making can be the deciding factor in a writer's success. Don't get flustered by contracts and agreements. Smile, they are simple and a good sign that your publisher is going to cover your back.

PUBLISHING CONTRACTS EXPLAINED

First, never sign anything without understanding it. The goal of these documents is to make a deal legally binding. Negotiate things before you take on the awesome responsibility of signing a contract … or present one for someone else to sign.

There are some general provisions covered in all basic publishing contracts. Mine were pure simplicity, just two pages long, but they covered all the bases. Not all publishers trust plain talk. They hire a lawyer who works by the hour, stretching it out into a fifteen-page monstrosity.

Sometimes, attachments, like an eight-page marketing questionnaire or a three-page author questionnaire, may accompany your contract. From one-page release forms to monolithic contracts that bleed legalese, publishing contracts consist of only twelve items:

1. Parties to the Contract
2. License of Rights
3. Terms and Termination
4. Author Warranties
5. Publisher Indemnification Warranties
6. Permission and Releases
7. Use of Author's Name and Likeness
8. Publisher Bankruptcy
9. Notices
10. Governing Law, Venue, and Attorney's Fees
11. Arbitration
12. Entire Agreement

1. *Parties to the Contract* – This is you, hereby "The Author," and them, hereby "The Publisher," for the rest of the contract.

2. *License of Rights* – This is the most important part of the agreement. If you grant all rights, then the publisher has exclusive control over the material. That's okay if you have a publisher who does everything you want. I encountered one who published eBooks only, and if that paid for itself, then they'd produce a print edition. I couldn't talk them into advancing into formatting a print version (with orders for copies for several local libraries)! This meant I had to negotiate a new license authorizing a third party to format the book for print and wrangle the publisher to agree to the terms. Save yourself the trouble, get everything you want, then sign.

3. *Terms and Termination* – This defines how long the license will last. It could be for life or be limited. Four typical options are:

- Exclusive, but only for one year
- Exclusive for a specific number of years, but the author can terminate at any time, giving written notice within a specific number of days (usually 30 – 60)
- Nonexclusive for a specific number of years, and the author can cancel at any time.
- Exclusive for the full term of the Copyright and renewal thereof (that one lasts about 70 years after your death).

4. *Author Warranties* – Basically, you, the "Author," promise to make original work, and not violate any laws or someone else's rights with your writing. There are eight author warranties you can be asked to grant:

- "Author is the sole author and proprietor of the work."
- "Author owns all rights to the work free of any liens and encumbrances and has full authority to enter this agreement."
- "The work is original and has not been previously published."
- "For work not in the public domain, legally effective written licenses have been secured."
- "No part of the work, including the title, contains any matter which is defamatory, unlawful, or which in any way infringes, invades, or violates any right, including privacy, copyright, trademark, or trade secret of any person."
- "The Publisher doesn't breach any oral or written agreement the author has made with anyone else."
- "The representations and warranties will be in full force and effect on the date of publication."
- "The warranties survive the term of the Agreement."

5. *Publisher Indemnification Warranties* – Basically, this is where the "Author" promises to cover legal expenses if the publisher gets sued for any false things you wrote. There are typically three ways of saying this in legalese:

- "The author indemnifies and holds the publisher harmless from any losses, expense, or damages arising out of, or for, the purpose of resolving or avoiding any suit, demand, etc., as a result of the author's breach of the representations and warranties."
- "The publisher can extend the benefit of the author's representations, warranties, and indemnities to any party affected by the author's breach."
- "Author has to pay legal fees, costs, etc., to defend any claim brought against the publisher as a result of the author's breach of any representations or warranty."

6. *Permission and Releases* – This one is pretty easy; it lays the responsibility on the "Author." You agree to obtain any permissions to use a quote or segment of writing.

7. *Use of Author's Name and Likeness* – Just because you grant the publisher permission to use your writing doesn't mean that you've granted them permission to use your pictures and name. It's stupid legalese red tape. That's why there's a clause that usually reads something like this, "The author grants the publisher and its licensees the right to use the author's name and likeness in the sale, promotion, and advertising of the work."

8. *Publisher Bankruptcy* – Everyone hates this. As a bankrupt publisher, I'll tell you from experience it's not a fun time (especially when all your assets are jammed up due to a rogue editor). This clause protects the author. Upon filing bankruptcy, and sometimes the sale of the company, the license is terminated, and all rights return to the author.

The problem is that the clause may not be enforceable due to the Automatic Stay provision of the bankruptcy section of the US Code (11 U.S.C. § 362(3)), which states that the stay applies to any act to obtain property from the estates or to exercise control over it. The good news is that most trustees will return all rights to authors; if they didn't, you'd have to file a motion in court as an unsecured creditor -the author.

9. *Notices* – If you keep things friendly with your publisher, you can just write, email, or fax (anything that acts as a record) and work out changes in your agreement. Maybe you have an offer from another publisher or competitor, just call them up and table the idea of writing it. Maybe you would like a different royalty invoice, call 'em up and explain why.

However, if you have a rough relationship with your publisher, then you have to go to greater lengths to work out day-to-day needs. It's all about official records, or communications that will hold up in court (if everything goes wrong) – like sending things via certified mail, or from an attorney. The contract will detail any special methods the publisher prefers.

10. *Governing Law, Venue, Attorney's Fee* – In order to satisfy certain states' requirements, legalese cites state and federal laws that grant various powers in contracts. You'll see stuff like this:

- Governing Law: "This Agreement will be construed and controlled by the laws of the State of New York ..."
- Venue: "… and each party consents to the exclusive jurisdiction and venue by the state or federal courts sitting in the State of New York, County of Norfolk."
- Attorneys' Fees: "If either the publisher or the author employs attorneys to enforce any rights arising out of or relating to this Agreement, the prevailing party will be entitled to recover reasonable attorneys' fees and costs."

11. *Arbitration* – This is the same thing as going to a marriage counselor; you may be able to work things out, or you may not, but it's best to have a legal head in the room while you figure it out. Usually, a contract refers to the American Arbitration Association (AAA), but I've never met anyone who used them, nor have I ever relied on them. For all I know, a flair sent up to the AAA would go unnoticed or land back in my lap stamped "Return to Sender."

12. *Entire Agreement* – This clause wraps up the contract. This is the part where you can stand your ground and hammer out the final details before you sign. When it's right, you sign, and you're done. It usually reads like this:

- "This Agreement constitutes the entire Agreement between the publisher and the author with respect to the subject matter hereof and supersedes all prior written or oral agreements by the parties. This agreement may not be modified or amended except in writing and signed by both parties."

There may be some extra legalese thrown into the end of your contracts. Most of these terms are simply ways of getting into things specified in black and white in the license. Most of it is unnecessary, because if you and your publisher are going to work together, you can get things done without overwrought "gotcha" terms like these:

- "Author may not assign this Agreement of any rights or obligations hereunder, by operation of law or any other manner, without the publisher's prior written consent, such consent which will not be unreasonably withheld."
- "If any term or provision of this Agreement is illegal or unenforceable, this Agreement shall remain in full force and effect and such term or provision shall be deemed deleted or curtailed only to such extent necessary to make it legal or enforceable."
- "No modification, amendment, or waiver shall be valid or binding unless made in writing and signed by all parties hereto."

MAKE A DEAL

It's obvious when a publisher is out to screw you over and when they are not. The power to negotiate is always in your grasp; no one can stand up for what you want better than yourself. The stuff you'll ask for is pretty basic: royalty percentages on net profits (High = 50% on e-book, 30% on print), payment schedules with statements (quarterly or annually), and the way your name appears in the book. Other options are a little harder to negotiate. Stuff like cooperative marketing and guarantees of minimum advertising.

There are seven "options" you barter to get the deal you want. Most publishers want "all rights," which isn't a bad thing, but you aren't obligated to give them more than they need. The Copyright Law that went into effect January 1, 1978, states writers are primarily selling one-time rights to their work unless they and the publisher agree otherwise in writing. Here are the subsidy rights you own with each manuscript you create:

1. *First Serial Rights* – These are sought after by newspapers and magazines; it's a one-time publishing agreement for shorter work. Which is good because you get paid if you convince another publisher to run the same piece later. This is likely to happen in a different market; that's why this right is divided into "North American," "International," and "All Formats."

2. *One-Time Rights* – These are non-exclusive rights, meaning you can license them to multiple publications at the same time. Good luck convincing them, though. This only occurs with a mix of online and print-based publishers, or with a mix of publications that cater to widely different readers. You could also just not tell a publisher that a piece will appear in multiple publications, but that's a little unethical.

3. *Second Serial (Reprint) Rights* – Nonexclusive, but valuable, this right allows another magazine or newspaper to run your work after it in a rival's publication. This right follows the old-time parable of "If you can't beat 'em, join 'em!"

4. *All Rights* – They want everything – A pint of your blood, your first-born son, and uttered sacred vows. Writers seem to need a little "selling" on this option, but it makes sense to take it. As a publisher I've found confidence in knowing I can profit from promoting my author's work, when it leads to a movie deal or a series, I am getting paid to develop their work. Without All Rights, I'm reluctant to go all in and may lose opportunities because of it. As a writer, I feel blessed when a publisher does this for me, especially after working on both sides. That said, not all publishers will make use of your subsidy rights. If you have distribution models to do so, you stand to make more income exploiting them independently.

5. *Electronic Rights* – Pretty much everything pixels and audio. Yep, we're talking phone apps, DVDs, games, and whatever else seems to have a shot at selling.

6. *Subsidy Rights* – This covers a lot of ground, from translations to serialized TV, movie, and audio rights. It also extends to advertising products, T-shirts, posters, and coffee mugs. If your work has the potential to appeal to customers in this way, it's a good thing to manage this right as tightly as possible.

7. *Dramatic, TV, and Motion Picture Rights* – Exactly what it sounds like. Just be prepared to receive a small check; most "movie deals" net under $10,000. Since most scripts are never produced into a film, it's questionable whether it's worth the time to negotiate a royalty on tickets, DVDs, and downloads. If you get offered a check, it might not be a bad deal.

THE ART OF THE DEAL

Of the seven subsidy rights, the more options you withhold, the more control you have, and the more value remains for bartering over the terms in your contract. Bear in mind that the art of deal-making is making it clear that you have more to offer. Subsidy rights are only one thing you can trade, because as a writer, you have more value than you realize.

Perhaps you can assist a writer in finishing or improving their book for a publisher. Depending on your market, you can design reports that expand on the subject of your book or actively scout new talent for your publisher. If your writing has the potential to become popular (like a series), or can be used as a marketing tool (annual editions and advertising space) then tell publishers you'll give them first "right to refuse" before you shop it around.

Let your publisher know what you can do. The promise of delivering something valuable puts any writer in a better position to negotiate the terms they want. Just be sure to get everything in writing, just in case.

🖉 **Writers Manifesto No 27 – Paper is nine tenths of the law.**

RESOURCES

Identity Theft Solutions
- Federal Trade Commission
  ID Theft Clearinghouse
  600 Pennsylvania Avenue, NW
  Washington, DC. 20580
  ftc.gov/idtheft

Credit Reporting Agency Fraud Departments
- equifax.com
- experian.com
- transunion.com

Better Business Bureaus
- Council of Better Business Bureaus, Inc
  42000 Wilson Boulevard, 8th Floor
  Arlington, VA. 22203
  bbb.org

Legal Document Templates
- nolo.com
  (A good source for Non-Disclosure, License, and Work agreements)

Chapter Thirty

"I'm all in favor of keeping dangerous weapons out of the hands of fools. Let's start with typewriters." – Frank Lloyd Wright

CONSEQUENCES OF FREE SPEECH

When you're out there promoting your work and researching your next piece, it's easy to say some things, to borrow stuff, and do things that'll get you the wrong kind of attention. Freedom of speech really isn't a freedom; it's a guideline. You need to know how far you can legally push things. Where do Judges side on the issue of the First Amendment and Copyright Law? And how do you diplomatically disengage when you've crossed the line?

Most importantly, you need to prepare yourself, so when you hire a lawyer, it's not as bad as it sounds. You've probably heard some of this before. Good advice can save you some trouble. If you've got issues with taking advice, then stop and think a moment about how smart you feel when following it saves you face: eat your vegetables, fill up the tank when it's a quarter empty, don't plug in too many Christmas lights into the wall socket.

Ignore this good advice at your own peril. Know your rights. That means study them, or at least read this section a couple of times, turn every paragraph yellow with a highlighter, and memorize the facts like John the Baptist.

WHERE DO RIGHTS COME FROM?

Give our Founding Fathers some credit. Thanks to a little dust-up in the Colonies, things like journalism or the right to freedom of speech were a cornerstone of the U.S. Constitution. The First Amendment. Along with that freedom comes a whole train wreck of legal nightmares. Like ethics, fair use, and libel, and we're the lucky ones!

"Paper, any paper, is about the most precious article for a political prisoner, for the urge to write is almost irresistible." Wrote Ngugi wa Thiong'o, a Kenyan writer who has frequently been subjected to imprisonment, in his memoir *Detained*. Similar contempt is heard from Chinese activists and members of PEN's International Offices who fight persecution by getting their words out there. The freedom of expression can be a life-or-death issue in most countries. Just look at what happened at the Parisian office, where terrorists killed several cartoonists working in the same office as the artist who drew depictions of the Prophet Mohammed for their comics.

America's speech for everyone offers great power. Quoting Uncle Ben Parker, "With great power comes great responsibility." Stuff like copyright. Disclaimers. Journalistic privileges. Commanding a basic knowledge of what lines you can and cannot cross is as critical to writing and getting paid as focused writing.

THE FIRST AMENDMENT

The U.S. Constitution and the First Amendment originated from a new idea that the press could criticize the government. It was rebellious and fittingly matured in the early American colonies. It peaked in 1734 when John Peter Zenger's *New York Weekly* criticized colonial policies and led to his arrest under charges of "seditious libel." During the trial the following August, the judge instructed jurors that, according to the definition of seditious libel, truth afforded no protection against libel of the government.

Zenger's attorney, however, made a stirring argument just like Johnnie Cochran did in the O.J. Simpson trial. His position was "The liberty both of expressing the opposing arbitrary power... by speaking and writing truth." The jury decided that Zenger was innocent. Due to the allowance of such criticism, revolutionary literature was easier to print. The seeds of the American Revolution were planted with those words by authors like Thomas Paine.

Because of this, Freedom of the Press was guaranteed in the First Amendment of the U.S. Constitution. But Freedom of Speech has been a struggle for U.S. citizens ever since. Just eleven years after the ratified constitution was signed by America's forefathers, a political conflict led to the Sedition Act. Under federalist president John Adams, twenty-five people were arrested and ten convicted for "false, scandalous, and malicious writing" against the government.

The act was allowed to lapse under Thomas Jefferson's presidency in 1890. The adversarial role resumed in 1971, when the Supreme Court conceded that the *New York Times* had a constitutional right to publish the Pentagon Papers, which were top-secret government documents. The next year, Washington Post reporters covered the Watergate scandal, which led to the resignation of then-President Richard Nixon.

Journalism remains one of the great taste-testers of free speech; in the early 2000s, it expanded to the internet. Bloggers fed us real-time "news" about the Iraq invasion, circumventing the filtered news coming from embedded reporters with U.S. military units. The trend turned more and more radical as the fifth estate became the playground of figures like Julian Assange and WikiLeaks. Because of the politicized notion of "national security," our Freedom of Speech is no less controversial today than it was in the colonies.

ETHICS MATTER, REALLY

With all that freedom, exploitation, stupidity, and errant abuse isn't anything new. The late 19th century was the most colorful example of how American Journalism could push the 1st amendment to the breaking point. In many cities, newspapers competed using tough tactics. Nowhere was this more evident than in New York, where two newspaper barons, Joseph Pulitzer and William Randolph Hearst, vied for the lucrative market. The two owned rival papers, Pulitzer the *New York World*, while Hearst bought the *San Francisco Examiner* and the *New York Journal*. They engaged in a competition in which each owner sought to out-sensationalize the other.

Hearst hired away several of the *World's* star reporters, and both papers cut prices to a penny. Their stories and stunts were significant. At the apex, these magnates caused the furor that led the U.S. into the Spanish-American War in 1898.

This style of rabid sensationalism was labeled "Yellow Journalism," derived from a comic strip called "The Yellow Kid" that, naturally, both papers believed was their sole right to publish. Such journalism sold, both newspapers regularly sold 1 million copies a day. Eventually, "Yellow" tactics drew disdain from contemporary papers, and Pulitzer tired of it as well, later founding the well-known Pulitzer Prize for exceptional journalism.

Yellow Journalism lives on, however, raising ethical questions about where we should draw the line or categorize certain speech. Commercial news networks are the biggest offenders, packaging news as entertainment and competing for ratings by politicizing or sensationalizing current events. This is second only to the ironic "fake news" bloggers serving readers with a crossroads, ranging from the gonzo satire of *The Onion* to crafty counterfeiters.

LINE IN THE SAND

If writing is deemed "obscene" or "radical," it can lead to censorship of the author's work. This is what Allen Ginsburg experienced when his novel was deemed "obscene" by San Francisco authorities in the 60s, pulling Ginsburg into a trial. The trial was well publicized, causing the empowered "flower power" generation of beatniks and hippies to rally outside the courthouse steps. The ruling came down that Ginsburg's work (it's just sex and drug use) was not obscene. With that ruling, the floodgates were opened to embrace the sexual revolution of the sixties.

Times were changing. In the early 60s, there was a loosening grip of censorship over airing profanity on TV or depicting a married couple getting into the same bed together. The Comic Authority Code of the 50s, which silenced horror comics, and the Parental Advisory Stickers of the 80s have lost their teeth over the years as societal change gave way to more freedom. Furthermore, Eminem changed our perspective of "obscenity" in the 90s and YouPorn forever altered access to pornography.

While the lines are constantly shifting, certain loopholes in The First Amendment aren't in your favor, for example, it doesn't cover verbally abusive language if it is distinguished as a threat. The "fighting words" provision in most states' statutes authorizes punishment for whoever "directs at another person in a public place offensive words which are likely to provoke violent reaction on the part of the average person addressed." The details were outlined in *Chaplinsky v. New Hampshire*, 315 U.S. 568 (1942), where the U.S. Supreme Court held that one of those limited categories of unprotected speech is "insulting or fighting words" that by their very utterance inflict injury or tend to incite an immediate breach of the peace.

Things like the "fighting words provision" can hamper certain artists' range of expression, especially since the legal definition of "public place" now encompasses social media. Far more worrisome is a form of "incitement speech." Which means that any rhetorical statement that a reasonable person might believe may incite violent acts, such as an order to followers on social media to "commit a massacre at a preschool," implies both the followers' existence and a potential threat. In the case United States v. Wheeler, BL 12083, 10th Cir. Wheeler was prosecuted under 18 U.S.C. 875 (c) and received a 40-month sentence. Further, in Brandenburg v. Ohio, 395 U.S. 444 (1969), the court's opinion removed stringent rules which allowed defendants to take shelter in the First Amendment, "Simply by phrasing threats as exhortations," which would make the states powerless against the ingenuity of certain creations.

LIBEL

The rules are the same for everyone, until they aren't. Money and power are the "get out of jail free card" that never seems to come the way of laypeople. Like George Orwell's classic book Animal Farm, where the farm animals revolt in a communist takeover, but their principles turn from "All animals are equal" to "Some are more equal than others" with the development of the power-hungry pigs.

Libel is a great example of how things can be right if you have enough money to throw at lawyers. Libel is known as "slander" or defamation. Black's Law Dictionary defines defamation as "The offense of injuring a person's character, name, or reputation by false and malicious statements." In this case, many "experts" advise us to tuck our tails and take the advice given to us as children, in a Disney movie of all places (Bambi), "If you don't have anything nice to say, then don't say anything at all."

The next technique is to critique. Indirectly check your sources really carefully, then quote people with their own words. Or leave that person out and say, "some people will argue," or "many authorities believe," and tear up their opinions, not them personally. It is a good defense against being sued for libel, but it isn't nearly as satisfying as sticking it to someone.

LIABILITY

Getting sued is a reality for certain types of writers. Writers can be held liable for publishing something, anywhere. A reader could claim a book misled them, to their great damage. In most cases, the courts have found books not to be "products," so publishers are not strictly liable for their content. It must be proven that the publishers and the author knew or should have known of any inaccuracies. The best defense is to be prepared, root out facts, and note that your book is not the reader's only source of information.

WHEN THINGS BEGIN TO FALL APART

From the American Revolution to the religious fanatic who sniped *Hustler*'s founder, Larry Flint, and his lawyer, the power of words can incite individuals and the government to take action. All it requires is a person getting their feelings hurt over something you write. This happened in 1983 when *Hustler Magazine* published a parody featuring the Reverend Jerry Falwell, the well-known fundamentalist minister. The parody featured the Reverend describing his "first time" having sex as occurring in an outhouse with his mother and saying that he always gets "sloshed" before sermons. At the bottom of the page, in small print, was the disclaimer "a parody not to be taken seriously."

An outraged response was organized by the Moral Majority Inc., an ultra-conservative political lobbying group. They sent out mailings signed by Falwell, containing a passionate plea to over 500,000 contributors to fund a lawsuit to help Falwell "defend his mother's memory." It included a wholesale copy of the parody. They collected $680,000 in a week.

What had started off as a libel issue now became more complicated. Here's a chronology:

- *Hustler* sued Moral Majority Inc. for copyright infringement in *Hustler Magazine Inc. v. Moral Majority Inc., 729 F. 2d 1148 (9th Circuit* 1988).
- The appellate court carefully deliberated and found that there simply was no unfair exploitation of *Hustler's* work (more about the decision and the four-factor test for Fair Use in the next chapter).
- Larry Flint and his supporters believed they'd been "railroaded" by the court system because the judges were all self-identified "Christians" who sided with Falwell on theological identity.
- Flint's argument didn't win the case.

Pumped up by his victory, Falwell pressed his luck and sued Hustler for libel and inflicting emotional distress, see Hustler Magazine Inc. v. Falwell, 485 U.S. 46 (1988). This case went all the way to the Supreme Court, and *Hustler* prevailed. The magazine prides itself as a champion of First Amendment freedoms. And you know what? They are champions. Regardless of whether it's the government or religious demagogues, no one has the right to stomp on the right of free expression.

WRITERS IN PRISON

✎ Writers Manifesto No. 28 – Don't write about the crime if you can't do the time.

You know my story, and as an incarcerated author, I deal with plenty of First Amendment issues. My battles have already been fought, but that doesn't stop guards from acting like "RoboCop" and trying to shut off my writing career. They say, "You can't publish anything under your own name because you're a prisoner," or "You can't sign a contract because you're a prisoner," or "You can't profit from your crime because you're a convicted felon," and they all believe it. They are also dead wrong.

At times, it is the most ridiculous barrier imaginable. One time, I donated three cartons of my self-help book *Life With A Record* to every unit Counselor (12 of them) and Reentry Affairs officials at the federal prison in Forrest City, Arkansas. All but one welcomed the books as a tool to help inmates prepare for getting out of prison. One staff member who gave me chaff said, "What you are doing is illegal. You can't publish a book from prison. You can't get paid while you are in prison." I stood silent, letting him finish as I prepared to play the broken record of educating a prison official.

He reached for his radio and was about to call the Special Investigation Service guards to lock me up in the "Hole" and begin an investigation. I told him flat out he was an idiot, and that I'd love for him to infringe on my First Amendment rights, because I'd file a lawsuit immediately through my publisher's attorney. I cited the dozen or so cases that irrevocably guarantee my rights are protected (*Mumia Abu Jama v Price* says it all about where the Supreme Court stands on a prisoner's right to write). He stared at me for a moment, then accepted the book as a donation for the prison library. He later offered me a job.

It's been so bad at times that laws have been passed that would limit the right of prisoners to write about their experiences, in effect, to prevent them from profiting from their crimes. The nickname of these laws is the "Son of Sam Laws," which came after rampant speculation suggested that David Berkowitz, the infamous New York serial killer from the late 70s, was getting huge offers from publishers to tell his story. The original "Son of Sam" law was enacted in New York in 1977. It was deemed unconstitutional in 1991, in a case regarding the publication of the book *Wiseguys* by Nicholas Pileggi, which became the basis for the classic film Goodfellas.

If you visit Berkowitz's religious website, called "Arise and Shine," which is updated with the help of outside supporters (he's never getting out of prison), you'll face the reality. Even a serial killer's First Amendment rights are guaranteed. On the site, he offers advice for parents and troubled teens. On one part of his website, an "apology" is declared: "I am deeply sorry for the pain, suffering, and sorrow I have brought upon the victims of my crimes." If something like that is protected, guess what, it all is.

It took the Supreme Court until 2007 to make free speech officially open to federal prisoners; their conclusion was:

- A Federal Bureau of Prisons (FBOP) policy that was similar to most "Son of Sam" laws was deemed unconstitutional by a federal court.

- The court opinion claimed it violated not only the plaintiffs' freedom of speech, but also "The speech of more than 198,000 other federal inmates."

- For whom the only way "to be certain to avoid punishment is to not submit an article to the news media for publication."

What's sad, and what ends this section on a soaring note, is that this fight for our rights isn't anything new. My right to share these stories with you has been under assault for a very long time. But here it is in front of you. When I get chaff from guards (and I get it often), I shut them down with the law, then I open them up with morals. During a case in 1974, which struck down California Department of Corrections policy to censor "inflammatory" ideas from inmates, Justice Thurgood Marshal said:

"When the prison gates slam shut behind an inmate, he does not lose his human quality: cease to feed on a free and open interchange of opinions: his yearning for self-respect does not end, nor is his quest for self-realization concluded. If anything, the need for identity and self-respect is more compelling in the dehumanizing prison environment."

Knowledge about where rights come from is the key to unlock the internet of otherwise embattled and easily infringed-upon entitlements. When an author's work sparks a First Amendment lawsuit, however, they usually gain a lot of free publicity. That said, the fewer issues you face, the more time there is to write. It doesn't apply very often to novelists, or even most nonfiction, but authors should remain mindful about what they publish online and in all forms of journalism. Guard accordingly.

Chapter Thirty-One

"What is originality? Undetected plagiarism." – William Ralph Inge

PROTECT YOURSELF WHILE WRITING

When you visit a Mom and Pop hardware store, you'll see a couple of different signs. They are cute, like "Beware of Owner" with a fisted 44 magnum revolver pointing at you. Many signs have the charm, but none are equal: "A lack of planning on your part doesn't constitute an emergency on mine." No one could say it better when talking about the problems you could find yourself in as a writer. When faced with fixing a First Amendment problem I always turn to the Yokel's philosophy, "My Prices – $5 an hour for me to fix it, $10 if you watch, $15 if you worked on it first."

Here is how to prevent 99% of inconveniences to yourself by:

- Register your material with the U.S. Copyright Office
- Cover yourself with a Disclaimer
- Get permission to use copyrighted material

My experience has shown that most problems can be resolved without going to court. The idea is to write what pays, minus any interruptions like getting bled by lawyers and drawn-out litigation. But to do that, you've got to prepare ahead of time.

REGISTER YOUR WORK WITH THE U.S. COPYRIGHT OFFICE

Though it costs less than $100 to copyright a book, many writers who consider registering their work for the first time decide to try what is called a "poor man's copyright." There is no such thing. Mailing your work to yourself and using the postmark as proof of the work's creation is inadmissible as evidence in a court for the following logic:

1. It is easy to place materials in the envelope before or after the postmark (just steam the glue strip with an iron).

2. Because of the ease of changing materials, the possibility of scamming becomes a very real consideration.

3. The work lacks a notarization, similar to the one you get from a Pubic Notary but issued by the Registrar of the Copyright Office.

The website for the U.S. Copyright Office, located at copyright.gov, explains, "Your work is under copyright protection the moment it is created and fixed in a tangible form so that it is perceptible either directly or with the aid of a machine or device." This is true, but it still won't hold up in court until you have filled out the forms with the Copyright Office and have received a registration number for your work.

A certificate of registration documents the title of the work, its author, the name and address of the copyright owner, as well as the year of creation. Furthermore, it records whether the work is published, has been previously registered, or includes preexisting materials.

Write & Get Paid

Registration offers several other advantages:

- Before an infringement suit can be filed in court, registration is necessary.
- Registration establishes "prima facie" evidence of the validity of the copyright when made before or within five years of publication.
- When registration is made prior to infringement or within three months of publication, a copyright owner is eligible for statutory damages, attorney's fees, and costs.
- Registration permits a copyright owner to establish a record with the U.S. Customs and Border Protection (CBP) for protection against the importation of infringing copies.

It's really easy to do. Here is a sample form, filled out, for you to get the hang of it. You can download copies from the U.S. Copyright Office website and find additional tips and tricks in their excellent informational database.

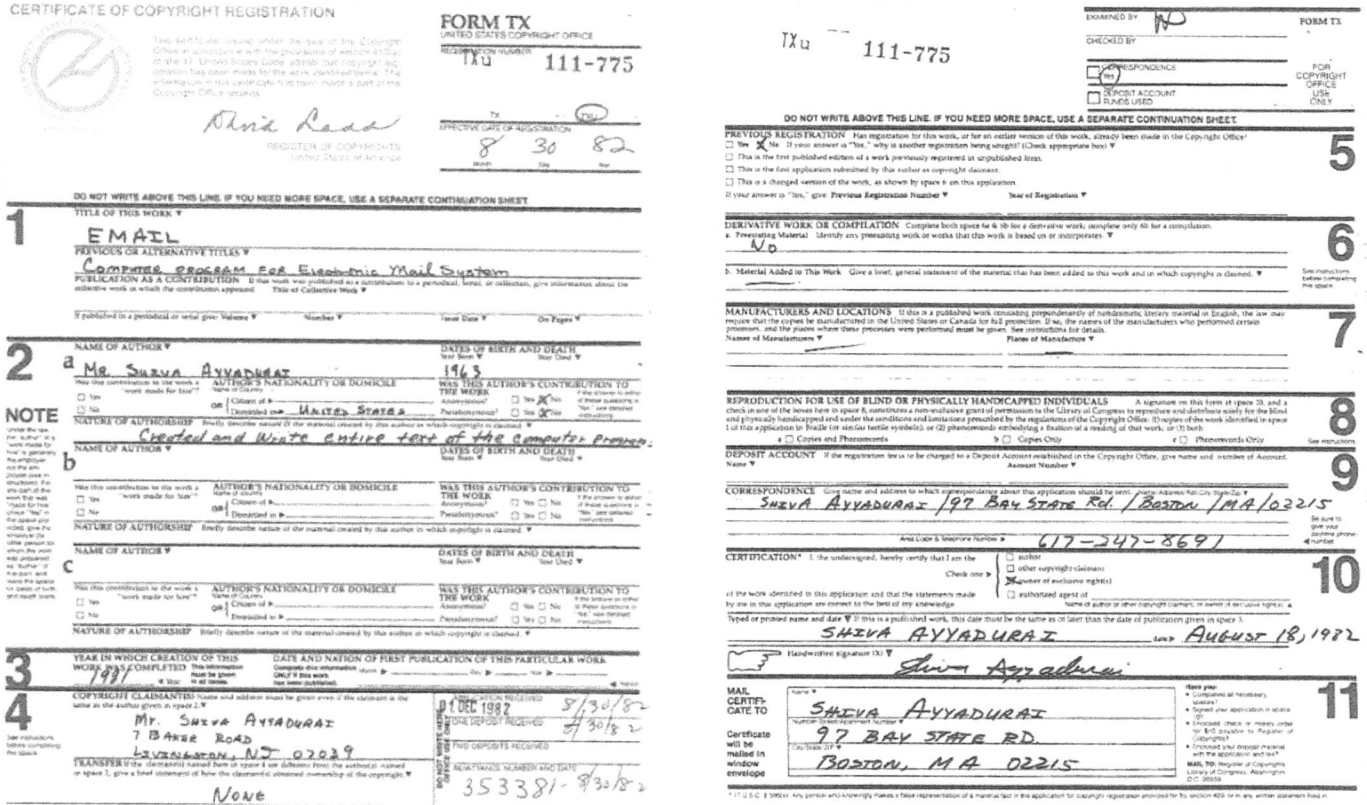

You can write to them and ask for a copyright package or fill out a request called "Copyright Forms By Mail" on their website.

Copyright Forms by Mail

To file a claim to copyright in your work, we recommend you use the Copyright Office online system. If you prefer, fill out the form below to request U.S. Copyright Office forms be sent to you by mail. Note that there is a higher fee for paper filings than for online registration.

Name:	
Street Address:	
Address Line 2:	
City:	
State:	Select
ZIP or postal code:	
Country, if not U.S.:	
Your e-mail address:	

Select forms below:

Form TX - For published or unpublished non-dramatic literary works	Quantity 0
Form TX with Instructions	Quantity 0
Short Form TX - Simplified version of Form TX	Quantity 0
Form PA - For published or unpublished works of the performing arts	Quantity 0
Form PA with Instructions	Quantity 0
Short Form PA	Quantity 0
Form SR - For published or unpublished sound recordings	Quantity 0
Form SR with Instructions	Quantity 0
Form VA - For published or unpublished works of the visual arts	Quantity 0
Form VA with Instructions	Quantity 0
Short Form VA	Quantity 0
Form SE - For serials (newspapers, magazines, newsletters, annuals, journals, etc.)	Quantity 0
Form SE with Instructions	Quantity 0
Short Form SE	Quantity 0
Form SE/Group - For registration of a group of serials	Quantity 0
Form G/DN - For registration of a group of daily newspapers	Quantity 0
Form RE - For claims to renewal of copyright	Quantity 0
Form RE with Instructions	Quantity 0
Form RE/CON - Continuation form to be used only in conjunction with RE application form	Quantity 0
Addendum to Form RE - For all works published between January 1, 1964, and December 31, 1977, that were **Not Registered** during their first 28-year term	Quantity 0
Form MW with Instructions - For registration of mask works which are fixed in a semiconductor chip product	Quantity 0
Form MW/CON - Continuation sheet to be used only in conjunction with MW application form	Quantity 0
Form CA - To correct an error or amplify the information given in a registration	Quantity 0
Form CON - Continuation sheet to be used only in conjunction with basic application Forms CA, PA, SE, SR, TX, and VA **only**	Quantity 0
Form GR/CP - An adjunct application to be used for a group of contributions to periodicals in addition to an application Form TX, PA, VA	Quantity 0

Registration can be made at any time within the life of the copyright. If you register before publication, you do not have to register when the work is published, although you can do so with the published edition, if desired. Prepublication costs $140 and is only accepted online.

Most publishers wait to copyright a book until after publication. It currently costs $85 and is accepted by mail or online. This has numerous benefits: 1) it protects the work where it really needs protection, namely, out in the public where piracy routinely occurs, 2) authors can submit a copy of the book to the Copyright Office, meeting their "best copy" requirement. This means the actual book will be placed in the Library of Congress and not just a loose-leaf manuscript. This means researchers and reporters may review it (in room LM-404 of the James Madison Memorial Building) more easily in the future.

Another benefit is that it makes the publisher's job easier since they don't have to register an original manuscript and then register the edited version. Once you have the registration number, you can create a "Copyright Page" in the design of your book, at the front. Being registered gives it teeth, should you ever find yourself in a dispute over who owns the rights to your words. A copyright page simply states, "Copyright 20___," the word "copyright" can be spelled, but the "c" is necessary for international protection. The full paragraph should read like this:

"© 20___ Author Name. All rights reserved. No part of this book may be reproduced except for the inclusion of a brief quotation in a review."

COVER YOURSELF WITH A DISCLAIMER

✏ Writers Manifesto No. 29 – If it's simple to write but it gets you paid, then it isn't stupid.

A disclaimer is a short statement that absolves you from most libel and slander. In short works, you can detach yourself from possible libel by quoting a professional instead of writing your own opinions. In a longer work, like a book, you must add a "Disclaimer page" in the front.

Disclaimers are crucial for protecting yourself, especially in memoirs and true crime books. Both genres are presented as "factual," so if you defame actual people, they may sue you for libel or defamation. Your options are to just change the characters' names so much that they are no longer factual, like making your cross-dressing uncle your aunt instead. Or you can muscle forward and write a simple disclaimer, such as:

"Any similarities to actual events or people are purely coincidental."

It's even worse if you're in a position to consider writing a book about your life, which depicts criminal acts. You could get sued for slander and libel in cases where you were the victim, like in Augustan Burroughs memoir *Running with Scissors* (which alleges rape, medical malpractice and routine child abuse while living with his mother's psychiatrists' family). In other circumstances, victims of a crime can sue for "revictimization," which is a fancy way of saying you're emotionally messing up their heads by forcing them to relive the traumatizing events. All of that is avoidable with a simple statement like this:

"Names and distinguishing characteristics have been changed to preserve the identity of individuals."

This disclaimer doesn't always hold up in initial court proceedings, but the nuance of a lawsuit usually leads to victory on the side of the author, since it boils down to a First Amendment issue. That's what got Jimmy Lerner into a world of trouble. Lerner drove a taxi after getting out of prison, and published a memoir called *You Got Nothing Coming*, which outraged his victim's sister, Donna Seres. In the book, he depicted his friend as a big, muscular type who attacked him. The guy was much smaller than Lerner, and the circumstances presented in his memoir were questionable. The two had holed up in a Las Vegas hotel and fell out over gambling debts.

Donna Seres was furious, understandably, but she couldn't sue for libel since A) the depiction wasn't about her, and B) the book's basic disclaimer absolved Lerner of any liability. So instead, she filed suit under Nevada's Son of Sam laws, which prohibited criminals from profiting from their crimes. Lerner appealed the case and in December 2004 gathered before a panel of Supreme Court magistrates, the "Son of Sam" law was deemed unconstitutional and the case was dismissed. The book remains on Amazon after his death, thanks in no small part to a *disclaimer*.

The alternative to writing a "factual" book, which may contain details of unprosecuted criminal activity, is to change the work significantly. Various techniques will change the work and make details refuse to line up with reality: the dates are off, the characters are inventions, and the crimes are dramatized. Of course, if you've had a wild criminal lifestyle that no one knows about, it may be best to publish it as a "Novel" and depict it as factually as you want.

Charles Bukowski did this in many of his books, *Women, Ham on Rye, Post Office,* etc. He called them novels, but they were obviously based on his life. A disclaimer attesting to the fictional representation of events is important in this work. Something simple will work, even as simple as this:

"This is presented as a work of fiction."

GET PERMISSION TO USE COPYRIGHTED MATERIAL
You must attribute your sources, whether they are from other books, interviews, music, or speeches. Sometimes you need permission to use (reprint) portions of someone else's work. Luckily, the Copyright Clearance Center (CCC) can provide permission to use song lyrics, quotes, and other references. The CCC is a nonprofit central clearinghouse established in 1977 by publishers, authors, and users, which acts as an agent for the publisher and grants permissions for a fee.

CCCs electronic database allows writers to search close to 100,000 published and approximately two million registered works. Some permission can be had immediately; otherwise, the CCC will locate the copyright holder and facilitate a deal.

You may also contact publishers personally and ask them to grant you permission. All you have to do is explain how the work will be used, where it will appear, and maybe some personal stuff to smooth over the request. Don't fret about "what if they say no," because you won't say no if someone contacts you for permission, right?

We all want to increase visibility, and getting your work cited in other publications is a great way to do that. To prevent issues, simply attribute the material you use to its creator. Wherever their work is cited or referenced, include a mark (usually a numeral) and provide the full source, either at the bottom of each page as a footnote or gather them at the end of a book as a bibliography. Here's an example:

So why is this decision paralysis? Let's be clear, choosing your path in life is like choosing from 100 flavors of doughnuts. Mr. Snodgrass was uncertain about what to do with his life as surely as he would be confused by a 7-11 shelf stuffed with 24 flavors of Doritos. (1) "Analysis of Paralysis," Dan Heath and Chip Heath, Fast Company, 2009.

Citing your sources allows you to use work without getting permission for every little thing; it's called "Fair Use." According to experts, Fair Use means what and how much authors can quote from someone else's work and avoid getting sued. There is a four-factor test and a large body of court cases that offer concrete examples of the nuances of Fair Use and how it applies to what you write.

Remember the *Hustler* case in the last chapter (*Hustler Magazine Inc. v. The Moral Majority Inc.*), in which Fair Use saved Falwell. The appellate court carefully applied four factors in Section 107 of the Copyright Act, otherwise known as the Doctrine of Fair Use, to test *Hustler*'s claim that the Moral Majority had infringed on its work.

The four factors are:

1. The purpose and character of the use. For example, is it for a commercial nature or a nonprofit purpose?

2. The nature of the copyrighted work.

3. The amount and substantiality of the portion used in creating the copyrighted work as a whole.

4. The effect of the use upon the potential market for or value of the copyrighted work.

The reason the court sided with the Moral Majority is this: the value of the work had not been diminished. If anything, Hustler got a lot of free publicity out of it. Basically, there are very few instances where "creative" use of small portions of copyrighted work will result in a court's decision against you. Just be careful and try to get permission to use it ahead of publication.

TOUGH NEWS, WHEN YOU CAN'T SUE
Don't flip out if you find yourself (or the characters in your work) the target of a parody. Copyright can definitely take a joke. Courts have uniformly held that humorous adaptations are a form of "comment" and "criticism," which are allowed under fair use laws. Courts favor works that draw recognizable characters rather than copying images wholesale from the parodied work. Also, context is an important factor, such as whether the parody diminished the value of the copyrighted work.

All you have to do to see the master at work is pick up an issue of *MAD Magazine*. The great jester Alfred E. Neuman has headlined a million parodies in *MAD*. These "spoofs" are based on copyrighted work, including Disney characters, TV sitcoms, major films, popular products, and celebrities. They are rarely sued because the work is original and doesn't attack the copyrighted material; it merely satires it.

Some satire crosses the line. While Disney turns a blind eye to *MAD,* they almost ruined a small underground magazine when they duplicated Disney characters in a parody that made reference to sexual and drug-related activities. They sued them on the basis of copyright infringement (*Walt Disney Productions v. Air Pirates*, 581 F. 2d 751, 9th Circuit 1978) and won.

There are exceptions, though. Ironically, the Disney Corporation considered suing another small magazine called The Realist, which published a "degenerate" cartoon after Walt Disney's death. It consisted of the following: Mickey shot up heroin, Goofy had intercourse with Minnie on a combination bed and cash register, Dumbo simultaneously flew and crapped on an infuriated Donald Duck. Meanwhile, Huey, Duey, and Louie peeked up Daisy Duck's dress as she watched the Seven Dwarves Grope Snow White and on and on.

Paul Krassner, editor of *The Realist*, knew exactly why Disney passed up the lawsuit: "They (Disney) realized *The Realist* was published on a proverbial shoestring and besides, why bother causing further embarrassment?" But there was a strong possibility that a court would decide in *The Realist*s' favor, under the Doctrine of Fair Use.

Criticism is also considered Fair Use, subject to the four-factor test. In 1990, the Second Court of appeals had to take a look at a book called *A Piece of Blue Sky: Scientology, Dianetics and L. Ron Hubbard Exposed*, about the founder of the controversial Church of Scientology.

The author was a former disenchanted member of the church who referred to Hubbard as an "arrogant, amoral egomaniac" and a "power-hungry, petty sadist." To add credibility, he borrowed liberally from Hubbard's work, reproducing entire paragraphs. The court held that the critical nature of the biography fit "comfortably within" the boundaries of Fair Use and noted that the "scope of fair use is greater with respect to factual rather than non-factual works." Furthermore, the work did not diminish the value of

Hubbard's. All that to say this, when it comes to copyright infringement, it takes more than just hurt feelings to make a lawsuit stick.

WHEN YOU CAN SUE, THE OPTIONS
Kevin Bullock has fifteen eBooks published under his small publishing company, Iseness. His sister manages things while Bullock pumps out new books. Fans followed him from his original publisher, Triple Crown, to Amazon. His bestselling book, *Daddy Dearest,* launched his career, and with family consensus, he made the decision to make more money by publishing himself. His fans agreed, filling chat lines with free reviews of his work and driving sales onto the Amazon best-seller list in 2014.

His sister ran the company for him, and despite having a life, raising kids, working, and walking her pet, she stumbled on a startling discovery. It was an infringement, plain and simple. Someone was selling hardcover, gold inlaid "collector" editions of his best-seller, *Daddy Dearest*. The infringer was using eBay to sell them for $80 a pop.

I'd met Bullock a few months before and enjoyed picking his brain, but when I saw him that day, he was coming unglued. Instead of typing straight from his crammed, hand-written pages, he just leaned over the small typing pad and projected an aura of rage. I approached him, we shook hands, and getting him to spill the beans was easy. After I looked at the proof his sister had sent, I told him he was lucky.

> "Why am I lucky?"

> "Because this is easy to stop."

> "Yeah, I'm writing a letter telling him I get out of prison in 12 months, and he better stop."

> I held out my palm in a 'stop' gesture, "Don't send that letter. There's a process for this whole thing."

> "What is it, like a Cease and Desist?"

> "Much better than that."

The proof of infringement was clear. That's the first step to stopping the problem. In fact, there is a three-part test to prove copyright infringement, which I explained to my friend.

    1. *Does the Work Qualify for Copyright Protection?* Since Bullock had registered Daddy Dearest with the Copyright Office after dissolving his original contract with Triple Crown Publishing, this satisfied the first requirement.

    2. *Has the Work Been Copied?* In Bullock's situation, he held up a screen-print from eBay with a thumbnail of the hardcover books, clearly offering "*Daddy Dearest* by Kevin Bullock." Since there was no attempt to conceal the infringement, it was open and shut proof.

    3. *Is it Fair Use?* The pirate had no license to copy Bullock's work, and he wasn't citing small portions in criticism, parody, or commentary. In fact, he was selling the entire book page-for-page. It was not fair use by any court's definition.

I told Bullock that when it comes to copyrights, imitation is the sincerest form of flattery, and the surest sign of liability. I stepped in as an advisor, instructing Bullock to communicate with the infringer and make a deal. A letter, not a lawsuit, might get them both something they want. It took Bullock some time to calm down and see the wisdom in this. If he negotiated a license fee with the infringer, then they both could make money from these $80 Collector's Editions. If a polite letter didn't work, then he could take the gloves off and sue.

The civil statute of limitations for copyright infringement is three years, anyway. All you have to do is file a grievance as a plaintiff (and pay the $300 filing fee), but it is advisable to hire an Intellectual Property lawyer once things go that far. And we all know how expensive lawyers are.

Even a successful lawsuit isn't very satisfying. If you have to take an infringer to court, they're probably too buck wild for a court order to control their behavior. All a court may provide are basic remedies:

- Injunction
- Actual damages and actual profits the infringer has earned
- Attorney fees
- Statutory damages, which vary wildly.

Copyright enforcement can sometimes be a waste of time and money. This was the situation in a case over a quarter of a century old. In 1993, Universal Studios argued that it should receive $50,000 for each bootleg copy of *Jurassic Park* that the Defendant, Ahmed, had made and sold with the ferocity of concert tickets. The studio's logic was "that the average price of a movie ticket is $7.50 (and) each (counterfeit) film could be viewed on a daily basis by 25 (or more) people, times 365."

The court decided that this was a stretch and determined the amount would apply to the work infringed, not each individual copy. The defendant paid about $30,000 in the end. That means Universal Studios paid a lawyer bill for nothing. While a big corporation can absorb the costs, we little guys are forced to be a little more creative.

LEVERAGING DEALS

As his advisor, I directed Bullock through the deal and got him paid. It was easy since the infringer was clearly an opportunist. After talking over all the options, Bullock agreed to the plan. That's when the fun really started.

Bullock's infringer was doing business online. I gave him a crash course on the copyright enforcement tool all writers should know about: The Digital Media Copyright Act (DMCA). It contains the Safe Harbor provision, which established a notice-and-takedown system for removing infringing works online. Countless DMCA notices have been filed to remove everything for illegal MP3s and movies, to plagiarized poems since its introduction in 1999.

The DMCA stemmed from the World Intellectual Property Organization Copyright Treaty. Under DMCA, copyright holders and their agents can demand the removal of allegedly infringing content. To do that, they must provide a complete takedown notice. Under the law, the notice must have a signature of the copyright owner, identify the work being infringed, a statement that use is not authorized, and a statement that all information presented is accurate.

The European Union (EU) has a similar system for online copyright infringement called the European Directive for Electronic Commerce. Other countries like India and Canada do not have notice-and-takedown systems. Though there is no such thing as an "international copyright," most countries offer protection of foreign works through international treaties and conventions. When filing a takedown notice with an ISP in another country, it is best to check the laws that exist there and ensure that your notice is compliant with their terms: some international takedowns can be initiated with a request, while others require a court order.

Usually, all you have to do is file the notice, and they act on it instantly. A phone call may take place, but you can expect the infringer's site to be shut down within 24 hours. For example, once the internet host received Bullock's complete notice, they disabled the infringer's account immediately. Then the host contacted the "client" to give them an opportunity to respond. The infringer could have issued a counter-notice, but he had no way to identify a good-faith agreement or any ownership. If that had been the case,

Bullock would have had to settle things in a Federal District Court in the judicial district where the service provider was located.

As predicted, it didn't require all that. Bullock shared the instructions for the DMCA with his sister, and I wrote a proposal on Bullock's behalf, politely educating the infringer. The next day, his eBay account was disabled, and he received an email:

"I thought you might like to hear from the copyright holder of the book you are selling without a license. This is called copyright infringement and is enforceable by law; it is illegal, and we must resolve this matter immediately. There are three options for us."

Those three options are pretty tough.

1. Cease and desist, destroy all copies, and send evidence.
2. Ignore this and get sued in Federal court.
3. Sign a license agreement with the copyright holder, and you both continue to make money.

I followed up with Bullock, and within two weeks, his devilish grin had returned. The infringer had taken the license agreement, and they were both back to making money again. Bullock was back to his old self, hammering away pages on his next novel. And that, in a nutshell, is the best outcome you can hope for.

If you encounter a similar situation, bear in mind that some infringers are really stupid. They will disappear and try to scam other authors. The DMCA will usually scare them out of your life. Like all dramatic events, utilize them, write about the experience, and help other writers avoid these nightmares.

A LITTLE PIRACY IS NORMAL

🖋 Writers Manifesto No. 30 – Prepare to get sued, it's good publicity.

You can read, you're educated, so don't think that you can work a miracle and make money by suing infringers. Also, don't copy people's work expecting to make a bunch of money from it. The truth is, we all steal a little, and we all get ripped off a little. A little bit is acceptable.

Here are some highlights from experience.:

- My account, username, and byline were used by a scammer to sell reviews on *Huffington Post* for $300 a pop.
- My byline has been printed on a short story called "Seeker of the Dead" (yeah, they ripped off Orson Scott Card) published in *Cosmic Cupid*. I didn't write it.
- Three poems have been published without a license agreement by two University Presses (names withheld).
- Portions of a review copy of one of my novels, called Cookie Crumbles, have been circulated online without permission.

There are some dirty things I've done.

- Quoted, on the bleeding edge of the Doctrine of Fair Use limitations, a combined 1,000 words from articles and reports in my book "*Life With A Record.*"
- Reprinted entire government documents and correspondence without approval.

- Broke Federal Prison policy (Correspondence Between Inmates) with dozens of articles in 3 major e-newsletters.
- Reprinted portions of correspondence without permission.

The reason I haven't been sued is that I attribute everything to whoever I borrow from. No one's hands are completely clean. But at least I haven't used my powers to try to "shake down" anybody. Anyone I've ever threatened to sue had it coming, and so far, the matters have always been resolved without going before a judge. It goes to show that if you can just behave, things can work themselves out in the least dramatic fashion, and you can go on your way writing toward another paycheck.

RESOURCES
Copyright Registration
- Library of Congress
  U.S. Copyright Office
  101 Independence Avenue SE
  Washington, DC. 20559 – 6000
  copyright.gov
  202-707-3000 (8:30 – 5:00 M–F)

U.S. Copyright Office
- Circular 1, *Copyright Basics*
- Circular 2, *Copyright Registration*
- Circular 3, *Copyright Office Fees*

Copyright Clearance Center
- ccc.com

PART 9
THE END

Chapter Thirty-Two

"There is probably no hell for authors in the next world – they suffer so much from critics and publishers in this." – Christian Nestell Bovee

LIFE AS AN AUTHOR

Publishing did not excite me anymore. Also, a 90-day binge had failed to resuscitate any creative abilities. People found out I'd relocated, and letters came in. Some were memorable enough to add to my portfolio: it's a hard-bound affair with clear plastic sleeves. I've kept letters from stalkers, fans, one convicted murderer, and only the very best exchanges with editors. Once the book was closed, however, back out of sight it went.

Unexpectedly, an editor set up a deal with Ozzy.com; they wanted a personal biography about my past. Though my heart wasn't in it, and the prose was a little rusty, it still got published. It was like a cosmic reminder to keep creating, which was ignored. The next thing I got was a royalty check for $500. It vanished like smoke in the air.

At work my office was a broom closet so tight I bumped knees with visitors. There was a line outside, as usual, but it shrank gradually. Clients pressed with typical questions about clearing up traffic tickets, child support, education, and employment. A small-framed, wiry-haired Vietnamese man walked up. He rubbed his hands together nervously.

> "Oh! Wow! I feel like I know you!"

> "Really?"

> "I've read everything you've written."

> "What you've read is only half the story."

The Mr. Tinsman he'd conjured was based on the noble figure in blogs, essays, and articles about heavy stuff like actual rehabilitation. In a rush of fear, the saying, "Never meet your heroes," came to mind, as it always does. But I stood my ground, determined to go with the momentum that had led up to this point. We shook hands and chatted.

No one can tell you how to feel about a thing. That reader humbled me, especially when he asked, "What's your next project?" Unfortunately, the new book languished on a computer screen. The experience was a punch to the gut, which absolutely rekindled that incurable disease: graphomania – the lust to write. Instantly, publishing was vital to the bigger picture. The goal wasn't to satisfy an editor's expectations; on the contrary, the motivation was to live up to the image readers hope for. Within days, after a round of emails, I'd squeezed an advance out of my publisher to finish the book. Since then, life has brightened up quite a bit.

ECCENTRICITY IS OKAY

Jack London (author of classics like *White Fang*) is said to have been an alcoholic and socially awkward. As was Tom Wolfe. As were many other "literary superstars" like F. Scott Fitzgerald, Truman Capote, and

Edgar Allen Poe. Lesser-known writers, like you and me, are anticipated eccentrics. It's in our blood. Wolfe especially, who wrote nonstop for 36 hours, then drank whiskey and caroused through Greenwich Village until he collapsed in a stupor of exhaustion and relief. These "outbursts" are the result of a very internal life that only writers fully understand.

In the stagecraft, there's truth. It's normal to see fame-starved C-listers acting foolish to just get some attention. This is different than the honest eccentricity of creative people. You'll see it in the drive of some authors, who've taken their income to the next level, as well as their possessiveness, by starting a business. By contrast, the outward manifestations of neurotics are emulations of something not understood.

Allie Brosh, author of *I Need to be Famous by Thursday* and *Hyperbole And A Half*, is only half joking in her bio, which says that she "lives in her bedroom." She's turned dark stuff like depression and suicide plans into hilarious comics, a blog, and several books. While on tour, she's a dynamo; some readings have lasted 7 hours. But while at home, "I'm going to take three weeks to just play Magic: The Gathering and reread *The Hitchhikers Guide to the Galaxy*. I need my hermit time."

We are not all Tony Robbins types, with his ice box multi-day seminars, up-selling memberships, and fire walk cultism. By nature, writers are individuals who aren't afraid to spend time alone in a room with their thoughts. Don't be afraid to unplug from the world. Allie Brosh once took an 18-month break from her blog; it's time to work, think, and strategize. You need it, too. The mind can't take in information nonstop; it needs time to do the synaptic voodoo that produces original thought, to sort, shuffle, and smear.

Barbara Tuchman was working as hard as ever the summer she was finishing *The Guns of August*. Her daughter Jessica remembered, "She was behind schedule and desperate to catch up. To get away from the telephone, she set up a card table and a chair in an old dairy attached to the stables – a room that was cold even in summer. She would go to work at 7:30. My job was to bring her lunch on a tray at 12:30, a sandwich, V-8 juice, and a piece of fruit. Every day, approaching silently on the pine needles that surrounded the stables, I'd find her in the same position, always engrossed. At 5 pm or so, she stopped."

The opening paragraph of *The Guns of August* took her 8 hours to complete, or two full days in the stables. It paid off because the book went on to win the Pulitzer Prize. Once, after she was famous, her daughter Alma told her that Jane Fonda and Barbara Streisand wanted her to write a movie script. She shook her head. "But, Ma," said Alma, "don't you even want to meet Jane Fonda?" "Oh, no." Said Tuchman, "I don't have time. I'm working."

Writers are permitted a fair amount of eccentric behavior. They bounce from isolation (where all the writing happens) to exhibition (where all the living happens). These things feed on one another, driving the appetite to live life to the fullest. It's a free pass to act badly and should be exploited to the legal maximum. Whatever antics you concoct can only imitate the luminaries who came before you. Sample Charles Bukowski's diet of dive motels, wine, and tramps. Dabble in Hunter S. Thompson's belief in the right to use drugs. Walk in the shoes of John McPhee's epic beer guzzling strolls across campus each morning. People are expecting it, and you know what? It feels pretty good in moderation.

EVERYBODY HAS HATERS
Plenty of people won't ever think of you. When authors get on people's radar, they bear the extremes of celebrity status. It brings a lot of perks, but also disrespect, envy, and cruelty. David Morris, author of 17 books including *First Blood* (yes, the one with John J. Rambo), was boycotted by many bookstores because of the misconception that he was a right-wing nut job. Little changed even after the Saturday morning cartoons (Rambo was animated, didn't kill bad guys, and talked to small forest animals).

Morris was a regular guy. He worked hard to hustle harder than the next man. Once he brought doughnuts, juice, and coffee to some of the book warehouse's staff. The manager took him into his office and

talked for half an hour while Morris tried to talk him into prioritizing shipments of his books. The revealing moment came when the manager took Morris (who was a celebrity, after all) on a guided tour of the warehouse, which was toasty warm despite a snowstorm outside. They reached the back of the warehouse, where flames flickered, and a roar grew louder. They had come to the source of the warehouse's toasty warmth: a massive, open-doored furnace.

To understand the point of this story, you need to be aware that back then, the book business allowed its wholesale and retail outlets to return all unsold stock for a full refund. For hardbacks, warehouses and stores must return the actual book. For paperbacks, only the book's cover needed to be returned in order to receive a credit.

That's what Morris was looking at. Pile after pile of coverless paperbacks are being thrown into the furnace to heat the warehouse. "This is where your books will end up some day, too," the manager told Morris. Years later, he could still not imagine his motive for saying that. Was he trying to be funny? Was he by nature cruel? When you meet haters, remember that you can stare into the metaphorical mouth of that furnace and see all your books on fire, but don't let it stop you.

TAKE WHAT YOU NEED

✎ Writers Manifesto No. 31 – Being a celebrity author is the frosting, not the cake.

Time, motivation, and money: all these things are crucial to making things last. There are exceptions, like one homeless writer who produced while living in a roach-infested apartment until his savings ran out and then continued writing on the streets. Literally, he wrote an excellent essay about sifting food from dumpsters, including such gems as to avoid pizza shops because they routinely poison the throwaways. Other memorable scenes include the way his dog would bark at the ground and dance when fire ants had beaten them to good food. Few writers can pull this off. The rest of us need at least a roof over our heads.

So, let's review the priorities of living one more time.

    1. *Time* – Since total focus is impossible to maintain without distractions, authors must establish a dedicated place to achieve their word diet. It could be a professional home office or library, but if your lifestyle affords it, lists of retreat centers can be found online (awpwriter.org and pw.org). You can also, of course, create your own retreat for a day, a weekend, a week, or longer by renting a place by yourself or ideally with others. Vacation rentals by owner (VRBO) is an excellent resource for finding reasonably priced rentals (vrbo.com).

    2. *Money* – It's true, most writers work a day job and make supplemental income through writing. Financial I.Q., a game plan, and steady income go a long way, but emergencies happen. The zealots will try to convince you that there are opportunities for financial support for writers. But you are better off going to the bank and asking for a vacation loan.

If you feel lucky, check out the clearinghouse (fundsforwriters.com/grants.htm) for the grants available. You can bypass the waiting period by getting involved with various organizations. The odds are still low that it'll work (seriously, a loan from a bank is easier, or crowdfunding). But if you get into a position, you might charm the pants off a board member of the NEA ($20,000), the Guggenheim ($25,000), or the Whiting Foundation ($30,000).

3. *Motivation* – It's easy to feel "used up," you've used all your material, plumbed all your memories, and reflected on everything there is to write about. When this happens (and it happens to all of us), you must remember that it will come back. You may simply need a "near-death experience."

There are so many anecdotes, vignettes, and quotes on this topic that the entire self-help industry has drained the well and left me with none to give you that you haven't probably heard already. I'll settle for this, what the Zen masters call "beginner's mind," open to all possibilities. If you need some reason to get you off your backside and out of a slump, then go practice that "open mind." Fresh eyes can give you back the perspective good writing needs.

PAY THE MAN
No one wants to hear about paying taxes, but it's necessary. I put it at the end because after reading the ins and outs of a bunch of tax code, you'll want this book to be over, too. Taxes are a part of life, even when you spend your life avoiding them.

Whether they are state or federal, the Boy Scout in all of us warns, "You better pay your taxes." That's all good and fine, but we've all done work for cash and "failed to report" small sums of money. Even the royalties from book sellers (direct deposit from Amazon) can fly under the radar if they aren't too big. But at some point, your income is going to attract attention.

1. *Federal Taxation* – Writers who get paid a large sum from clients have it easiest, since they can file a regular 1099 for payments below $1,000 or file a Schedule C for larger payments (ask a professional if you qualify for Schedule E, it has better rates). Tax consultants or Taxpayer Advocate Services (TAS) can help with contacting the IRS and preparing a tax return.

As with any business, you should keep a full record of all receipts (electronic and print). Accounting software like Excel or QuickBooks makes things a breeze to manage. Armed with good records, your tax consultants can help report deductions and expenses related to freelance writing. Almost everything counts – phone, postage, copies, gas, and the costs of operating a home office (yes, groceries too). Write off everything you can.

Visit the IRS website (irs.gov) and look under "Forms and Publications" and get Publication 334, which outlines business deductions. It isn't that complicated; like most things, it's all about getting organized. For additional clarity, check out these IRS booklets:

- Publication 533, Self-Employment Tax
- Publication 505, Tax Withholding and Estimated Taxes
- Publication 535, Business Expenses
- Publication 463, (discusses travel and entertainment deductions)
- Publication 538, Accounting Periods and Methods

2. *State Taxation* – When you travel (tours), it can get messy selling your books without a Business License or Sellers Permit for each state (and sometimes for certain regions within each state). If you work through a Speakers Bureau, share your accounting balance after each event, and they'll take care of the rest. After they've processed the taxes, you get a check.

If you're traveling on your own and intend to sell print copies of your book (or other merchandise), then it's time to obtain a seller's permit. It's not complicated. The Secretary of State has a remittance process for you to collect sales tax for them. Complete the application online, answer a few questions, pay a fee (in 50 states, the cost ranges from $50 to $500), and you can be ready to go in a day or two. Familiarize yourself with each state's Sales Tax Procedures; they'll want payments sent to specific offices: usually either immediate payment upon collection, or payment on a quarterly schedule. Or skirt the law by selling books for hard cash and stuff it in your pocket.

THANK GOD THAT'S OVER

Death and taxes are life considerations where preparation plays a critical role in success. At the end of this chapter, you'll find resources for ways to protect your writing after you pass. You should talk to a lawyer about creating an estate, a trust, or simply transferring ownership. You can bequeath a copyright by will or pass it along as personal property under applicable state laws. For more legal advantage, such a transfer can be "recorded" with the Copyright Office through its Office of Public Records and Repositories, for a fee. Ultimately, these methods hand over the potential of your words to your descendants. Now, a message for us, the living.

KEEP GETTING PAID

The world is changing all around us. The self-publishing revolution and electronic publishing model have dissolved barriers between authors and publication in ways that were unthinkable only a decade ago. Printing on paper has become a novelty, large publishing houses have shrunk to the size of most university presses, and online venues rule consumer interest, ads, and content. It is a wonderful time to freelance.

This is the era of universal graphomania. The internet is a river of content: tweets, Facebook blabber, and hook-ups on Plenty of Fish. Stay ahead of these distractions. Listen to what the experts are saying. When you detect an opportunity, jump all over it. It could be the next phase of social media or a major shift in readers' appetites. Pivot to test markets and subdivide your ideas, but above all else, learn as you go.

Skilled authors who write with focus and work hard hold the key. The industry continues to mature with new features, technology, and consumer expectations. Unlock the potential to get published, get paid, and have the success you desire by updating your approach again and again. Before you know it, writing may reward you beyond your wildest dreams.

"As practice is to policy, so style is to belief. Style is merely a consequence of what we believe, of what is in our hearts." – Max DePree

RESOURCES

Writers Retreats Directories
- awpwrite.org
- pw.org
- vrbo.org

Writers Grants and Awards Directories
- fundsforwriters.com/grants.htm
- pen.org/grants-and-awards-for-writers

Authors
- Kristine Rusch – Estate Planning series of articles – bit.ly/1nXwYKU
- J.A. Konrath – Death and the Self-Published Writer – bit.ly/1rMYJkh
- The Passive Voice – What happens when an author dies – bit.ly/1+OI98D

U.S. Copyright Office
- Circular 12 *Recordation of Transfer and Other Documents*

Chapter Thirty-Three

GOOD HELP AND WHERE TO FIND IT

Reference Books and Organizations:

1. For financial support and project financing information:

    - "Grants and Awards Available to American Writers"
      PEN American Center
      58 Broadway
      New York, NY 10012
      pen.org

    - Directory of Literary Magazines
      Council of Literary Magazines and Presses
      154 Christopher Street, Suite 3C
      New York, NY 10014

    - The Associated Press Stylebook and Libel Manual
      Addison-Wesley Publishing Co., Inc.
      Jacob Way
      Reading, MA 01867

    - Low Residency and Nonfiction Programs
      On Cloud Nine: Writers' Colonies, Retreats, Ranches, Residencies, and Sanctuaries
      Poets & Writers, Inc.
      72 Spring Street
      New York, NY 10012
      pw.org

2. For annual information about publishing companies and writing trends:

    - Writers Market: Where and How to Sell What You Write
      1507 Dana Avenue
      Cincinnati, OH 45207
      writersmarket.com

- National Society of Journalists and Authors
  1501 Broadway, Suite 302
  New York, NY 10036
  nsja.com

- Works of Authorship: A Guide to Understanding Copyrights
  Buchanan Ingersoll P.C.
  412-562-8800

- Writers' Conferences and Festivals
  P.O. Box 102396
  Denver, CO 80250

Reading List

1. For regular information about the writing community:

   - Poets & Writers Magazine
     72 Spring Street
     New York, NY 10012
     poetsandwriters.com

   - Writer's Digest
     F & W Media
     writersdigest.com

2. For essays and profiles of the finest creative nonfiction writers:

   - Creative Nonfiction
     P.O. Box 81536
     Pittsburgh, PA 15217
     creativenonfiction.com

For Prisoners

- Freebird Publishers
  221 Pearl St., Ste. 541
  North Dighton, MA., 02764
  774-406-6682
  Diane@freebirdpublishers.com
  Self-publishing, book promotion, and more. Works with inmates and their families. Publishes annual inmate resource directory, *Inmate Shopper*. Highly recommended.

- Prisons Foundation
  1600 K. ST. NW, #501
  Washington, DC., 20036
  202-393-1511
  prisonsfoundation.org
  Electronic publication of prisoners' manuscripts. Book length: 100 pages. Poetry and comic books: 20 pages. Write for submission guidelines and a permission questionnaire.

- PEN Prison Writing Program
  PEN American Center
  588 Broadway, Suite 303
  New York, NY 10012

212-334-1660
pen.org
Sponsors an annual writing contest for poetry, fiction, nonfiction, journalism and more. Manuscripts should be no more than 20 pages long. Publishes free book "*Handbook for Writers in Prison*." Highly recommended.

- Midnight Express Books
  P.O. Box 69
  Berryville, AR 72616
  870-210-3772
  mebooks1@yahoo.com
  Offers self-publishing services to prisoners.

- The American Prison Writing Archive
  198 College Gill Road
  Clinton, NY 13323
  315-859-4125
  dhinitiative.org/projects/apwa
  An internet archive of essays that offer firsthand testimony about living and working conditions in prisons. 5,000 words max. Write a permission questionnaire that must accompany all submissions.

- The Cell Block
  P.O. Box 1025
  Rancho Cordova, CA 95741
  Send SASE when you write to them.
  Publishes an annual resource directory.

The Write & Get Paid Quiz

How do you stack up as a writer? Can you hold your own against the upstanding professionals and drug-crazed pirates that have filled paper with ink throughout the ages? Find out where you rank by taking this exclusive quiz.

1. How often do you write?
   - Not this month -5
   - Once a week 0
   - Every couple of days +2
   - Up to 2 hours a day +5
   - Up to 4 hours a day +10

   Score _____

2. How much do you get paid?
   - I pay -5
   - Quarterly royalties below $50 +2
   - 3 cents a word +3
   - Quarterly royalties above $500 +5
   - Up to 15 cents a word +10

   Score _____

3. What does your biography look like?
   - Nude picture 0
   - Less than 100 words +2
   - 2 pages long -2
   - One major credit listed +2
   - 3 major credits listed +5

   Score _____

4. What is your current project?
   - Nothing 0
   - The same novel for the past six years -2
   - My new blog +2
   - Another book-length manuscript +5
   - The editor has their foot on my neck for this one +10

   Score _____

5. How reasonable are you when considering critique?
   - My work is flawless -5
   - I'll follow about 10% of suggestions +1
   - The more eyes the better +5
   - I enlist help after each major revision +10

   Score _____

6. Your self-promotion includes.
   - Direct mail advertising 0
   - A website +2
   - Email marketing -2
   - I don't promote myself -5
   - SEO, social media, you name it +10

   Score _____

7. How well do you work with editors?
   - I don't have one 0
   - As I need to +2
   - I'm open to rational suggestions +5
   - They don't respond to my messages -5
   - Working with one today +10

   Score _____

8. Your platform resembles:
    - Empty space 0
    - A landfill for bad reviews -10
    - A message thread from Facebook +2
    - Brand new site on WordPress -5
    - A theme park bustling with crowds and attractions +10   Score _____

9. These documents are in your safe:
    - None 0
    - Copies of all correspondence between me and the publisher +10
    - A copy of my publishing contacts +5
    - Rejection letters -3
    - Rejected manuscripts -10
    - Original releases, contracts, and agreements +10   Score _____

10. Reading anything?
    - One book, like a year ago 0
    - Radical newspapers -5
    - The newspaper +3
    - Wikipedia +2
    - Contemporary authors +5
    - Textbooks, journals, manuals +5   Score _____

11. The last time you were published was...
    - Never 0
    - Last year +2
    - Five years ago, -2
    - This year +3
    - Too often to recall +10   Score _____

Total Score _____

Your Stats:
1-25   It's only up from here.
26-45   Finish getting organized.
45-65   Be kind to your editor and they'll be kind to you.
66-85   You might be making more money than the writer who created this quiz.
86-100+   When, exactly, will you be speaking next?

Notes:

The Writers Manifesto

1. Don't let perfection interfere with what's possible.
2. Original doesn't equal interesting.
3. Choose a lot of role models; it gives you more people to steal ideas from.
4. All those submission guidelines were meant for someone.
5. Deliver your manuscript like a dozen roses, smile a lot, be funny, and get down to business.
6. The only form of harassment not recognized in a court of law is that of a writer demanding payment.
7. Quickening interest is nature's way of telling you to take more notes.
8. The best stories choose you; you don't choose them.
9. You'll get to The End many times before you're finished.
10. The art will happen when you aren't editing.
11. All the jobs you bid high will be easy, and all the jobs you bid low will be difficult.
12. The stuff you write on the side, you should probably write full-time.
13. Your contract was made by the lowest bidding attorney.
14. Agents are 95% hope and 15% commission.
15. Edit, because it's less expensive to put ink on paper than to take it off.
16. The secret ingredient in magic formulas is "the gift of gab."
17. The path of least resistance is paved by reading with purpose.
18. If the feeling doesn't fit, try a new form.
19. Your 10,000-word manuscript will probably read better at 2,000.
20. A sucked in bank account is nature's way of telling you to engage some readers.
21. When in doubt, repeat what readers say is working.
22. If bookstores were a good business model, they might be able to pay their bills.
23. All book titles are come-ons.
24. The first forms of organized crime were business, government, and publishing.
25. Gimmicks don't sell books; hustlers who use all the gimmicks sell books.
26. No one ever made a statue of a book critic.
27. Paper is nine-tenths of the law.
28. Don't write about the crime if you can't do the time.
29. If it's simple to write but it gets you paid, then it isn't stupid.
30. Prepare to get sued, it's good publicity.
31. Being a celebrity author is the frosting, not the cake.

Write & Get Paid

About the Author

Anthony Tinsman is a multiple award-winning author with numerous books available through online retailers. When not developing his next book, the green-technologies enthusiast enjoys studying new systems. Tinsman lives in Texas.

WE NEED YOUR REVIEWS ON amazon

Rate Us & Win!

We do monthly drawings for a FREE copy of one of our publications. Just have your loved one rate any Freebird Publishers book on Amazon and then send us a quick e-mail with your name, inmate number, and institution address and you could win a FREE book.

FREEBIRD PUBLISHERS
221 Pearl St., Ste. 541
North Dighton, MA 02764

www.freebirdpublishers.com
Diane@FreebirdPublishers.com

FREEBIRD PUBLISHERS

Thanks for your interest in Freebird Publishers!

We value our customers and would love to hear from you! Reviews are an important part in bringing you quality publications. We love hearing from our readers-rather it's good or bad (though we strive for the best)!

If you could take the time to review/rate any publication you've purchased with Freebird Publishers we would appreciate it!

If your loved one uses Amazon, have them post your review on the books you've read. This will help us tremendously, in providing future publications that are even more useful to our readers and growing our business.

Amazon works off of a 5 star rating system. When having your loved one rate us be sure to give them your chosen star number as well as a written review. Though written reviews aren't required, we truly appreciate hearing from you.

Sample Review Received on Inmate Shopper

 poeticsunshine

☆☆☆☆☆ **Truly a guide**
Reviewed in the United States on June 29, 2023
Verified Purchase

This book is a powerhouse of information. My son had to calm/ground himself to prioritize where to start.

GRAPHIC IS ONE IMAGE OF OUR BOOK COVERS. NOT THUMBNAIL PHOTOS

Freebird Publishers

CURRENT FULL COLOR CATALOG

98 Pages filled with books, gifts and services for prisoners

We have created four different versions of our new catalog A: Complete B:No Pen Pal Content C:No Sexy Photo Content D:No Pen Pal and Sexy Content. Available in full Color or B&W (please specify) please make sure you order the correct catalog based on your prison mail room regulations. We are not responsible for rejected or lost in the mail catalogs. Send SASE for info on stamp options.

CATALOG ONLY $5 - SHIPS BY FIRST CLASS MAIL
ADDITIONAL OPTION: add $5 for Shipping and Handling with Tracking

NO ORDER FORM NEEDED CLEARLY WRITE ON PAPER & SEND PAYMENT TO:
FREEBIRD PUBLISHERS 221 Pearl St., Ste. 541, North Dighton, MA 02764
www.FreebirdPublishers.com Diane@FreebirdPublishers.com Text/Phone: 774-406-8682
We accept all forms of payment. Plus Venmo & CashApp! Venmo: @FreebirdPublishers   CashApp: $FreebirdPublishers

FREEBIRD PUBLISHERS

Only $25.99
plus $7 S/h with tracking
SOFTCOVER, 8" x 10", 360 pages

Only $22.99
plus $7 S/H with tracking
SOFTCOVER, 8" x 10", 240+ pages

Only $24.99
plus $7 S/H with tracking
SOFTCOVER, 8" x 10", 210+ pages

Things don't magically change after you get kicked out of prison. Life starts all over again but there's a catch, having a record impacts almost every part of your life. With this book you'll find out how to prepare for life as an ex-offender. Filled with insights, advice, contacts, and exercises the information strikes legal, personal and professional levels. A real world guide for minimizing disruptions and maximizing success. Life With A Record helps make sense of the major challenges facing ex-offenders today. Ten hard hitting chapters outline the purpose of makinga Strategic Reentry Plan and making peace with supervisors, family, your community and your future.
Inside you will find: How to rebuild your credit, halfway house rules and terms, special grants and loans to finance education, job training or start a business, legal tips for dealing with discrimination, hundreds of reentry contacts and so much more!

Don't let a prison cell keep you from interacting with the world. Jailhouse publishing is possible! In fact, our new book gives authors the blueprint for first time to full time success.
In 30 information-dense chapters you'll DISCOVER how to turn your way with words into wads of cash.
- How to brainstorm, outline and then write your book.
- What to negotiate for in publishing agreements and other binding documents!
- Learn to write one book but sell it in multiple formats.
- Effectively make yourself irresisstable to editors–who'll stay on your team for years.
- What to do once you get published so your readers keep coming back.
- Learn self-publishing tools on Amazon, iTunes, Scrivener and beyond.
- Find useful creative writing advice
- How to design a press kit that empowers your publicity campaign
- And more!

U.S. law is complex, complicated, and always growing and changing, and many prisoners spend days on end digging through its intricacies. Pile on top of the legal code the rules and regulations of a correctional facility, and you can see how well the deck is being stacked against you. Information is the key to your survival when you have run afoul of the system. Whether you are an accomplished jailhouse lawyer helping newbies learn the ropes, an old head fighting bare-knuckle for your rights in the courts, or an inmate just looking to beat the latest write-up – this book has something for you. Freebird Publishers has drawn from the best legal offerings of the Lewisburg Prison Project, to put together this comprehensive guide to your legal rights.

Learn about: Litigation, First Amendment, Status, Due Process in Prison, Cruel and Unusual Punishment, Medical Care, Post Conviction and much more!

No Order Form Needed: Clearly write on paper & send with payment of $24.99 to:

Freebird Publishers 221 Pearl St., Ste. 541, North Dighton, MA 02764
Diane@FreebirdPublishers.com   www.Freebirdpublishers.com
We accept all forms of payment. Plus Venmo & CashApp!
Venmo: @FreebirdPublishers   CashApp: $FreebirdPublishers

2 MUST HAVE BOOKS FOR PRISONERS

$29.99
Includes Shipping/Handling with Tracking

$26.99
Includes Shipping/Handling with Tracking

INMATE SHOPPER

EVERY ISSUE CONTAINS:
- Non-Nude Girls
- Pen Pal Resources
- Social Media
- Magazine Sellers
- Text/Phone
- Catalogs to Order
- Sexy Photo Sellers
- Typists
- Personal Assistants
- Gift Shops
- Publishing Services
- LGBTQ Resources

GET BOTH FOR JUST **$47.99** INCLUDES PRIORITY S/H WITH TRACKING

ORDER THE COMBO AND SAVE! $$

THE BEST 500+

INCLUDES MANY RESOURCES:
- Legal: Innocence, Research, Advocates, Copies
- Newsletters
- Educational
- Health & Healthcare
- Reentry & Jobs
- Family & Children
- Veterans
- Sentencing Issues
- LGBTQ Resources
- Newsletter & Books
- & Much Much More!

No Order Form Needed: Clearly write on paper & send with payment to:

Freebird Publishers 221 Pearl St., Ste. 541, North Dighton, MA 02764
Diane@FreebirdPublishers.com   www.Freebirdpublishers.com
We accept all forms of payment. Plus Venmo & CashApp!
Venmo: @FreebirdPublishers   CashApp: $FreebirdPublishers

www.ingramcontent.com/pod-product-compliance
Lightning Source LLC
Chambersburg PA
CBHW080918170426
43201CB00016B/2189